T0295622

Engraved
on Our
Nations

Engraved on Our Nations: Indigenous Economic Tenacity
© The Authors 2024

28   27   26   25   24   1   2   3   4   5

University of Manitoba Press
Winnipeg, Manitoba, Canada
Treaty 1 Territory
uofmpress.ca

Cataloguing data available from Library and Archives Canada
ISBN 978-1-77284-064-3 (PAPER)
ISBN 978-1-77284-063-6 (PDF)
ISBN 978-1-77284-062-9 (EPUB)
ISBN 978-1-77284-061-2 (BOUND)

Cover photograph by Fred Elcheshen, 8 May 2005
Cover design by Drew Gonsalves
Interior design by Sarah Peters, Galley Creative Co.

This book has been published with the help of a grant from the
Federation for the Humanities and Social Sciences, through the Awards
to Scholarly Publications Program, using funds provided by the
Social Sciences and Humanities Research Council of Canada.

The University of Manitoba Press acknowledges the financial support for
its publication program provided by the Government of Canada through
the Canada Book Fund, the Canada Council for the Arts, the Manitoba
Department of Sport, Culture, and Heritage, the Manitoba Arts Council,
and the Manitoba Book Publishing Tax Credit.

Funded by the Government of Canada | Canadä

Engraved
on Our
Nations

INDIGENOUS ECONOMIC TENACITY

EDITED BY

Wanda Wuttunee
and Fred Wien

UNIVERSITY OF MANITOBA PRESS

CONTENTS

PREFACE

✦

Exploring Indigenous Economic Tenacity in Canada

✦

Wanda Wuttunee and Fred Wien

For the past several decades, academic literature, reports of inquiries, and media features have chronicled the disadvantaged and unequal position of Indigenous peoples in Canada. While often accurate in terms of substance, these narratives have contributed to a deficit perspective that is deeply discouraging to elected leaders, their administrations, and civil societies that on a daily basis engage in the struggle to improve community conditions. A deficit perspective also ignores the tremendous resilience of Indigenous communities that have survived despite extreme hardship.[1] It downplays the strengths of their political leadership as well as the tenacity and innovativeness of their business class, and the lessons that might emerge from a study of strength and resilience are submerged. Such a perspective fails to inform government policy and programs, neglects to give hope to those working on the front lines, and misinforms students who are seeking better answers for the future.

The historical record also teaches us that during much of the 1800s and 1900s, governments largely responded to evidence of hardship and petitions for relief by grudgingly, if at all, providing charity to those most in need.² By the middle decades of the twentieth century, Canada was becoming sufficiently prosperous that the expanding components of the welfare state such as social assistance, unemployment insurance, and pensions could be extended to Indigenous communities as well. While these individual-focused measures served to put in place a badly needed income floor more or less on a par with what people in the rest of Canadian society received, they failed to take the more difficult path of rebuilding Indigenous societies and economies, recognizing Indigenous Aboriginal and treaty rights, and accepting the right of Indigenous peoples to govern themselves.³

On the economic front, there were some exceptions to this pattern, for example the sporadic, limited, and ultimately misguided efforts to replace traditional hunting and fishing with agriculture. More successful was the increasing investment made in areas such as housing and education, also an individual-focused strategy. Yet even these measures were overwhelmed by other policies that had the effect of undermining and destroying what Indigenous collectivities had managed to achieve. One thinks of the profoundly negative implications of measures such as the policies to centralize communities into fewer locations (Nova Scotia) or induce populations into settlements (Inuit), the incursions on promised lands and subsequent dispersal of populations (Red River Métis), removals to make way for hydroelectric projects (Manitoba and elsewhere), the impact of residential schools, and the external controls imposed by legislation such as the Indian Act and its enforcement by the Department of Indian Affairs.

Despite these almost insurmountable obstacles to individual and collective well-being, an economy based in part on traditional fishing, hunting, trapping, and handicraft production has survived, although not so much in some areas as in others. Additionally, a "modern" business sector has emerged, and it did so even before government programs became available to support entrepreneurship and business development.

Indigenous authors, for their part, have been less inclined to buy into a picture based on deficits. The contributors to the book *Hidden in Plain Sight: Contributions of Aboriginal Peoples to Canadian Identity and Culture* recognize the blind spot that exists when Canadians consider Indigenous peoples, and their writing highlights the many contributions that Indigenous existence has in fact made to enrich the lives of Canadians.[4]

Economic development encompasses a wide range of dreams, visions, and choices for Indigenous communities that have identified the important parameters of economic efforts. While hidden in plain view, Indigenous people have made economic choices a reality through their tenacity. The chapters offer insight into how individuals and communities survived through tough times and continue to meet diverse challenges in a variety of initiatives that are important to them.

In the book's introduction, David Newhouse provides an overview of economic history and some of the specific realities that Indigenous Canadians faced in different historical periods. Looking at Indigenous economic history through the lens of tenacity, he underlines the importance of adapting to change, seeking to regain control, and bringing Indigenous perspectives to economic development strategy.

Four sections follow the introduction, each with its own introduction that explains the theme of the section as well as how the included chapters elaborate on the theme. Part One focuses on strategic leadership, which is illustrated by Mary Beth Doucette and Fred Wien's case study of Membertou First Nation and its impact well beyond reserve boundaries, by Daniel Millette's examination of the complexity of carrying out economic development involving multiple stakeholders, as in Tsawwassen First Nation, and by Charlotte Bezamat-Mantes's account of a First Nation pursuing Treaty Land Entitlements to develop an urban reserve in Saskatchewan.

The chapters in Part Two examine cases that are "culturally on point." Isobel Findlay describes a fur trappers' organization seeking to maintain a traditional way of making a living, Clifford Atleo reflects on whether capitalism can be Indigenized, and Judith Sayers discusses the debate around energy resource projects in the context of climate change and sustainable community development.

Part Three's chapters illustrate the importance of family and community connections to the success of Indigenous economic development projects. Chris Googoo, Catherine Martin, and Fred Wien pay tribute to entrepreneurs in the Atlantic region who have been awarded lifetime achievement awards by the Ulnooweg Development Group for their vision and tenacity in sustaining their businesses at a time when there were few programs available to support them. Family and community support was vital to their success. Wanda Wuttunee describes a Métis electrical contracting business that was established and thrived despite the odds in the Northwest Territories. Wuttunee also gives an account of a community development project in the North End of Winnipeg that aimed to build skills among people from marginalized communities while also working toward strengthening Indigenous food security.

The final section, Part Four, features two projects that illustrate the theme of partnering for success. Jerry Asp's chapter features the Tahltan First Nation and the business partnerships it developed on the way to success in developing housing, mining, and hydropower projects. Wanda Wuttunee describes partnerships that developed between individual municipalities and First Nations in pursuit of joint projects, as supported by the Council for the Advancement of Native Development Officers (Cando) and the Canadian Federation of Municipalities.

The volume concludes with the editors reflecting on the themes and lessons that have emerged from the chapters, especially from the point of view of Indigenous tenacity in the economic realm.

The cover art has been chosen to illustrate the message of *Engraved on Our Nations*: one of tenacity and hope, based on a proud history of resilience shared by the First Peoples. The hands are those of an older man, representing all the wisdom that is shared in this work. The eagle staff, drumming stick and rattles, and ribbon shirt establish the proud traditions and cultural elements important to many Indigenous peoples. The brown tones in the background evoke grounded perspectives provided by the land and by the persistence of individuals and communities. Above all, the story is one of hope and joy for the future as borne out in the bright colours.

NOTES

◆

1   Jennifer S. Dockstator, Eabametoong First Nation, Misipawistik Cree First Nation, Opitciwan Atikamekw First Nation, Sipekne'katik First Nation, T'it'q'et, Lillooet BC, Gérard Duhaime, Charlotte Loppie, David Newhouse, Frederic C. Wien, Wanda Wuttunee, Jeff S. Denis, and Mark S. Dockstator, "Pursuing Mutually Beneficial Research: Lessons from the Poverty Action Research Project," *Engaged Scholar* 2, no. 1 (Spring 2016): 17–38.

2   Hugh Shewell, *Enough to Keep Them Alive: Indian Welfare in Canada 1873–1965* (Toronto: University of Toronto Press, 2004).

3   Royal Commission on Aboriginal Peoples, *Report of the Royal Commission on Aboriginal Peoples*, vol. 1, *Looking Forward, Looking Back* (Ottawa: Minister of Supply and Services Canada, 1996).

4   Cora J. Voyageur, David Newhouse, and Dan Beavon, eds., *Hidden in Plain Sight: Contributions of Aboriginal Peoples to Canadian Identity and Culture* (Toronto: University of Toronto Press, 2005).

Engraved
on Our
Nations

INTRODUCTION

◆

Indigenous Economic History as the History of Tenacity

◆

David Newhouse

From the earliest times to the first part of the twenty-first century, Indigenous economies developed through a spirit of tenacity. Prior to the 1970s, economists, governments, and Indigenous leaders had not conceived of something called "Indigenous economies." Indigenous individuals were expected to assimilate and participate in the larger Canadian economy as wage labourers. There was simply no sense of an Indigenous economy that needed to be developed. In the early part of the twenty-first century, we now conceive of "Indigenous economies" as the object of Indigenous and Canadian government policies and programs and something that can be developed.

What follows is not an analysis of Canadian government policy as it pertains to the economic development of Indigenous peoples[1]—their nations, communities, and individuals—although this is part of the history. Instead, the focus rests on the efforts of Indigenous peoples to regain the stewardship of this aspect of their lives. This involves negotiating new social contracts with Canadians to regain control over lands and territories to use as homelands and capital, to secure assistance from governments to educate and train individuals, to establish and operate businesses, and to maintain a set of economic support institutions. Economic development is now linked to nation building, pride, and cultural revitalization and resurgence.

Transformation

One of the central notions of Indigenous thought is transformation. The world is animate and in a process of constant transformation. It takes great strength of character and confidence to live in this type of world. It also requires creativity, innovation, and a belief in one's own knowledge to adapt and live well. Living in a powered universe requires great tenacity. This chapter sketches some of the changes Indigenous peoples have encountered, especially in economic aspects of life, and ends with an analysis of the economic development strategies that Indigenous leaders and communities have been following for the last half century. As a story of economic tenacity, the focus is on Indigenous thought and action rather than government thought and action.

Across the western hemisphere, 1492 marked the beginning of change for Indigenous peoples. Over the next 500 years Indigenous peoples were subjected to assaults on their cultures, lands, and territories. They were dispossessed of their lands, often moved away from their traditional territories, and had their access to lands and waters and the resources they contained severely restricted. Trade among Indigenous nations was disrupted and eventually almost entirely replaced by trade with the newcomers and production to meet market demands. Indigenous leaders saw their ability to sustain healthy nations diminished. In what would become Canada, Indigenous economies were disrupted, and Indigenous peoples were expected to make the transition to a new economy, which required new ways of life and doing things. Indigenous peoples were expected to adjust to the world of markets and to think of land as a commodity and a source of capital.

The transition from a web of traditional self-directed and self-sustaining economies to participation in a market economy has been a difficult and challenging process for Indigenous leaders, particularly when it was clear that the terms of participation required assimilation. The emergence of Indigenous economies in the early part of the twenty-first century is a testament to the sheer determination and tenacity of Indigenous leaders to create good lives for their nations and communities in a changed world. The notion of a good life encompasses more than just economic aspects. A good life means that one can live well in accordance with one's own cultural precepts and understanding and that the economy supports culture and language and governance activity, not the reverse.

Indigenous Economies

It is fair to say that historically, there was not a single Indigenous economy but rather a set of interrelated economies that were rooted in the particular places where Indigenous people lived. Extensive trade routes provided connections among the economies and were a source of goods and ideas as well as mutually beneficial relationships. Initially, Indigenous leaders sought to incorporate the newcomers into these economies and networks through mutually beneficial activities such as trade and barter. As the newcomers came to understand the bounty of the land and waters (furs, game, fish, minerals, trees, and rich soil), they sought to remove Indigenous peoples and to claim these resources for themselves. As the number of Europeans grew over the nineteenth and twentieth centuries and as European-informed nations and economies were established, Indigenous peoples understood that their ways of life were being severely challenged and that they had to find ways to participate in this new economy.

The conventional way of looking at Indigenous economic history is to frame it through the lens of deficit and loss, to focus exclusively on dispossession and marginalization. That these things occurred is beyond doubt. However, focusing only on these outcomes masks the consistent philosophy and efforts of Indigenous leaders to ensure that their nations and communities were able to live well in a changed world. One can describe their efforts through the lens of tenacity: since Confederation, Indigenous leaders have consistently worked to advance their own communities' well-being.

Indigenous economies developed along lines that were different from those of Europeans. Most economists, anthropologists, and Indigenous Elders describe traditional Indigenous societies as non-market societies. The production, distribution, and consumption of goods was performed according to long-standing traditions and had to be seen to support Indigenous social and political structures. Most of the functions that we would describe as economic were embedded in the social roles of individuals. What was produced, how it was produced, how it was distributed, and how it was consumed evolved over time and became part of a shared history and way of doing things. The economy supported society rather than society supporting the economy. These societies then developed and established a moral and social order, which influenced the behaviour of individuals and institutions. The moral order indicated which goals were good and hence were supported, which types of social behaviours were acceptable, and the nature, ends, and workings of social institutions. Moreover, this order provided the glue that kept society together. One could say that these societies had a moral commitment to this particular social/

political/economic system. The system they had developed produced, in their view, the greatest good for the greatest number.

During the early encounters with Europeans in the seventeenth and eighteenth centuries, Indigenous peoples and leaders acted upon their understanding of the world and engaged in trade to secure goods, to build and maintain trading relationships, as well as to maintain peace. They based their activities upon the fundamental ethic of mutual benefit and sharing.[2] As Europeans sought to meet a growing demand for animal furs, Indigenous people served as harvesters and trappers. Some demonstrated market savvy through the development of a network of harvesters as well as in negotiating skills when it came to getting a good deal with the English and French traders. Indigenous people also worked in the fur-trading posts as labourers and in clerical and supervisory jobs, in addition to continuing in their roles as hunters and trappers (primary producers). Indigenous labour was essential to the fur trade. Indigenous people were able to continue their traditional activities, learn how to participate in a market economy, provide for their communities, and learn how Europeans think. As European settlements increased, Indigenous people also became skilled craftspeople who contributed to the building of churches, business establishments, and houses.

The continued settlement of Canada in the 1800s led to an increase in the number of European settlements and the need for land for them. Indigenous peoples began to be perceived as obstacles to development. Europeans began to find ways to remove Indigenous peoples from their lands and waters and to acquire title to the land so they could legally, or with good conscience, develop the land. Indigenous leaders, cognizant of the changing world, sought to use the treaty process to secure their access to traditional lands and gain resources to participate in the new economy. Treaties contained provisions for continued access to hunting and fishing territories as well as funds to assist participation in local economies, particularly as farmers. More often than not, the provisions of these sharing agreements were not honoured.

Frank Tough, in *As Their Natural Resources Fail*, points out the important roles played by Indigenous people in the Manitoba fur trade and the transition that Indigenous trappers made from production for use and consumption to production for market, at which they proved remarkably adept.[3] Sarah Carter, in *Lost Harvests*, points out the emergence of Indigenous ranchers across the prairies,[4] and in *Indians at Work*, Rolf Knight describes a growing but fragile Indigenous participation in the Canadian industrial economy of the early twentieth century as day labourers, farmers, and fishers.[5] The historical evidence suggests that despite the barriers Indigenous people in the early twentieth century encountered, they were starting to participate in the emerging market economy.

Indigenous participation in the Canadian economy was derailed by the Great Depression of the 1930s. As the last ones in, Indigenous peoples were the first ones out and as a result became almost totally dependent upon government assistance to survive. The government put into place an extensive system of welfare and income security. The approach to development in this period was to foster the participation of Indigenous individuals in local economies, although racism and discrimination inhibited this approach. The idea of an Indigenous economy that needed to be developed was not part of the mindset of economists or public policy makers during the first two-thirds of the twentieth century. The use of Indigenous lands and waters as the basis for such an economy was similarly not part of the thinking. Indigenous rights to these resources were limited. The approach to development of Indigenous economies was dominated by government policies and strategies, elaborated largely by economists working through a modernization framework that ignored issues of Indigenous culture.

Modernization had no place for Indigenous rights, Indigenous land-holding regimes, Indian reserves, community, history, and tradition:

> The future moreover was envisioned largely as a world dominated by European thinking, not one that recognized or accommodated Indian cultural values. Implicit in this thinking was the belief that Indian emphasis on special rights was basically a reaction to their being denied equal status—a defence mechanism based on their exclusion. Indians were viewed as poor "aspiring whites" who preferred what they did not have. To the extent that Indian cultural systems were recognized, they were cast in the past tense and viewed as outmoded. The importance of these cultural systems to Indians, no matter how acculturated, was simply not understood.[6]

Indigenous cultures were seen as obstacles to development.

Indigenous economic futures were envisioned as looking similar to those of mainstream economies: largely urban settings where Indigenous peoples, after appropriate education and training, would participate in local wage economies. Indigenous peoples would be encouraged to move from rural and reserve locations. A 1958 plan[7] for modern Indian economic development included relocation of Indigenous communities, using urban foster homes as places for Indigenous children and the integration of Indian children into provincial school systems.

The future as envisioned by Canadian policy makers began to be challenged. Indigenous leaders experienced a growing frustration, confirmed by their experiences in the Second World War, with a government approach to development that was widely perceived as not working. With the changed political consciousness surrounding the 1969 White Paper, Indigenous leaders began to forcefully put forward their ideas about the development of their communities as *Indigenous communities*. They built on earlier articulations of the foundational elements of Indigenous economic development. In 1963 the National Indian Advisory Board advised the Canadian government that "the planning forces should begin at the local level, reflect local needs, respect local needs, and represent the desires of Indians."[8] Indigenous leaders insisted upon a local community-based approach and made it the centre of their desired development process. This was supported in part by the Hawthorn Report (1966), which argued for a comprehensive approach to economic development.[9] This plan included education and training to enable Indigenous peoples to participate in the mainstream economy. It did not consider local Indigenous communities as viable for development. The future was in the cities.

Wahbung: Our Tomorrows (1971), coming from the Manitoba Indian Brotherhood (MIB), challenged this premise and represented the preferred Indigenous development approach: community self-sufficiency based upon the notion of rights emanating from sovereignty as a nation of people. Government support should enable Indigenous peoples to engage in self-determined, not government-determined, actions. *Wahbung* called for a comprehensive approach to the development of Indian communities as economies and as communities central to Indigenous life. The Manitoba plan had three elements:

1. A plan to help individuals and communities recover from the pathological consequences of poverty and powerlessness. This meant a focus on individual and community health and healing. Adequate health services and community infrastructures were needed for this task.

2. A plan for Indian people to protect their interests in lands and resources. This meant ensuring that treaties and land claims were recognized.

3. A concerted effort at human resource and cultural development.[10]

The MIB plan had at its heart the idea that if change were to lead to increased self-sufficiency, it ought to be directed by Indian peoples themselves, so that they could consider both individual and community interests. It called for the development of Indigenous institutions that would serve as a foundation for the economy and community. These institutions were to be developed by Indigenous peoples and pursue goals and objectives determined by Indigenous peoples themselves. The foundation of Indigenous development efforts was sovereignty, a finding supported two decades later by the Royal Commission on Aboriginal Peoples[11] and the Harvard Project on American Indian Economic Development.[12]

In the same time period, the Council for Yukon Indians released Together Today for Our Children Tomorrow,[13] the first comprehensive land claim statement from an Indigenous organization. It asserted that Indigenous development must be based on a foundation of Indigenous rights to land and waters: "Without land, Indian People have no soul—no Life—no Identity—no Purpose. For Indian Yukon People to join in the Social and Economic life of Yukon, we must have specific rights to lands and natural resources that will be enough for both our present and our future needs."[14] Indigenous leaders grasped the basic idea necessary for effective participation in a capitalist economy: they needed capital if they were to effectively participate and develop their communities. Indigenous leaders were also unwilling to see their culture as a development obstacle.

The early 1970s laid the foundation for the development strategy that Indigenous leaders would advocate for and follow over the next half century: a comprehensive approach grounded in community-developed plans. Social, cultural, economic, and political development are intertwined and impossible to separate. Development must support Indigenous lives in all of their aspects. It must enable Indigenous peoples to exercise their inherent sovereignty over their lands and support a wide variety of Indigenous economic activities, ranging from traditional activities to individually and collectively owned businesses.

Indigenous peoples faced an enormous challenge in executing their strategy. They had been systematically removed from their traditional territories, seen the agreements they made for sharing land repeatedly ignored or interpreted very narrowly, and faced discrimination when they participated in the mainstream economy as farmers or labourers or business owners.

The challenge was mitigated by changes in Canada's approach to economic development. Canada's economic development had been based upon Rostow's stages of economic growth,[15] which focused on large-scale national infrastructure projects with benefits that would trickle down and improve people's lives in all sectors of society. This tactic did not result in significant benefits to Indigenous communities. Development based upon small-scale, people-centred projects began to inform Canada's national approach to development.[16]

For more than 100 years, Indigenous leaders had been protesting their treatment and the loss of their lands. For example, European settlement in British Columbia in the 1800s had pushed many Nisga'a off their lands and prevented them from accessing their territories and its resources. The Nisga'a began to push back in 1887, and in 1973, the Supreme Court in the Calder decision recognized that Aboriginal title existed. Indigenous leaders were quick to capitalize on this recognition, and Canada was forced to respond with a land claims policy that attempted to correct the wrongs of the past.

Recovery of the land became central to Indigenous development efforts over the half century since Calder. Land, in Indigenous thought, is a multi-faceted concept. It is more than earth; it is the source of life and identity. It is the entire ecosystem of land, water, air, and all of the life within it. Land informs culture, social systems, relationships, spirituality, and is the basis of law. Land is more than property. The loss of land leads to an existential crisis and is a direct attack on sovereignty.

Indigenous leaders vigorously pursued claims through new land claims policies and new institutions (the Indian Claims Commission and its successors, the Canadian Indian Rights Commission, the Indian Specific Claims Tribunal) established by the federal government. The Cree of Quebec negotiated the first modern treaty, the James Bay and Northern Quebec Agreement, in 1975. This agreement centred economic life on the community and created a new land management regime that protected traditional activities while enabling development in some areas. The hearings for the Mackenzie Valley Pipeline in 1976 also provided an opportunity for Indigenous leaders to present their ideas about development. Support for a comprehensive approach began to build. In 1979, Jack Beaver, a Mohawk business leader, released his report on economic development, titled *To Have What Is Our Own.*[17] He also argued for a policy of self-direction as the fundamental basis for economic development of Indian communities. He insisted that the development of Indigenous economies should be under the guidance of Indigenous peoples.

In 1983, after an extensive set of presentations from Indigenous leaders, the Penner Report on Indian self-government advanced the same argument about economic development.[18] Coming after an intense period of constitutional discussions regarding the definition of Indigenous peoples, their rights, and their place in Canadian society, the report also recommended the establishment of a new relationship with Indigenous peoples. A key element of this new relationship would be the recognition of Indian self-government. One of the authorities of Indian governments—now called First Nations governments—would be to direct the development of their local economies. The Penner Report was adopted by the House of Commons in a show of all-party support in November 1985. And in 1996, the *Report of the Royal Commission on Aboriginal Peoples* recognized that jurisdiction over Aboriginal economies was a core area of authority for Aboriginal national governments; indeed, the commission went further and linked the development of Aboriginal economies as one of the keys to making progress on Indigenous self-government.[19]

Since 1973, twenty-four comprehensive land claims agreements have been signed that recognize Indigenous jurisdiction over 40 percent of the land mass of Canada. Ken Coates, in a 1995 report for the Ministry of Aboriginal Affairs in British Columbia, concluded that "treaties have provided Indigenous groups with the financial and administrative means to begin to chart a new economic future for their people and their regions. . . . Indigenous peoples have used the land claims process as a basis for participating more fully in the broader economy and, typically, have become more heavily involved with the non-indigenous population as a result of the treaty."[20]

Indigenous leaders also pursued land claims through the courts, resulting in a series of landmark cases that set out Aboriginal rights and how they might be exercised to protect lands and waters as well as enable their use in economic development activities: Calder (1973), Guerin (1984), Sparrow (1990), Van der Peet (1996), Delgamuukw (1997), Marshall (1999), Mitchell (2001), Tsilhqot'in (2014), Mikisew Cree (2018), and Williams Lake (2018), to name a few.[21]

Self-government agreements are used as vehicles for the development of Indigenous communities. As of 2018, there were twenty-two signed self-government agreements involving twenty-six Indigenous communities. Eighteen of these agreements are part of comprehensive land claims agreements. These agreements, also known as modern treaties, contain provisions that deal with issues such as land ownership and resources, harvesting and wildlife, and economic development as well as transfer of capital. A 2013 review of the implementation of the Inuvialuit Final Agreement concluded:

> Modern treaties provide a number of mechanisms through which they support economic development. The formalization of property rights helps individuals derive full benefits from the ownership of resources, which allows for the maximization of gains from trade and supports other transactions in the economy. In addition, modern treaties provide for direct capital transfers to beneficiary organizations, which have the potential to support investment activity as well as social and educational initiatives with possible long-term economic benefits. These benefits represent significant progress towards the modern treaties' immediate expected outcomes. Specifically, the agreements provide structures for clear and formalized land ownership leading to well understood rights regarding management and access. In addition, the formalization of property rights also provides certainty of ownership and contributes to a more stable economic environment.[22]

The Standing Committee on Indigenous and Northern Affairs in 2018 investigated the challenges involved in implementing Indigenous land rights. While documenting the issues First Nations faced in securing land and the rights to use land in ways that are consistent with their own traditional values, customs, and development objectives, the committee observed that land claims, whether comprehensive or specific, enabled Indigenous peoples to take their place in the Canadian economy. These new treaties, as the agreements came to be called, "when honourably implemented are a successful mechanism for the protection and reconciliation of Indigenous rights and can generate significant economic benefits for Indigenous peoples as well as for the local, regional, provincial, and Canadian governments and their communities."[23]

Indigenous leaders have consistently argued that the collective— community or nation—is the appropriate focus of development, that Indigenous governments ought to have jurisdiction over lands and resources and the capacity to direct development within their territories, including the ability to devise and develop their own economic institutions. They argue that governments have a responsibility to ensure that their efforts are supported. Leaders have emphasized that Indigenous cultures are not obstacles to development. This approach is reflected in the research findings of the Harvard Project on American Indian Economic Development, which uses the term "nation building" to frame development initiatives.[24] A nation-building approach is based upon the idea that economic development is intended to strengthen Indigenous nations, operates in accordance with Indigenous cultural imperatives, and develops institutions for the effective governance and operation of Indigenous national economies.

Indigenous advocacy over the last half century has brought a broadening of government support for Indigenous economic effort, as Indigenous leaders advanced the idea that First Nations ought to be developed as communities and economies. Support was initially seen through the lens of business development through the establishment of business loan and assistance programs as well as training and labour market preparation programs. Programs were created that supported Indigenous participation in sectors of the Canadian economy such as mining, forestry, fishing, oil, and gas. Gradually, governments came to accept the vision that Indigenous leaders were advancing, and community economic development approaches came to be supported through programs like the Canadian Aboriginal Economic Development Strategy (1993), the National Aboriginal Economic Development Program, the Federal Framework for Aboriginal Economic Development (2009), and the Aboriginal Economic Development Strategic Partnership Initiatives (2010), among others.

The advances of the last half century have been based upon the determination of Indigenous leaders to ensure that development of Indigenous communities and economies occurs under Indigenous jurisdictions, using Indigenous values, and reflecting Indigenous ideas of the economy and society. The basic strategy as set out in *Wahbung: Our Tomorrows* in 1973 has been tenaciously followed.

The Change

In the twenty-first century, the idea of Indigenous economies has been established. Indigenous economies are now considered part of larger provincial and Canadian economies and are seen as entities to be developed through Indigenous, provincial, and national efforts. This fundamental change is one that Indigenous leaders have created over the last half century. The 1969 White Paper proposed that Indigenous peoples be assimilated into Canada and that Indigenous peoples' futures follow a trajectory similar to that of immigrants: social and economic integration.[25] Indigenous peoples rejected this trajectory and with great tenacity advocated for a different future: one based upon self-determination as distinct peoples within the Canadian federation, with restored lands and governments and government support.

The performance of Indigenous economies is now reported on through the National Indigenous Economic Development Board. The board measures economic progress through the Aboriginal Economic Benchmarking project, which uses thirty-one different measures to track social and economic well-being.[26] Indigenous economic effort is now seen as a small but significant aspect of the Canadian economy. It has been estimated that reducing the economic gap between Indigenous and non-Indigenous peoples would result in a 1.5 percent increase in the Canadian gross domestic product.[27]

Over the last half century, the old idea that economics and business are not part of Indigenous cultures has waned. Excellent studies have been completed by Frank Tough, a University of Saskatchewan professor who wrote an economic history of Native people in northern Manitoba; Rolf Knight of the University of British Columbia, who wrote a history of British Columbia Indians in the labour force around the turn of the century; Sarah Carter, who documented the trials and tribulations of prairie Indian farmers in the last century; Fred Wien of Dalhousie University, who wrote of the economic history of the Mi'kmaq in Nova Scotia; and Douglas Elias, who wrote a history of Aboriginal economic development. Wanda Wuttunee of the University of Manitoba has written of the growth of an Indigenous small business sector as well as on Indigenous community economic decision-making processes.[28] The *Journal of Aboriginal Economic Development*, published by the Canadian Association of Native Development Officers (Cando) since 1999, is a peer-reviewed journal dedicated to exploring various aspects of Indigenous economic development through research and experience. Volume 2 of the 1996 *Report of the Royal Commission on Aboriginal Peoples* described in full detail the challenges relating to land, resources, and economic development.[29] These works are part of the economic history and life of Indigenous peoples. They are a start in our journey to understand aspects of Indigenous history as well as helping to inform future development efforts.

There is now a vigorous critical debate among Indigenous scholars about the nature of Indigenous economics and the course that Indigenous economic development ought to follow. I have described what I call "red capitalism"; Robert Miller uses the term "reservation capitalism"; Duane Champagne calls it "tribal capitalism"; and Wanda Wuttunee uses the term "community capitalism."[30] Clifford Gordon Atleo wonders whether resistance to Western capitalism is indeed futile.[31] Elizabeth Rata writes of "neotribal capitalism" to describe the emergence of revitalized Maori economies in New Zealand.[32]

The last half decade has also seen the development of an infrastructure of institutions whose purpose is to further Indigenous economic development: Aboriginal Financial Institutes facilitate access to capital; the Centre for First Nations Governance supports effective governance; the National Aboriginal Capital Corporations Association assists businesses, including community-based social enterprises; various business-support organizations such as the Indigenous Business and Investment Council, and the Council for the Advancement of Native Development Officers (Cando), which offers a certificate program for development officers working in Indigenous communities. Aboriginal Chambers of Commerce have emerged in several Canadian cities. Indigenous economic development corporations have become a common feature of Indigenous development. Cape Breton University has established the Purdy Crawford Chair in Aboriginal Business Studies to focus research on how to foster successful Aboriginal businesses. The National Consortium for Indigenous Economic Development, an initiative at the University of Victoria, assists Indigenous peoples in developing their own economies and their own approaches to economic self-sufficiency, sustainability, and success. The Canadian Council for Aboriginal Business, an organization of Indigenous businesses, describes its mission as promoting, strengthening, and enhancing a diverse and prosperous Indigenous economy.

Robert Anderson, University of Regina, and his colleagues at the
First Nations University argue that there is an Indigenous approach
to economic development. This approach is "predominantly a collective
one centred on [the] First Nation or community." The development
objectives, they outline, are directed to "attaining economic self-
sufficiency as [a] necessary condition for the preservation and
strengthening of communities," exercising "control over activities on
traditional lands," improving the socio-economic circumstances of
Aboriginal peoples, and "strengthening traditional culture, values and
languages and the reflecting of the same in development activities."[33]

Anderson describes three sets of activities that are the basis of
development for Indigenous nations and communities:

1. creating and operating businesses that can compete profitably
   over the long run in the global economy in order to exercise
   control over activities on traditional lands; building an economy
   necessary to preserve and strengthen communities and improve
   socio-economic conditions;

2. forming alliances and joint ventures among themselves and
   with non-Aboriginal peoples to create businesses that can
   compete profitably in the global economy; and

3. building capacity for economic development through
   iv. education, training, and institution building; and
   v. the realization of Treaty and Aboriginal rights to lands
   and resources.[34]

Indigenous Entrepreneurs

While many communities are pursuing collective strategies, there has
also been a rapid growth in individual entrepreneurs starting businesses
both on- and off-reserve. During the 1970s and early 1980s, organizations

like the National Indian Brotherhood (now the Assembly of First Nations) "warned against promoting private enterprise at the expense of the entire community."[35] Rochelle Coté reports that "Indigenous entrepreneurship has grown at a rate five to nine times the pace of the general population in Canada," citing reports from the Canadian Council for Aboriginal Business and Statistics Canada.[36] The Conference Board of Canada in 2020 found a similar rise in Indigenous entrepreneurship as well as the emergence of an infrastructure of institutions intended to support further growth and success of Indigenous entrepreneurs.[37] Both collectively and individually owned enterprises are now important aspects of Indigenous economic development strategies and efforts.

In a report on First Nations Small Business for the First Nations Governance Centre, Warren Weir concludes: "Aboriginal small business is a relatively new and interesting growth industry in Canada. And creative, independent, committed, culturally astute, and hard-working Aboriginal entrepreneurs are adding value to the Canadian economy, while making a difference to them individually, as well as contributing to their families and communities . . . an entrepreneurial spirit is alive, well, and prospering in Aboriginal communities located across Canada."[38]

Indigenous economic development has emerged as a complex area as communities and individuals navigate the territory defined by Indigenous cultural values, mainstream business and economic values and practices, emerging and new areas of business, as well as new ways of doing business in a diverse Canadian economy. Developing and supporting Indigenous economies require innovation, creativity, perseverance, and a willingness to see Indigenous nations, peoples, and individuals as economic actors. The fundamental change that has occurred over the last half century is a willingness to frame Indigenous economic development as being as foundational to Indigenous self-determination as Indigenous self-government is.

A strategy set out forty years ago and pursued diligently and tenaciously by Indigenous leaders has provided a foundation for the rebuilding of Indigenous nations and economies. It is remarkable what can be achieved with determination and tenacity.

NOTES

◆

1   This chapter uses the term "Indigenous" to describe the original inhabitants of North America. Over the half-millennium period of contact, other terms have included Native, Indian, and Aboriginal. These collective terms mask the diversity of Indigenous peoples, much as "European" masks the diversity of peoples living in Europe.

2   John Borrows, *Law's Indigenous Ethics* (Toronto: University of Toronto Press, 2019).

3   Frank Tough, *As Their Natural Resources Fail: Native Peoples and the Economic History of Northern Manitoba, 1870–1930* (Vancouver: University of British Columbia Press, 1996).

4   Sarah Carter, *Lost Harvests: Prairie Indian Reserve Farmers and Government Policy* (Montreal: McGill-Queen's University Press, 1993).

5   Rolf Knight, *Indians at Work: An Informal History of Native Labour in British Columbia, 1858–1930* (Vancouver: New Star Books, 1996).

6   Peter Douglas Elias, *Development of Aboriginal People's Communities* (Toronto: Captus Press, 1991).

7   Hugh Shewell, "'Bitterness behind Every Smiling Face': Community Development and Canada's First Nations, 1954–1968," *Canadian Historical Review* 83, no. 1 (2002): 58–84.

8   Elias, *Development of Aboriginal People's Communities*, 6.

9   Harry B. Hawthorn et al., *A Survey of the Contemporary Indians of Canada: A Report on Economic, Political, Education Needs and Policies in Two Volumes* (Ottawa: Indian Affairs Branch, 1966).

10   Manitoba Indian Brotherhood, *Wahbung: Our Tomorrows* (Winnipeg: Manitoba Indian Brotherhood, 1971).

11   Royal Commission on Aboriginal Peoples, *Report of the Royal Commission on Aboriginal Peoples* (Ottawa: Minister of Supply and Services Canada, 1996).

12   Stephen E. Cornell and Joseph P. Kalt, *Reloading the Dice: Improving the Chances for*

Economic Development on American Indian Reservations, Harvard Project on American Indian Economic Development 59 (Cambridge, MA: Malcolm Wiener Center for Social Policy, Harvard Kennedy School, Harvard University, 1992).

13   Council for Yukon Indians, *Together Today for Our Children Tomorrow: A Statement of Grievances and an Approach to Settlement by the Yukon Indian People* (Whitehorse, YU: Council for Yukon Indians, 1973).

14   Ibid., 31.

15   Walt W. Rostow, *The Stages of Economic Growth: A Non-Communist Manifesto* (Cambridge: Cambridge University Press, 1965).

16   Katherine Graham, Carolyn Dittburner, and Frances Abele, *Dialogue and Soliloquy: Public Policy and Aboriginal Peoples, 1965–1992* (Ottawa: Royal Commission on Aboriginal Peoples, 1996).

17   Jack Beaver, *To Have What Is Our Own* (Ottawa: National Indian Socio-Economic Development Committee, 1979).

18   House of Commons, *Report of the Special Committee on Indian Self-Government* (Penner Report) (Ottawa: House of Commons, 1983).

19   Royal Commission on Aboriginal Peoples, *Report of the Royal Commission.*

20   Ken S. Coates, *Summary Report: Social and Economic Impacts of Aboriginal Land Claims Settlements: A Case Study Analysis* (Ottawa: ARA Consulting, 1995), 10.

21   *Calder et al. v. Attorney-General of British Columbia*, [1973] SCR 313; *Guerin v. The Queen*, [1984] 2 SCR 335; *R. v. Sparrow*, [1990] 1 SCR 1075; *R. v. Van der Peet*, [1996] 2 SCR 507; *Delgamuukw v. British Columbia*, [1997] 3 SCR 1010; *R. v. Marshall*, [1999] 3 SCR 533; *R. v. Mitchell*, [2001] SCC 33; *Tsilhqot'in Nation v. British Columbia*, [2014] 2 SCR 257; *Mikisew Cree First Nation v. Canada* (Governor General in Council), [2018] 2 SCR 765; *Williams Lake Indian Band v. Canada* (Aboriginal Affairs and Northern Development), [2018] 1 SCR 83.

22   Aboriginal Affairs and Northern Development Canada and Inuvialuit Regional Corporation, *Evaluation of the Impacts of Comprehensive Land Claims and Self-Government Agreements—Federal and Inuvialuit Perspectives* (Ottawa, 2013).

23   Standing Committee on Indigenous and Northern Affairs, *Indigenous Land Rights: Towards Respect and Implementation* (Ottawa: House of Commons, 2018), 27.

24   Stephen Cornell and Joseph P. Kalt, "Sovereignty and Nation-Building: The Development Challenge in Indian Country Today," *American Indian Culture and Research Journal* 22, no. 3 (1998): 187–214.

25   Department of Indian Affairs and Northern Development, *Statement of the Government of Canada on Indian Policy, 1969* (White Paper) (Ottawa: Queen's Printer, 1969).

26   National Indigenous Economic Development Board, *The Aboriginal Economic Benchmarking Report* (Ottawa, 2012).

27   National Aboriginal Economic Development Board, *Reconciliation: Growing Canada's Economy by $27.7B* (Ottawa, 2016).

28   Tough, *As Their Natural Resources Fail*; Knight, *Indians at Work*; Carter, *Lost Harvests*; Elias, *Development of Aboriginal People's Communities*; Fred Wien, *Rebuilding the Economic*

Base of Indian Communities: The Micmac in Nova Scotia (Montreal: Institute for Research on Public Policy, 1986); Wanda Wuttunee, *In Business for Ourselves: Northern Entrepreneurs* (Montreal: McGill-Queen's University Press, 1992), and Wuttunee, *Living Rhythms: Lessons in Aboriginal Economic Resilience and Vision* (Montreal: McGill-Queen's University Press, 2004).

29   Royal Commission on Aboriginal Peoples, *Report of the Royal Commission on Aboriginal Peoples*, vol. 2, *Restructuring the Relationship* (Ottawa: Minister of Supply and Services Canada, 1996).

30   David Newhouse, "Modern Aboriginal Economies: Capitalism with a Red Face," *Journal of Aboriginal Economic Development* 1, no. 2 (2000): 55–61; Robert Miller, *Reservation "Capitalism": Economic Development in Indian Country* (Santa Barbara, CA: Praeger, 2012); Duane Champagne, *Social Change and Cultural Continuity among Native Nations* (Lanham, MD: Altamira Press, 2007); and Wanda Wuttunee and Stelios Loizides, "Creating Wealth and Employment in Aboriginal Communities," University of Illinois at Urbana's Academy for Entrepreneurial Leadership, Historical Research Reference in Entrepreneurship, 2005, https://papers.ssrn.com/sol3/papers.cfm?abstract_id=1509973.

31   Clifford Gordon Atleo, "Aboriginal Capitalism: Is Resistance Futile or Fertile?" *Journal of Aboriginal Economic Development* 9, no. 2 (2015): 41–51.

32   Elizabeth Rata, "The Theory of Neotribal Capitalism," *Review* (Fernand Braudel Center) 22, no. 3 (1999): 231–88.

33   Robert Anderson, Robert Kayseas, Leo Pal Dana, and Kevin Hindle, "Indigenous Land Claims and Economic Development in the Canadian Experience," in *Surfing the Waves: Management Challenges, Management Solutions, Proceedings of the 17th ANZAM Conference*, ed. Alan Brown (Joondalup, WA: Edith Cowan University School of Management, 2003).

34   Ibid., 635.

35   National Indian Brotherhood, Statement on Economic Development of Indian Communities, quoted in Elias, *Development of Aboriginal People's Communities*, 17.

36   Rochelle Coté, "Networks of Advantage: Urban Indigenous Entrepreneurship and the Importance of Social Capital," in *Well-Being in the Urban Aboriginal Community*, ed. David Newhouse et al. (Toronto: Thompson Educational Publishing, 2013), 74.

37   Conference Board of Canada, *Support for Success: Indigenous Entrepreneurship in Northern and Remote Canada* (Ottawa: Conference Board of Canada, 2020).

38   Warren Weir, *First Nations Small Business and Entrepreneurship in Canada* (National Centre for First Nations Governance, 2007), https://fngovernance.org/wp-content/uploads/2020/09/warren_weir.pdf.

PART ONE

✦

Strategic Leadership

What does it look like when community leadership has a broad economic vision that leads to self-determination and meaningful governance, as described in David Newhouse's introduction? The three chapters in Part One offer examples where leaders have changed the story through tenacity in the face of every kind of obstacle.

Mary Beth Doucette and Fred Wien present a model of community economic development carried out by Membertou First Nation, located on Cape Breton Island in Nova Scotia, that over time has had major positive impacts within the community, rippling out to the region and beyond. Consistent leadership by the Membertou Chief and Council over thirty years has been particularly fruitful and offers lessons that are broadly relevant to any community wanting a way out of poverty, using strategies that are culturally sensitive and professionally solid in the highest degree.

On the opposite coast, Daniel Millette documents the experience of Tsawwassen First Nation, British Columbia, as an example of effective land use planning for communities undergoing rapid change. In a bold and innovative process stewarded by the chief and a sharp team, major economic projects have been undertaken in a context of multiple jurisdictions and stakeholders. The benefit to the community lies at the heart of the effort, with an unwavering focus on the interests of all the stakeholders. In a daunting and complex environment, tenacious leadership has driven a very successful process that acknowledges a culturally important past and an economically viable future.

On the prairies, Muskeg Lake Cree Nation's early success in establishing a vibrant economic development zone in Saskatoon, Saskatchewan, is detailed in Charlotte Bezamat-Mantes's case study. A strong network of project support at the top leadership levels in the municipal, provincial, and federal governments developed over the course of building a business park. This project demonstrates how a strong and dedicated team took advantage of an opportunity to represent their community's interests, using an approach that made the project a win-win for all involved.

CHAPTER 1

◆

How Does First Nations Social
and Economic Development
Contribute to the Surrounding Region?
A Case Study of Membertou

◆

Mary Beth Doucette and Fred Wien

As many of the other chapters in this book demonstrate, First Nations communities are starting to come into their own again. After three centuries of resisting colonial pressure to adapt to European standards and decades of pressure to accept modern-colonial Canadian ideals, many First Nations from coast to coast to coast have become economic change leaders, practising self-determination with increasing success. However, as Wanda Wuttunee and Jerry Asp suggest in the final part of this volume, Indigenous economic development is not a one-sided transformation. As Indigenous economies adapt and transform, so too must those who are co-located in the spaces they inhabit as participants in various social and cultural networks, locally and nationally.

Membertou is a case in point. As a Mi'kmaw community that in the past has faced serious socio-economic issues, Membertou has increasingly built a thriving economic base while constantly reinvesting

in efforts to build toward the community's goals for self-determination.
The Membertou case reflects the central notions of Indigenous thought
discussed in this book's introduction: the community has consistently
embraced a transformation approach that has demonstrated tenacity
and resilience. Numerous academic studies have documented the
economic decisions and strategies that have led to its current influential
and perhaps enviable economic position.[1] However, the kinds of transformation displayed in the Membertou case also required transformation
of the relationships the community has had with others.

Membertou can now be legitimately regarded as a growth centre
in the local and regional economy, which has itself been struggling
with economic depletion for decades.[2] The Membertou story has been
recognized regionally, nationally, and internationally as a model of
First Nations economic development and nation building.[3] Despite the
recognition, the success of Membertou, like that of other First Nations
communities, tends to be framed exclusively as a model for other First
Nations.[4] First Nations' approaches are rarely framed as models of
community economic development with wider applicability, and only
rarely are they framed as models for Canadian or settler communities.[5]

In this case study, we highlight narratives of resilience and tenacity
that are reflected in voices of Membertou staff, adding these narratives
to those of their partners located in the wider region. The resilience
of the Membertou community has allowed it to survive a very challenging history for more than a century. The ongoing displays of
resilience and tenacity exhibited by the current chief and those who
work with him have led to a transition from high levels of poverty,
unemployment, and welfare dependence to being a community with
a strong, self-reliant economic base on the reserve. These efforts have
also changed local social perceptions about Indigenous communities.
The narrative reflected by the Membertou case study challenges the

familiar narratives of Aboriginal economic development as well as narratives of mainstream Canadian economic development that tend to undervalue the level of tenacity and resilience required to achieve the degree of change displayed by the Membertou case.

In this chapter we expand the discussion of partnership beyond corporate and typical economic initiatives to consider how non-Indigenous "partners" describe Membertou's transformation and the impacts it has had on various local relationships, whether they be social, political, or economic. We employ a mixed methods approach, where our analysis draws on primary and secondary, qualitative and quantitative data. To provide a sense of economic context, we refer to previously published studies about Membertou's approach to economic development. We include data from published policy documents, academic literature, and statistical data. At the same time, we consider this data in relation to the information and opinions provided through semi-structured interviews carried out in July and August 2019 with locally recognized Mi'kmaw and non-Mi'kmaw business and other leaders.

"Aboriginal" Economic Development and Asset-Based Community Development

The academic literature on Indigenous economic development has not been voluminous and, until recently, has tended to focus on the consequences of colonization. It has documented the poverty, lack of development, and inequalities of outcomes in relation to surrounding populations. Baseline indicators of employment and income levels are used to compare Indigenous development with that of Canadians. The focus of these analyses highlights gaps between the two populations with the goal of achieving parity. However, moves to achieve parity in the context of Membertou and the Cape Breton Regional Municipality

(CBRM), discussed below, would still mean economic decline and out-migration. Various analysts through the years have advocated for normalizing other indicators that represent a broader conception, focusing on determinants of community health and well-being and paths to equity and economic justice. This approach is especially recommended among those who study Indigenous models of economic development.[6]

Though these advocates are increasingly heard today, they were less prominent in the late 1980s and 1990s, when the Harvard Project on American Indian Economic Development undertook one of the earliest comprehensive studies of economic development in American Indian tribes. The Harvard Project used descriptive case studies to attempt to isolate some of the determining factors that would help explain why some tribes were able to rise above their pre-existing circumstances while others were unable to do so. Some commonly accepted determinants such as resource wealth or location were found to be insufficient in explaining successful transitions, while other factors such as "sovereignty," action-oriented leadership, and the cultural match between a tribe's values and institutions were identified as being more important. The research struck a responsive chord in "Indian country" and spread as well to other settler countries such as Canada, Australia, and New Zealand.

Membertou arose as a case study of a Canadian First Nation that broadly fit the emerging framework set out by the Harvard Project. Membertou is an exemplar of First Nations in Canada that are changing the national dialogue by "proving they can hold their own at the negotiating table."[7] Among other successful models of economic development, Membertou displays a unique mastery in situations of economic change that require a balance of culture and leadership. University-based research centres in Canada have also documented stories that position Membertou as a model. Case studies have been written about Membertou's social leaders[8] and its business model.[9] Even the federal government has been interested in the Membertou model and has commissioned research projects to identify its characteristics.[10] All of these studies cite a variety of critical attributes of successful Aboriginal economic development. In keeping with the Harvard Project's findings, the most consistently listed attributes of success include leadership, accountability, participatory decision making, and human resource capacity, with strategic, comprehensive planning processes.[11]

Within this framework of nation building, Aboriginal economic development has emerged as something different, requiring additional social indicators that are culturally appropriate. Focusing on the action-oriented nature of the transformation processes of Indigenous communities, success is increasingly attributed to wise practices that are more aligned with the goals of Indigenous communities.[12] An additional dimension addressed in this case study is the perceptions of neighbouring Canadians—those who are also impacted by Indigenous transformation.

Membertou Transformation, Then and Now

A common narrative that ran through our interviews was a consensus that Membertou has built a vibrant economic base in the context of strengthening self-determination. The level of change and the impact that has been accomplished in Membertou over the past few decades is made all the more compelling because it is located in a regional economy that has also been struggling economically.[13] Thus, we consider Membertou not only as a success story in its own right but also in terms of its impact on the wider regional economy and society. It is now one of the three largest employers in the CBRM. As such Membertou contributes directly and indirectly to its surroundings in numerous ways.

We consider the economic and social impacts of Membertou's approach to nation building in the CBRM and beyond by first contrasting themes of historical separation with present descriptions of partnership. As we did in the interviews, we look at the transition that was accomplished from two perspectives, employing a two-eyed seeing approach to thinking about regional histories.

Historical Background: Placing Membertou in Context

Occurring over some thirty years, the kinds of nation-building efforts of Membertou and the examples described throughout this book clearly don't occur overnight, nor is success guaranteed. Change efforts have required considerable vision, determination, and tenacity. In this section, we suggest that economic changes have only been possible because they coincided with other shifts in social consciousness about First Nations perspectives of history and justice.

Cape Breton Regional Municipality
Membertou Reserve lands are located within the boundaries of the CBRM and, prior to municipal amalgamation, within the boundaries of the City of Sydney. The current situation and proximity between the two creates an interesting juxtaposition because while Membertou has been growing and expanding both its population and its economy, the surrounding CBRM communities have been facing steady out-migration and economic decline since the late 1970s. The CBRM has become a depleted community, a space that once had a clear economic purpose but is now in doubt about its role. Yet many people refuse to leave because of a strong attachment to the place, its people, and its culture.[14]

Cape Breton Island has great historical significance for Canada. Some of the earliest European settlements were established on the island as military outposts (the Fortress of Louisbourg) or as centres of fishing and trade in the 1700s and 1800s.[15] In the late 1900s and the early part of the twentieth century, the area in and around Sydney was booming. Rich with an abundance of coal, a deep harbour, and an eastern seaboard location, Sydney was ideal for economic development of the coal and steel-making industries. In the 1920s, at the height of the economic boom in Cape Breton, the community was continuing to grow, with population and immigrants arriving from countries all over the world.[16]

The downfall of this growth was the dependence of the economy on core industries that were losing their economic viability. In the 1970s, when the coal mines started closing and steel manufacturing struggled, transition plans were put in place by Canadian governments to help minimize the impact. Various regional development agencies were established to help create and support regional industry clusters, such as the Cape Breton Development Corporation, the Atlantic Canada Opportunities Agency, and the Enterprise Cape Breton Corporation.[17] Despite this federal involvement, the population began declining and with it, the economy. In 1995, the communities of industrial Cape Breton (the area surrounding Sydney) amalgamated to create a single CBRM. Since that time, the municipal government, with federal and provincial assistance, has been trying to address the socio-economic problems of the area, without much success.[18]

In 2003 the CBRM Council considered options for governance reform that would support economic development. All options intended to address multiple underlying issues. Significant change from the status quo would be required. Council was also advised that relying on old-style political approaches rather than grassroots, community-centred approaches would likely constrain new patterns of innovation.[19] After that report was submitted to the CBRM Council, little changed. There continued to be significant and worrying levels of out-migration. Out-migration is a common issue for many rural communities that make up the landscape of Nova Scotia, and the CBRM was facing the most serious challenges in this respect.[20]

Membertou First Nation

Although much has already been written about Membertou over the years, few sources document Mi'kmaw history as part of mainstream economic histories of the region.[21] To provide a sense of the historical relationship for context, we draw from information available through the Membertou Heritage Park. Developed with leadership of the Elders Advisory Committee, the Membertou Heritage Park presents historical narratives displayed through panels and living artifacts.

Membertou's history is initially that of a small group of fewer than 100 people who had established a relatively permanent residence in the mid-1800s along a harbour named Kun'tewiktuk, meaning "at the rock."[22] According to oral histories, it was a place of trade, exchange, and travel for the Mi'kmaq. The panels in the Heritage Park are displays of resilience, tenacity, and social values. They tell stories of workers who faced racism and social segregation with conviction and commitment to community. They make Membertou's perspective on historical relationships between Membertou and Cape Bretoners available publicly. They serve as a foundation for community-centred re-building projects by making Mi'kmaw history visible to anyone who wished to learn.

While the Cape Breton regional economy had experienced decades of growth, the social and political landscape in the 1920s was such that Membertou residents (Mi'kmaq) were largely excluded from work in steel making or coal mining. This limitation of work opportunities, due to the fact that "Indians" were seen as lower-class citizens, meant women often worked as housekeepers and men as general labourers in the area. Social separation was reinforced by racist public policies, like the Indian Act, that were created by the Canadian federal government to encourage enfranchisement of Indians by stripping them of their culture and heritage.

The following three vignettes highlight significant events and relationships in Membertou's history over the past century.

The Relocation of Membertou

Some of the earliest external records of Membertou seen from the outside reveal that Membertou first gained public attention around the 1920s. At that time, the small settlement of Mi'kmaq was located in an economically booming area in one of North America's most active harbours.[23] During that time, there was a move spearheaded by Sydney capitalists to forcibly remove Membertou members through a court-sanctioned process of the Exchequer Court. Membertou residents were forced from their homes, which were located on prime real estate along Sydney harbour, and resettled on some of the least desirable land in the city.[24] The racism of government policies successfully created a sense of separation and distrust between Mi'kmaq and Canadians.

This forcible move demonstrates the settler-colonial attitudes of the early twentieth century. Mainstream economic growth of the region would not include the Mi'kmaq. It also demonstrates the power of the networks of influential individuals who could manipulate federal and municipal systems to force exclusion. The story is now one of resilience and tenacity: in 2016 Membertou purchased the former reserve land, Kun'tewiktuk, and the Medical Arts Building that is now located on it. There are now permanent commemorative displays located throughout the property that tell the story of the community that once was there and its relocation.[25]

Out of Sight, Out of Mind: Social Separation

The following quotes provide impressions of the social relationships that existed decades later. The sense of Membertou's separation was further compounded by physical space, with those living on-reserve being out of sight, and the Mi'kmaq living off-reserve being unseen and misunderstood.

Our interviewees, looking at Membertou from the outside, say that they rarely gave it much thought. While physically located within the City of Sydney's boundaries, Membertou was not part of the municipal structure, being a reserve located on Crown land and governed through provisions set out in the Indian Act. Several interviewees reported that they had little reason to visit the community.

> But I would have to say that the perception at that time and probably in the early 1980s was that Membertou was a community outside of Sydney more or less . . . a community that was in, not decline so much as poverty, and really didn't have a lot going for it. (Cape Breton public servant)

> There was no reason to go to Membertou. Membertou was a reserve off Alexandra Street, self-contained in many ways and not integrated in the business mainstream. (Membertou public servant)

> As somebody from the broader community, I don't think there would have been anything to go there for. Shops, restaurants, commerce, other services and amenities like the [present-day] rink . . . and the bowling alley . . . none of these services would've been there. (Cape Breton CEO)

These quotations present the dominant social impressions of Cape Bretoners working in the local area. There was a similar sense of separation felt by those living in Membertou as well. Interviewees from within Membertou are more likely to describe the external picture in terms of the racism that was evident, and the fear that may have motivated some behaviour.

> When I grew up here, meaning going through the public school system and then working here, there was a pretty strong negative attitude toward Mi'kmaw people, and people of Membertou. You can call it racism; you can call it ignorance. You can almost at some point call it hostility. But it was definitely an invisible wall between Membertou and the rest of Cape Breton. (Membertou leader)

Very few outsiders would visit Membertou. Someone coming to Membertou from outside would do so for a noticeable event, and it must have been painful when even friends from school would be reluctant to visit. There was some intermarriage, but the fear of outsiders extended to these newcomers as well.

> Yeah, very few people came to Membertou. If anybody from the outside came to Membertou, everyone would just stare in amazement. . . . Every once in a while, somebody from Membertou would marry somebody from the outside, and that person would come to live in Membertou. That was quite an event, right? That was so strange. . . . Of course today, now, it doesn't matter. (Membertou leader)

Later, the interviewee described a turning point when Membertou Chief and Council decided to develop a business park on the reserve, despite their fear that business development would attract trouble.

> People were worried about who's going to come from
> downtown to play these machines. Are we inviting crime
> or inviting drugs or inviting bad people? (Membertou
> leader)

Clearly, in the past, the two communities were thought of as separate.

The Wrongful Conviction of Donald Marshall Jr.

While residents of Sydney were experiencing economic growth (boom) followed by rapid de-industrialization and economic decline, Mi'kmaq of Membertou were tackling issues of systemic racism. These issues were notably reflected in public discourse in the 1970s and 1980s as a result of the experiences of a young man, Donald Marshall Jr. The son of Mi'kmaw Grand Chief Donald Marshall was arrested in 1971 at the age of seventeen and imprisoned on a charge of murder. After eleven years in prison, he was acquitted in 1983. Marshall's acquittal brought to light the systemic racism present in the Nova Scotian and Canadian systems of criminal justice. It led to multiple public inquiries and eventually changed the relationship between the Province of Nova Scotia, the federal government, and the Mi'kmaw Nation. It was also a significant process for the Mi'kmaq because it demonstrated how the community would support a member who was abandoned by Canadian society, as were so many other Mi'kmaq and First Nation people. There's no doubt it was a turning point for social justice in the CBRM, Nova Scotia, Canada, and beyond.

In 2015 the Mi'kmaq-Nova Scotia-Canada Tripartite Forum held a Donald Marshall Symposium to review the changes and progress that had been made since. Chief P.J. Prosper was quoted as saying that "Donald Marshall Jr. was a catalyst for evolutionary change in the justice system," and that "through the empowerment of self, we empower the community."[26]

Membertou's Impact on the CBRM

In this section we describe several types of impacts Membertou's transformation has had on local communities. These important infrastructure and other investments and trends have an obvious and direct effect on Membertou itself. However, our interest in this section is to assess what kinds of impacts the developments associated with Membertou are having on the wider CBRM and beyond. We will review what have already been deemed to be critically important aspects of Membertou's development, then discuss what lies behind these outcome indicators—social relationships.

Baseline Economic Indicators

The purely economic and demographic changes in Membertou and their impacts in the Cape Breton region can be compared because there are common, universal indicators to measure them.

Table 1.1 uses Statistics Canada data from the last couple of decades to show relative patterns. Despite the much smaller size of the Membertou population in comparison with the CBRM, the data show a pattern of sharp population increase in Membertou compared with population decline in the Sydney area. The median age at Membertou is very young, almost half that of CBRM. The youth factor is likely one of the roots of the dynamism and energy that we document in this chapter (Table 1.2).

The direct economic impacts that our respondents mentioned emphasized the employment dimension, which is regarded as very significant. While it should be kept in mind that Membertou employees are only a small percentage of the Cape Breton labour force, the indirect

TABLE 1.1	Comparative Population Dynamics in Membertou and the CBRM		
Dimension	Year	CBRM	Membertou
Census population	2001	105,968	621
	2006	102,250	726
	2016	92,285	1,015
Percentage increase (decrease) 2001–16		(8.9)%	63.4%

Source: Statistics Canada, 2001 Census of Population; 2006 Census of Population; 2016 Census of Population.

TABLE 1.2	The Median Age of the Population, the CBRM, and Membertou		
Dimension	Year	CBRM	Membertou
Median age	2001	41.0	23.8
	2006	44.9	26.0
	2016	48.9	26.9

Source: Statistics Canada, 2001 Census of Population; 2006 Census of Population; 2016 Census of Population.

TABLE 1.3	Comparative Employment and Unemployment, the CBRM and Membertou		
Dimension	Year	CBRM	Membertou
Employment rate	2006	44.8	48.5
	2016	43.9	45.8
Unemployment rate	2006	15.9	25
	2016	17.4	20.2

Source: Statistics Canada, 2006 Census of Population; 2016 Census of Population.

impacts of employment are also significant. The employment rate is marginally higher in Membertou, meaning a higher proportion of the population is working than is the case for the CBRM. While the unemployment rate is still higher in Membertou than in the surrounding area, we note that it is decreasing rapidly (Table 1.3).

Direct Employment Creation

Almost all our respondents identified direct employment creation not only for Membertou residents but also for CBRM citizens as perhaps the most obvious form of impact. The Membertou Band employs some 672 persons, and many of these government and commercial jobs are filled by persons from outside the Mi'kmaw community itself.[27] As one director explained,

> Half of our employees are not from the [Mi'kmaw] community. And I think we're fortunate to have great paying jobs with good benefits. We're now a place where people want to work. I think that's an impact, because all those people, like myself, are buying homes, cars, and spending money and you know, getting our groceries and everything else not here on the reserve, but in town. (Membertou public servant)

> I know that they've welcomed people from outside their community to work here. And people are happy and successful and doing well. I know even in their management team they have folks from outside that aren't Indigenous, so I would say they've impacted employment in a positive way for the rest of the Cape Breton Regional Municipality. (Cape Breton public servant)

Spinoff Employment Effects

In addition to generating direct employment, the development projects have spinoff employment effects. In the 2017–18 fiscal year, for example, Membertou spent more than $13 million on new construction projects (Table 1.5). Project expenses include construction materials and professional services that are sourced from the broader CBRM community.

> The employment would be quite high and the impact . . . every new position that they create is another person who's working here, who's spending money in the broader economy of CBRM. It would be a great number to be able to quantify. (Cape Breton CEO)

The employment dimension is an important consideration in Cape Breton where unemployment, out-migration, and "the oil patch commuting" labour force is a social norm.

> It's become a place where everyone knows someone that works [in Membertou] or that is benefiting from [Membertou initiatives]. And they're okay with it now. People are less concerned about the competition between the [Mi'kmaw] community and CBRM and more grateful for all the opportunities our development has provided. I feel a lot more acceptance, and you see it in people's comments. You know, "Chief Terry for mayor."[28] (Membertou public servant)

Infrastructure and Contract Services

Local non-Indigenous economic developers and leaders spoke about Membertou's model of economic development in general terms, as part of the Cape Breton community. In these circles, people highlighted evidence of Membertou's economic development efforts, referencing visible infrastructure developments (Table 1.4) and the services it now provides to the Cape Breton region. When the first business centre opened in 2010, it created space for twelve non-Aboriginal businesses and created an estimated 100 jobs.[29] The second centre, the professional centre, opened across the street in 2013 for six additional tenants. Again, a significant proportion of these positions involve hiring from outside the community.

> And those developments obviously are built out of construction materials and supplies that they need, so the spin-off to the CBRM and probably outside of the CBRM is huge when you look at some of those developments. The new Wellness Centre itself is a wonderful facility. It takes a lot of work and effort, and steel, aluminium, concrete, and whatnot to build these types of facilities. (CBRM Councillor)

> Not all the housing at Membertou is constructed by Aboriginals, they had to use private contractors. . . . You know, the plumbing, the heating, the electrical, the infrastructure, the paving, the ditching, the piping, all that stuff. (Cape Breton education leader)

Table 1.4 provides a list of projects located primarily on-reserve, meaning the primary focus is to improve internal operations and benefit from any revenues from the operations. Over time, there has been an increase in projects and partnerships to broaden the focus to include infrastructure investments in locations off-reserve but that have strategic value to the goals of the organization and the community vision. The

TABLE 1.4	Annual Infrastructure Projects Completed
Year	Project
2005	Youth Centre /C@P (Computer Access Program Site)
2006	Entertainment Centre (bingo hall) Entrepreneur Centre Membertou Gas Bar
2007	Daycare (expansion)
2008	First Fisherman Seafood
2010	Business Centre (1) 201 Churchill Plaza Hospital Connector Road Unama'ki Economic Benefits Office and Entrepreneur Centre Incubator space
2012	Hampton Inn and Pedway Heritage Park and Petroglyphs (new location)* Highway 125 interchange (completed in 2016)*
2013	Membertou Insurance Brokers Memski Projects Inc. (Partnership with Eskasoni)* Professional Centre (204 Churchill Plaza) Wellness Home (Health Centre)
2014	New elementary school (triggering chain reaction—remodelling and moving the daycare, then the Elders Centre) Housing and Public Works Office (Caribou Marsh) Sydport Compound*
2015	Acquisition of Medical Arts Building, located on the Old King's Road Reserve* Acquisition of Sydney Health Park, located at the Cape Breton Regional Hospital*
2016	Sports and Wellness Centre (twin pad ice rink and satellite YMCA)
2018	Bowling lanes Membertou Harbour Front Development partnership with Riverside Development Ltd.* Membertou Partnership with CME (boat building)*

(*) Asterisks indicate infrastructure developments that are located on fee-simple land.

off-reserve projects in Table 1.4 are indicated by an (*). For example, Membertou Geomatics continues to operate from an office in Halifax, and Memski Projects Inc. is a partnership with Eskasoni, and the Highway 125 Interchange refers to the construction of an overpass on Highway 125 that created space for expansion on land that was otherwise physically inaccessible for development. Other real estate purchases like the Sydport compound located in an industrial centre with harbour access, the Health Park building, or the Medical Arts Building each reflect the purposeful effort strategically to move operations to places that make sense for expansion when building economies of scale.

Beyond Infrastructure Development

From 1996 to 2006, Membertou also developed commercial service operations on-reserve, such as the Membertou Gaming Commission, Membertou Market, Membertou Geomatics, Quality Management Services, and the Membertou Trade and Convention Centre. As indicated above, the interviewees appreciate the direct and indirect employment created by the infrastructure developments. However, there is also something about the Membertou approach to providing high-quality professional business services that they recognize.

> They've got a hotel. This is great for conventions. This is great for gatherings. They give a good product, they give good service, this is wonderful. (Cape Breton education leader)

> [They've] created world-class facilities that people want to be at, but I think it really all started under the leadership of the community and direction of Chief Terry Paul. I think [they've] really been able to accept nothing but the best and were able to overcome a lot of barriers to position

Membertou, to be that world-class destination that the rest of the country strives to be. (Cape Breton CEO).

It's a very desirable location . . . and these corporations are saying, "That is where we want to be, in Sydney." (Membertou public servant)

These quotes refer to infrastructure projects that support commercial development efforts, but, as Table 1.4 indicates, the band also invested in socially minded community infrastructure projects in fields such as education, housing, public works, and health.

TABLE 1.5	New Projects and Investments Made by Membertou, 2017–18
$6.5 million	Investment in development of Membertou's harbourfront property
$5.1 million	Construction of lanes at Membertou bowling facility
$1.5 million	Development of boat building facility

Source: Membertou, *Leading by Example: Annual Report 2017–2018* (Membertou, NS: Membertou Band Council, n.d.).

Annually published community reports highlight the strength and resiliency of the Membertou community, and the exercise of self-governance powers have contributed to the acclaim received by Membertou and its development model. The number, size, and diversity of the projects is seen by one interviewee as evidence that Membertou has the ability to sustain the operations it builds and to adapt to market and government changes.

So I think it's a positive thing and I think that Membertou has shown in the past that they can deliver on projects,

> that they create projects that are sustainable, that have economic benefits. So that can only be good for the rest of the island. (Cape Breton public servant)

Membertou's revenue base results in employment and new infrastructure development, but the scale of the impact is questionable as the impact has been relatively modest until very recently. There was a sense of caution about holding Membertou up too high as a saviour of the region. One respondent noted that unemployment rates haven't changed in the region overall, staying in the vicinity of 15 percent (Table 1.3) for several decades:

> So that would say no, unemployment hasn't been helped here in fifty years . . . obviously the Trade Centre employed people. The strip mall we're in employs people. . . . Has Membertou had an effect on employment? Yes, but in the overall picture—and I'll use Cape Breton as an example— for the most part I see Cape Breton having a 15 percent unemployment rate, and if it was 15 percent when I was twenty and it's 15 percent when I'm fifty-four, I don't see where there's been an employment gain there, although there's been jobs created. (CBRM Councillor)

Beyond the Baseline Economic Indicators: Governance and Planning for Transformation

The economic changes in Membertou are visible to many because they correspond to universally accepted indices of growth and parity. However, there are other generally accepted narratives of success that are less consistently defined and not often mentioned. Leadership, strategic planning, and accountable governance are three themes that we highlight as part of the wise practices of development that we discussed in the interviews.

Visionary Leadership

Visionary leadership identifies someone as a change maker, an individual. In Membertou's case, it's Chief Terry Paul. Various terms were used to describe Chief Paul and his leadership style: a diplomat, a supporter, and a visionary. People in the community follow his lead, and those from the CBRM and the broader region respect his opinion. Even after many years of his advocacy work, which involved challenging governments and negotiating contracts, he has their respect.

> I think [you see a] strong sense of leadership and direction under Chief Terry Paul. The support of [his] community in being part of that broader vision . . . being able to realize the dreams that they did have for the community and knowing the possibility, the art of the possible. . . . He's a big supporter of trying to get the municipal government and First Nation communities working together and I think that has had a significant amount of impact across the Island. (Cape Breton CEO)

The election, re-election, and tenure of Chief Terrance Paul have been at the core of Membertou's success. Terry Paul was hired first as an economic development officer in 1979 and was appointed to the role of Band Manager in 1981. He assumed the role of Chief in 1984 and has been re-elected every two years since then. Chief Paul is quite possibly the longest consecutively serving Indian Act chief in the history of Canada. There is an undisputed impression that Membertou has been an innovation catalyst because of Chief Paul's leadership and that of his team. The local business community recognizes the value that Membertou staff bring to the table. There is something about Membertou that displays the "art of the possible," an entrepreneurial spirit, and a magnetic force that draws people together, and they make it look easy.

Obviously, Chief Paul does not work alone.

> I got to know Chief Terry Paul very well and I have a great deal of respect for him. And over the years, of course, they've brought on very good people, they've taken some of their own residents that live here and elevated them and people are educated and trained. (Cape Breton public servant)

Membertou Chief and Council have an unusually low rate of turnover in band elections. This suggests it may be beneficial to look at the organizational governance and management strategies of Membertou over the years to consider if their talent management approach is an indicator of success.

Strategic Goal Setting for Community Building

This consistency of leadership has created an unusual opportunity for long-range planning and embedded institutional knowledge, both of which significantly reduce the need to train or re-train community leaders in the complexity of band and corporate governance. Membertou is drawn to projects that have strategic potential to support the vision of a self-governing Mi'kmaw community and a vibrant, prosperous region. The leadership of Membertou knows they will only be successful if the entire region is successful. Thus they have partnered on a variety of economic development projects and lent support to community causes like the regional library project and by sponsoring community events.

In this consistent leadership context, strategic planning, multi-year development projects, partnership building, trust, and institutional knowledge are encouraged. Change at Membertou has involved developing a strategic vision for the community, taking back control of band operations (self-government), repatriating highly qualified band members living and working elsewhere in Nova Scotia and Canada to key positions in the band's social and business-focused operations, and building a much stronger economic base. Membertou also displays an entrepreneurial spirit that appeals to investors.

Transparent Governance: Quality and Investment in Human Resources
Within Membertou and Mi'kmaw'ki, Chief Paul, Councillors, senior band administrators, directors, and advisors have a wealth of knowledge and flexibility due to own-source revenues necessary to operate at the speed of business and to their understanding of the legal and administrative complexity of the Indian Act system. This has allowed members to develop unique and specialized qualifications in specific public services and industry. Membertou worked to obtain and maintain ISO 9001 certification and created a corporate development arm of the community, maintaining a commitment to community values and achieving clarity of shared purpose. These efforts were continually reinforced through a narrative of self-determination and resistance, making Membertou a community development model whose wise practices can be replicated and adapted to achieve community-driven success.[30]

Strategic Influence Political and Business Investment
The bigger picture is the topic of this next section. Governments and commercial investors are used to talking about both the direct economic impacts and the spinoffs, and that is one reason why Chief Paul has their ear. Membertou has a proven track record of spending money

wisely for the benefit of many. As a result, Membertou now plays an outsized role in regional initiatives and decision making: the mayor comes for advice, Membertou's influence is sought after in getting projects approved, and it has strong relationships with other levels of government.

> And now because Membertou has a degree of prosperity, now people quite often ask Chief Terry or ask Membertou for support for various projects that they want to take to Ottawa or to the province. So now politically Membertou has a role where our voice makes a difference in what happens in Cape Breton or Sydney. (Membertou leader)

However, it would be incorrect to conclude that Membertou's influence is attributable to one individual and his network of contacts. The reputation that Membertou has is built on a track record of quality and strategic, thoughtful risk assessment. Membertou gives advice. Membertou also asks and expects others to be reasonable and professional.

> I think we are working very effectively with the groups and organizations. I mean the proximity now, the irony of it is to be moved off your original land to be positioned up in the undeveloped woods more or less. . . . And now it is the throughway and the centre of all the health care. Corporations are coming. We did an aerial shot and they said, "That makes sense. We're in the heart of it now." It took one hundred years, but now we're in the heart of the development of Sydney. (Membertou public servant)

The expectation of transparency and professionalism is at the heart of the organization, both in decisions about business development and in

public administration. Transparency and professionalism are achieved
through efforts to find consensus or at least keep disagreements within
the community (except for elections).

> There's only one time or one area where the Council really
> votes and that [is] in allocating houses. But every other
> decision is pretty well made by consensus. And consensus
> could mean positive affirmation of a decision. It could
> also mean people abstain. They don't disagree publicly or
> privately. They'll say what they think and leave it at that.
> When it comes time to make an agreement they just
> abstain. . . . But you're right, very rarely would somebody
> take an issue outside the community and go to the press
> or the media. Every once in a while that happens, but it's
> usually people who are seen as not in step with the com-
> munity. . . . Well, in Membertou although it's probably
> more known today, but that was always the way, as far as
> I can remember and I'm going back to the '60s and '70s,
> when we had only two or three members on Council. I
> mean . . . there was this almost inherent built-in way of
> deciding that you had to go out and get as much support
> as you could about your idea, including the Chiefs them-
> selves. They would have to get the support of their Council
> and their community. And so that really hasn't changed
> very much over the years. That's still pretty much the way
> the Council runs. (Membertou leader)

The professional attitude may explain why the Membertou business
model, in which Chief and Council act as the board of directors, has
been successful, with the usual caution to keep an arm's length between
business and politics.[31]

Investing in Relationships

When we asked people to comment on Membertou and the changing relationship between it and the CBRM, their top-of-mind responses tended toward a discussion of activity or leadership. Membertou has become a place of seemingly endless energy and activity: "There's always something happening in Membertou." As we probed the issue, discussions shifted to the various ways that Membertou has been an innovation catalyst. There is something about Membertou that displays the "art of the possible," an entrepreneurial spirit and a magnetic force that draw people together. One of the interviewees even referred to "magic" of Membertou. Zeroing in on the language of "art" and "spirit" and "magnetism" is our focus in this final discussion section.

Here, we strive to demystify the narrative of innovation, suggesting that because of its resilience and tenacity and a commitment to a vision of better social relationships, Membertou worked to build respectful professional and social relations. A strategic partnership approach goes beyond commercial and corporate relationships to relating to people as equals.

A Centre of Activity: Social and Cultural Impacts
Membertou was once a place where no one visited; now the community has become a centre of activity, the place where everyone goes for social events and high-quality business services. It has become a destination of seemingly endless energy and activity.

> People always tell me there's so much always going on in Membertou so it's built kind of an excitement in the whole region . . . I just think people in general . . . were saying, "My God, that's all we hear about when we're away is Membertou this, Membertou that." So, I think we're becoming a place of constant activity in positive news . . .

we're a beacon of positivity around here because really there isn't a lot of positivity around here. It's getting better but I think we'd be certainly at the forefront of it. (Membertou public servant)

Similar sentiments were expressed by those from outside Membertou: "There's always something happening in Membertou." It's a place where people want to go.

Membertou has become this destination. People go to Membertou, right? Whether it's to the Convention Centre, whether it's the rink, whether it's the bowling alley and now hospice. It's fascinating. (CBRM community leader)

Membertou is a place that I frequent with my kids on a daily basis for the facilities and amenities that are there, and we do a tremendous amount of work with Membertou. . . . From the community's perspective, I think Membertou has positioned itself as a destination. . . . I will use hockey as a perfect example. That is everyone's favourite rink to play at. It is the showcase, whenever there's a tournament, everyone wants to play there. (Cape Breton CEO)

It remains transformative, right? . . . You've gone from a place that people were reluctant to go, to a place where I can't wait to come, go to the gym or go to the Convention Centre or for a coffee or—a place that Sydney people are proud of, you know, let alone people that live in Membertou. (Cape Breton public servant)

It was an uncomfortable choice to be transformative. For example, the first time Membertou made a large monetary contribution to the local hospital, it was a controversial decision.

> Bernd really thought that we should begin to share some of our wealth. And I remember the first time he came to the Council he wanted to give $25,000, which for us was a whole bunch of money, to the Cape Breton Regional Hospital Foundation because they were having a big fund-raiser . . . I was on the Council at the time. . . . But he kept saying, you know, Membertou has to show that it's a leader, that it gives back to the community, that yes, we generate wealth from the community but we have to give back. (Membertou leader)

However, Chief Terry trusted the advice of his CEO and the rest of Council grudgingly supported the decision. The good will, the positive energy that was built from that first contribution has since become a central part of Membertou's approach to community development. The community of Membertou is a community of givers. The attitude reflects a philosophy, a culture of being a good neighbour.

> That we should help others when we can. So—and that was part of Terry's philosophy too, he felt we always should be a good neighbour. (Membertou leader)

Investments in Social Development

Membertou's on- and off-reserve investments have not been restricted to narrowly defined economic development projects. They have also involved social, community, or charitable investments. The data from the Membertou annual reports are informative. Each year they provide a bit of a narrative about Membertou as a whole, as a community and an organization. Table 1.6 itemizes investments made on-reserve in the 2015–16 fiscal year. While these investments are on-reserve, some would also have spinoff effects on the off-reserve economy.

Contributions were also made to organizations based off-reserve. Between 2007 and 2016, for example, the Membertou Entertainment Centre alone gave $1,141,000 back to charities in the CBRM.[32] Beneficiaries of these donations included the Kinsmen Club of Sydney, Big Brothers Big Sisters, MADD Cape Breton, Knights of Columbus, Sydney Minor Hockey, Rotary Club of Sydney, Two Rivers Wildlife Park, Cape Breton Crime Stoppers, and Children's Wish Foundation. But Membertou contributes in a variety of other ways as well.

> We don't share enough how much we give back to the community as well. There's barely a week that goes by that I don't get a request on my desk for something. And I think they do a really good job of giving back to the community. . . . I think the greater community sees us at things like being the Prime Ribber sponsor at RibFest. And not only sponsoring things that are in the community, but spending our money and giving to things that do not have a direct impact on Membertou. (Membertou public servant)

One way Membertou does share this kind of information is through its annual reports, synthesizing and presenting information in ways that communicate Membertou's core organizational value that community comes first. For example, Table 1.7 highlights many of the annual operational expenses, reflecting a portion of the millions of dollars that are spent directly within the CBRM and indirectly through employment and service contracts.

TABLE 1.6	Investments in Social Development in Membertou Programming, 2015–16
During the fiscal year, Membertou reinvested $5,133,575 back into the community, as itemized below:	
$ 616,069	Community support
$ 70,073	Seniors
$ 320,117	Sport and youth programs
$ 14,978	Membertou Pow Wow
$ 2,111,500	Annual community donation
$ 642,838	Housing rental subsidies to community members
$ 1,358,000	Housing repairs and maintenance
Overall, 2015–16 was a good year, with all of Membertou's financial objectives being met and the overall financial health of the community remaining strong.	
Source: Membertou, *We Have Arrived: Membertou Annual Report 2015–2016* (Membertou, NS: Membertou Band Council, n.d.).	

TABLE 1.7	Membertou Spending, Contributions within the CBRM Community
$3.43 million	Community and charitable support
$1.37 million	Education and training
$1.22 million	Health care
$7.52 million	Repairs, maintenance, and community infrastructure
$2.05 million	Tax and municipal service contributions to the CBRM
Source: Membertou, *Leading by Example: Membertou 2017–2018 Annual Report,* 19.	

Even to those who were imagining a shift, the degree to which the success of the CBRM has become entangled with the successes of Membertou is still surprising. One interviewee recalled stories of collaboration around events that would not have happened without Membertou's involvement, and of groups depending on its involvement.

> Just for instance we've got the TELUS Cup coming to Membertou the year after next, which is a major national hockey Canada championship for midget Triple A hockey players, right? That wouldn't happen without us. (Membertou public servant)

> The national police chiefs' convention, they even said, "If Membertou doesn't have their hotel ready by a certain day, we're going to have to move the conference to Vancouver." So I think we've added a lot of extra resources to the area that I don't know if the area could attract certain events without our, I'll call it horsepower, behind it. (Membertou public servant)

Despite the organizational transparency, it seems the impression from within the organization is correct—that the general public may not fully appreciate the amount of community giving that Membertou does, or the various ways that it contributes to Cape Breton's prosperity and beyond. This sentiment is reflected in this statement from a CBRM Councillor:

> But Membertou is involved in many different things that are off-island, on the mainland, and beyond Nova Scotia. And I don't know how much the general population really realizes how much Membertou is involved in that broader picture. (CBRM Councillor)

But perceptions are changing. The community development approach discussed above was possible because Membertou has gradually and consistently worked to create a better social relationship between two communities.

Efforts at Relationship Building: Engaging with Tension, Taking Risks

Though there may have been pushback in the early years, Membertou became involved with many projects with organizations that reflect the values and vision of a healthy prosperous community. These have included developing a satellite YMCA, organizing a police chiefs' conference, investing in youth hockey, and other projects on the horizon such as the building of a hospice centre.

Membertou's approach has not been without controversy. There were a few areas where the respondents expressed a range of opinions, reflecting the tensions that still exist in the relationship between Membertou and the surrounding area. Our interviews reflected long-standing Canadian myths and misconceptions about the nexus of economic development and Indigenous rights and policy issues deriving from self-government and land claims that require resilience and tenacity.

The tax situation. Some respondents referred to the argument that Membertou has an unfair advantage because it is believed (incorrectly) the community escapes having to pay any taxes. The tax argument usually fails to acknowledge the other systemic barriers that have disadvantaged and continue to disadvantage the social and economic well-being of Mi'kmaw communities. In fact, in 2015–16 Membertou paid $1.85 million to the CBRM for taxes and municipal service agreements, a figure that rose to $2.05 million in 2017–18. The following statement from a Membertou employee demonstrates the tax situation is complex and requires education and communication:

It just depends on the time and the purchase and the designation of the land. This was designated a commercial zoned property and owned, then what happens after that Membertou has the right to change those designations if they so wish and so on. But for now, when they acquire, the properties have two separate and distinct designations of whether it's Membertou commercial or Membertou reserve, and there are different business models that happen on each. (Membertou public servant)

So while Membertou works to navigate the complexity of multiple jurisdictional rules and government policies, it also educates its partners, suppliers, and vendors about the business implications of unfamiliar laws that only apply on First Nations reserves.

Small business owners, especially if we compete in [their] space, think that we have the upper hand because of taxation. Or—on the real estate side of things too they think that we can offer better rental rates because we don't pay property tax. But I think now the word is out, what we charge for class A space is pretty equivalent to what somebody would pay downtown plus the property taxes. So the only difference is the money is going into our pocket. . . . So yes, . . . sometimes [the tax situation] is why some-body wants to partner with us, obviously. (Membertou public servant)

Competition. Related to this is the question sometimes raised in the past of why something should go to Membertou rather than downtown, reflecting the perspective that social and economic development is a zero-sum game, a competition between jurisdictions. But not everyone sees it this way:

Some people off-reserve complain about the advantage Membertou has that they can't compete . . . so I think Membertou has an advantage. There's a part of me thinking they deserve an advantage. (Cape Breton community leader)

Growth is a good thing and if you can grow your conference space from smaller to medium-size to large-size because you have a newer space that can accommodate that, that's got to be good for everybody. It should be irrelevant where it's built, whether it's built in Membertou, built in North Sydney, built in Glace Bay, whether it's built in Port Hawkesbury. . . . If we can accommodate bigger events and larger opportunities to benefit our municipality and our island as a whole, that should be the goal. It shouldn't be about who's building it, where it's at and competition . . . you want the cluster to be able to be successful. (CBRM Councillor)

Scale of operations. We also heard the perception that Membertou can only achieve what it does because it is small. It has been suggested that Chief Paul could run for the municipal mayor's office, for example, but the view is also advanced that people are underestimating the complexity of municipal operations. However, as one interviewee demonstrated, it's all a matter of perspective:

And a lot of people say, you know, Membertou should be running the city, Membertou should be running the municipality. And I don't say this being disrespectful, but it's a whole lot different running an area the size of Membertou than running an area that's the size of the municipality. Not to say that Chief Terry Paul couldn't do that—

> absolutely, he's done a tremendous job here. But . . . the
> automatic assumption is, I think, that if they can move
> Membertou forward, then they could move everybody
> forward if they run the municipality. Hence, if they were
> premier, they could maybe move everything ahead in the
> province . . . I don't know that it's that easy. (CBRM
> Councillor)

Any comparison of Membertou and the CBRM also needs to recognize that the two jurisdictions are structured quite differently. The CBRM basically provides services to its citizens, such as policing, sidewalks, refuse collection, and the like. It has at most a facilitative role in promoting economic development by establishing industrial parks, providing water and sewers, and creating a supportive business environment. Membertou's government, on the other hand, as we have seen, goes well beyond service provision and plays a direct role in commercial development, serving as business owners, property developers, source of financing, and a host of other activities. This feature gives Membertou much more authority and flexibility over the economic developments that take place within and outside the reserve boundaries, even while a smaller private sector continues to exist and flourish.

We heard the sentiment expressed that the Province of Nova Scotia is not invested in seeing Cape Breton succeed, that provincial leaders make it difficult, put up barriers, and are only concerned about the Halifax Regional Municipality. Membertou, on the other hand, can be successful because the Province doesn't interfere.

> I feel optimistic, more so than I have in the past, of the
> opportunities that exist for that to start to work . . . [in]
> that way, but there has to be a change in how senior levels
> of government work with us, partner with us, and fund

us. And that's been an ongoing issue obviously for many
years, and I think that has to also change to be able to
change CBRM as a whole, to put us in the direction of
15 percent to 12 percent to 8 percent, or however at all
we can get our unemployment down. (CBRM Councillor)

The Cape Breton Development Challenge. Without a doubt, there is a sense
among people interviewed that Membertou is contributing to the
well-being of the broader community. And yet, when the question was
posed about the extent to which Membertou is impacting the employment rates on Cape Breton or in the CBRM, it was clear that Membertou
plays a small part in a much bigger challenge. The attitudes represented
by the quotes are also evidence of the social norms of Cape Breton.
A culture that some interviewees described as a dependency attitude,
it's also a culture born of long-standing frustration and tension with
the provincial capital of Halifax and the federal government in Ottawa.

The biggest problem we have in Cape Breton is the culture.
What I mean by culture is how we think and how we
behave and the fact that we were predominantly an industrial culture. So therefore, a one-horse town . . . and then
the government took us over. . . . So there's this whole
dependency. So when I say we're desperate, it's that dependency that makes us desperate. (Cape Breton community
leader)

From inside Membertou, the difference in results may be attributed to
a different approach.

The municipality is in a desperate state of help, help, help,
help, and they're coming in with that negative desperate
attitude. Whereas Membertou was brought in a couple of

> weeks ago to do an analysis on a potential new business
> venture, and it's sort of very relaxed, "Well, let's take a
> look at them. Does it make sense?" It just seems to be a
> much smoother, not so much desperate [approach] and
> when we meet in the middle, that's when the business
> community and so on are saying, "Who do you want to
> deal with?" (Membertou public servant)

The comparison between the scale of operations and discussions of
political clout are not new. However, it is helpful to look at the situations
and approach from multiple perspectives, and to think about Membertou
from an external vantage point.

> Yeah, and it's almost a desperate—"We have to do some-
> thing. We have to do it now," and it's not relaxed and
> they're making harsh and hasty decisions, and they're not
> looking at maybe it's something very simple that we could
> be doing. But the attitude, when Membertou comes to the
> table, it's a very relaxed professional and—the accounting
> and the financial end of it is well analyzed, and sometimes
> we have the resources to take a little bit more risk to get
> into this and if we do, let's give it a look. So the approach
> I think from the community is much different when it
> comes to Membertou. (Membertou public servant)

The way Membertou staff navigate government bureaucratic processes
that tend to take months was described by way of the following example.

> For example, we turned around a permit for our harbour
> project in eight days, which, you know, I know another
> group was waiting three and a half months. There was a

> lot of speculation about how did that happen. (Membertou
> public servant)

Addressing the assumption many people make that Chief Terry leverages political clout, the interviewee explained the process they followed to obtain approval for particular projects. It involved asking clarifying questions about the processes and decision points required to get approval. It also involved explaining the business plan and the risk of missing out on the opportunity if the decision was delayed. All the decision makers would be invited to meet around the table and discuss the opportunity.

> And it's a very last resort to have Terry pick up the phone.
> It's been done. Kind of to see where something is. . . . I
> don't believe the way we do things is about jumping over
> someone. Instead of jumping over someone, you can all
> come together and get it figured out. And I think that's
> worked well for us. Saved some time. (Membertou public
> servant)

A Different Model of Governance and Decision Making?

When we set out on this research project, we anticipated many of the impacts described in the previous section. However, what was surprising to us was the perception advanced by several of our interviewees that the impact of Membertou goes beyond jobs, investments, and social spending. Membertou also demonstrates a different approach to governance and decision making, a different model that the wider Cape Breton region and beyond could learn from. We summarize the essence of this approach by highlighting the simultaneous investments in both wise business practices and social relationships, or being neighbourly.

From a business and economic perspective, people are starting to realize that companies and governments alike are more likely to invest in or support a project if Membertou is at the table. It used to be because of government funding, but now it's because Membertou brings a sense of sophistication. It has a positive track record for doing things that are high quality. Local organizations approach Membertou for various forms of support because Membertou is generous with time and expertise.

> I think organizations look to us to help them with their causes. And I think that the Council's really giving in that regard. . . . And I think that's a really good quality for an organization to have. (Membertou public servant)

> We're doing it again very methodically. The business analysis is right on the mark. Does it make money? It doesn't, but it does make sense to get into it economically. (Membertou public servant)

And Membertou's approach to business relationships carries through to formal and informal social relationships.

> We got to know people from all across the province. I think opening up the corporate office in Halifax was one way of really reaching out to people, and meeting them in their own backyards and working with them directly. That was controversial because we were paying class A rent in downtown Halifax and we could pay for several houses on-reserve for the rent we paid each year. But we had the corporate office for ten years and during that time, I think we earned back our investment with the relationships, the reputation,

> the ability to meet people. . . . That's been a real learning
> journey for Membertou. (Membertou leader)

Changing Perceptions?

Existing conceptions of First Nations development tend to focus primarily on what is happening within the First Nation itself, on the
employment and businesses that are or are not created, on investments
in the community, and on barriers that stand in the way of progress.
The results of our interviews reveal that this perspective is too narrow.
There is an external dimension to First Nations development that is
extremely important, as the Membertou story illustrates. In fact, the
message is that First Nations development is good for the surrounding
region in many ways—as a source of jobs, contracts for services,
provision of on-reserve services that can be accessed by the wider
community, investments in off-reserve businesses, and charitable contributions. Rather than resisting the efforts of First Nations to get ahead
on the grounds that it will mean unfair competition, First Nations
should be encouraged to use the levers at their disposal (tax status,
set-aside programs, Aboriginal and treaty rights) because their success
will benefit not only the First Nation but also the surrounding area.

The Membertou story, and those of certain other First Nations in
the Atlantic region and across Canada demonstrate that even the First
Nations that have charted new paths to well-being are interpreted in
a narrow framework, deemed to hold lessons only for other First Nations
and not for Canadian society more generally. We began this chapter
by suggesting that exploring the Membertou case brings to light a shift
in social consciousness that has the potential to inform the national
dialogues in a significant way. Further, by considering not only the
social and economic influences Membertou has had on the region, but

also the way people describe these influences today, we can contemplate the potential this kind of Indigenous nation building has for the well-being of Canada as a whole.

The way people look at and speak of Membertou now is not the same as it was a century ago when the Mi'kmaw settlement along King's Road was seen as bad for business. We suggest that we review and accept the importance of what has been written by those who have studied Membertou's development approach in the past. There is much we can learn about Aboriginal Community Economic Development, using the lens of wise practices to consider the leadership, the tenacity and resilience of Chief Paul, and alongside him the Membertou administrative team and community who supported his vision. We also suggest that by focusing on changing the external perceptions in terms of business partnerships as well as in being a good neighbour, Membertou has gone beyond those practices that are typically discussed, envisioning a new long-term relationship between the Mi'kmaq and the rest of the CBRM.

Our interviews reveal that informed observers in the CBRM were inspired by the Membertou example, not only in terms of the business and other successes achieved but also in providing a picture of a different model of proceeding, a different style of governance and decision making that held hope and promise for jurisdictions outside of Membertou itself.

Finally, our interviews suggest that Membertou's success is a powerful driver of changed attitudes and perceptions. It has taken a long time—three decades or more—but there has clearly been a sea change in how Membertou is regarded by the outside world. Supporting First Nations transitions of the kind we have documented at Membertou is a powerful antidote to racism and related attitudes.

NOTES

✦

1   Keith Brown, Megan Finney, Janice Esther Tulk, Mary Beth Doucette, Natasha
     Bernard, and Isabella Yuan, "Membertou Always Wanted to Succeed: The
     Membertou Business Model," *Journal of Aboriginal Economic Development* 8, no. 1
     (2012): 32–48; Mary Beth Doucette, "Membertou Heritage Park: Community
     Expectations for an Aboriginal Cultural Heritage Centre" (research project, Cape
     Breton University, 2008); Harvey Johnstone, "Membertou First Nation
     Indigenous People Succeeding as Entrepreneurs," *Journal of Enterprising
     Communities, Bradford* 2, no. 2 (2008): 140–50; Bob Kayseas, K. Hindle, and R.B.
     Anderson, *Fostering Indigenous Entrepreneurship: A Case Study of the Membertou First
     Nation, Nova Scotia, Canada* (2006); Jacquelyn Thayer Scott, *Doing Business with the
     Devil: Land, Sovereignty, and Corporate Partnerships in Membertou Inc.* (Halifax: Atlantic
     Institute for Market Studies, 2004); Fred Wien, "Profile of Membertou First
     Nation, Nova Scotia," in *Growth of Enterprises in Aboriginal Communities*, ed. Stelios
     Loizides, Robert Anderson, and Conference Board of Canada (Conference Board
     of Canada, 2006), 19–20.

2   Harvey Johnstone and Doug Lionais, "Depleted Communities and Community
     Business Entrepreneurship: Revaluing Space through Place," *Entrepreneurship and
     Regional Development* 16, no. 3 (2004): 217–33.

3   Stephen Cornell, "Accountability, Legitimacy, and the Foundations of Native
     Self-Governance," in *Rebuilding Native Nations: Strategies for Governance and
     Development*, PRS 93-1 (Cambridge, MA: Malcolm Wiener Centre for Social
     Policy, Harvard Kennedy School, Harvard University, 1993), 1–34.

4   Frank Iacobucci, introduction to *Uneasy Partners: Multiculturalism and Rights in
     Canada*, ed. Janice Gross Stein (Waterloo, ON: Wilfrid Laurier University Press,
     2007).

5   Some instances of reframing First Nations' approaches to community economic
     development as possible models for non-Indigenous Canadian communities
     include Wanda Wuttunee, "Aboriginal Perspectives on the Social Economy," in
     *Living Economics: Canadian Perspectives on the Social Economy, Co-operatives, and Community
     Economic Development*, ed. J.J. McMurtry (Toronto: Emond Montgomery
     Publications, 2010), 179–201; and Fiscal Realities Economics, "Stage 2:
     Economic and Fiscal Benefits Generated in Urban ATRs," in *Improving the
     Economic Success of Urban Additions to Reserves* (Gatineau: National Aboriginal
     Economic Development Board, 2015), http://www.naedb-cndea.com/reports/
     IMPROVING-THE-ECONOMIC-SUCCESS-OF-URBAN-ADDITIONS-TO-
     RESERVES.pdf.

6   Robert B. Anderson, Leo Paul Dana, and Theresa Dana, "Indigenous Land
     Rights, Entrepreneurship, and Economic Development in Canada: 'Opting-In' to
     the Global Economy," *Journal of World Business* 41, no. 1 (2006): 45–55; Robert
     Hamilton, John Borrows, Brent Mainprize, Ryan Beaton, and Joshua Ben David
     Nichols, eds., *Wise Practices: Exploring Indigenous Economic Justice and Self-determination*

(Toronto: University of Toronto Press, 2021); Wuttunee, "Aboriginal Perspectives."

7   Stephen Cornell, Miriam Jorgensen, Joseph P. Kalt, and Katherine Spilde Contreras, "Seizing the Future: Why Some Native Nations Do and Others Don't," in *Rebuilding Native Nations: Strategies for Governance and Development*, ed. Miriam Jorgensen (Tucson: Native Nations Institute for Leadership, Management, and Policy, 2003), 296–320.

8   Gabrielle Donnelly, *Women of Membertou* (Indigenous Women in Community Leadership Case Studies, International Centre for Women's Leadership, Coady International Institute, St. Francis-Xavier University, Antigonish, NS, 2012), https://coady.stfx.ca/wp-content/uploads/pdfs/womensLeadership/IWCL_case_studies/Women_of_Membertou.pdf.

9   Rachel Starks, Janice Esther Tulk, Tamara Young, Mary Beth Doucette, Trevor Bernard, and Cheryl Knockwood, *Managing Land, Governing for the Future: Finding the Path Forward for Membertou* (Dartmouth, NS: Atlantic Policy Congress of First Nations Chiefs Secretariat, 2013), https://www.cbu.ca/wp-content/uploads/2019/08/FINAL-ManagingLandGoverningfortheFuture-FindingthePathForwardforMembertouMarch2014.pdf.

10   Keith G. Brown and Janice Esther Tulk, "Membertou Pedway: A Case Study of Challenges in Aboriginal Economic Development" (Purdy Crawford Chair in Aboriginal Business Studies, Cape Breton University, Sydney, NS, March 2012), https://cbufaces.cairnrepo.org/islandora/object/cbu%3A1924.

11   Janice Esther Tulk, *Guiding Principles for Aboriginal Economic Development* (Purdy Crawford Chair in Aboriginal Business Studies, Cape Breton University, Sydney, NS, 2013), https://www.cbu.ca/wp-content/uploads/2019/08/Guiding_Principles_for_Aboriginal_Economic_Development_sm.pdf; Wien, "Profile of Membertou First Nation."

12   Brian Calliou, "A Wise Practices Approach to Indigenous Law, Governance, and Leadership: Resistance against the Imposition of Law," in *Wise Practices: Exploring Indigenous Economic Justice and Self-Determination*, ed. R. Hamilton, J. Borrows, B. Mainprize, R. Beaton, and J.B.D. Nichols (Toronto: University of Toronto Press, 2021), 19–43.

13   Johnstone and Lionais, "Depleted Communities."

14   Ibid.

15   "Cape Breton, Nova Scotia—History," Fortress Louisbourg Association: Association de La Forteresse-de-Louisbourg, http://www.fortressoflouisbourg.net/Overview/mid/12 (accessed 24 October 2019).

16   Johnstone and Lionais, "Depleted Communities."

17   Gertrude Anne MacIntyre, *Perspectives on Communities: A Community Economic Development Roundtable* (Sydney, NS: University College of Cape Breton Press, 1998).

18   "CBRM Amalgamation—Twenty Years Later," editorial, *Cape Breton Post*, 30 July 2015, http://www.capebretonpost.com/Opinion/Editorials.

19 Wade Locke and Stephen G. Tomblin, "Good Governance, a Necessary but Not Sufficient Condition for Facilitating Economic Viability in a Peripheral Region: Cape Breton as a Case Study" (discussion paper prepared for the Cape Breton Regional Municipality, Memorial University of Newfoundland, St. John's, NL, 2003).

20 Nova Scotia Commission on Building Our New Economy, *Now or Never: An Urgent Call to Action*, Report of the Nova Scotia Commission on Building Our New Economy (Halifax: Nova Scotia Commission on Building Our New Economy, 2014), https://www.onens.ca/sites/default/files/editor-uploads/now-or-never.pdf.

21 William C. Wicken, "Moving into the City: The King's Road Reserve and the Politics of Relocation," in *The Colonization of Mi'kmaw Memory and History, 1794–1928: The King v. Gabriel Sylliboy* (Toronto: University of Toronto Press, 2012), 202–28.

22 "Kun'tewiktuk," Ta'n Weji-sqalia'tiek: Mi'kmaw Place Names Digital Atlas and Website, accessed 24 October 2019, http://mikmawplacenames.ca/.

23 Rannie Gillis, "Historical Significance," Novaporte, accessed 24 October 2019, https://novaporte.ca/sydney-nova-scotia/.

24 Brown et al., "Membertou Always Wanted to Succeed"; Scott, *Doing Business with the Devil*.

25 In October 2016, the Membertou Communications department issued an eight-page story titled "Kings Road Reserve 100 Years Later." They also held a public event on 23 October 2016 to celebrate the significant event.

26 Elizabeth Patterson, "Donald Marshall Jr.'s Legacy Continues," *Cape Breton Post*, 14 January 2015, http://www.capebretonpost.com/news/local/donald-marshall-jrs-legacy-continues-7940/.

27 Membertou, *We Have Arrived: Membertou Annual Report 2015–2016* (Membertou, NS: Membertou Band Council, n.d.).

28 Throughout the chapter Chief Terrance Paul is also referred to by his less formal title, Chief Terry.

29 Nova Scotia, Communications, "Membertou First Nation Opens Business Centre," news release, 23 June 2010, https://novascotia.ca/news/release/?id=20100623006.

30 Cynthia Wesley-Esquimaux and Brian Calliou, *Best Practices in Aboriginal Community Development: A Literature Review and Wise Practices Approach* (Banff, AB: Banff Centre, 2010).

31 Cornell, Jorgensen, Kalt, and Contreras, "Seizing the Future"; Scott, *Doing Business with the Devil*.

32 Membertou, *We Have Arrived*, 10.

CHAPTER 2

◆

Incremental Planning:
The Tsawwassen First Nation Experience

◆

Daniel M. Millette

I beg to introduce to you the bearer of this, the chief of the
Tchwassen village. He and His people are very anxious to
see their reservation staked out by the government.
Father L. Fouquet, Oblate Missionary, 1865[1]

S ituated within the Greater Vancouver region of British Columbia's
lower mainland, the Tsawwassen First Nation is poised to become
one of the area's principal actors in the realm of economic development.
Since the signing of the Tsawwassen First Nation Final Agreement—
the first contemporary urban treaty in the country—several economic
development activities have been negotiated, all within a comprehensive
land use planning strategy initiated by former Chief Kim Baird that
can only be referred to as "innovative" and "bold."[2] Several multi-
million dollar projects are in the works, including a $400 million
shopping mall, an inland port, and a series of subdivisions that will
eventually accommodate 4,000 new residents. In terms of community

planning in Canada, it can readily be argued that the Tsawwassen First Nation is undergoing one of the most challenging processes in present-day planning practice, demonstrating its tenacity. The planning process of integrating the First Nation lands within a peri-urban framework while maintaining a progressive, jurisdictional approach that places traditional values, transparency, and community well-being at the forefront of several important and at times competing planning tenets is ambitious, to say the least. The objective, for Chief Baird, was to create an economy that welcomes investment while attracting families, within a First Nations regime that is fair to all stakeholders despite the challenges.

The journey has been a long one, having its roots in early colonial times, with the former Chief's great-grandfather's eventual address to the McKenna-McBride Commission, adhering to the British Columbia Treaty Commission's Treaty Process, becoming a signatory to the Framework Agreement on First Nation Lands Management, and culminating in what would arguably be one of the most significant urban treaties in Canadian history. The Tsawwassen First Nation Final Agreement (TFNFA) has provided for a complex blend of lands whose uses together must satisfy needs that extend from the culturally important past into an economically viable future. The land use planning process for this very special set of lands and stakeholders was therefore not straightforward, having required an incremental approach that is novel and worth consideration for other communities undergoing rapid change.

By the time the above-quoted letter of Oblate missionary Fouquet reached the Lands and Works Department in New Westminster in 1865, colonial activities were already shaping what would become the Tsawwassen reserve. We get a glimpse of some of the difficulties from as early as 1860, when settlers were removing official markers of Indian lands. A letter by the Chief Commissioner of Lands and Works, R. Moody, for example, refers to an incident during which parcel boundary posts that had been installed on a previous day were removed by a settler who installed a fence to mark the same lands as his own.[3] Father Fouquet certainly saw urgency in establishing a set parcel of land for the Tsawwassen people: pre-emption, the mechanism through which lands could be appropriated by colonials, was rapidly locking away lands around the traditional Tsawwassen village near the southern reaches of the expanse between the mouth of the Fraser River and Point Roberts.[4] The process of pre-emption was closed to Indigenous peoples and as lands became tied to others, it became urgent for an official survey of the reserve to be carried out. The reserve's external boundaries were set in 1871 and the Tsawwassen reserve formally established at 290 hectares,[5] without any detailed consideration for site actualities or community needs (Figure 2.1). This was typical of reserve surveying, leaving descendants of Aboriginal populations across Canada to fight for land rights for generations to follow.

Later, in 1914, Tsawwassen Chief Harry Joe appealed to the McKenna-McBride Commission for additional lands but was refused. Chief Joe would not live to see the results of what he had initiated, but in the early

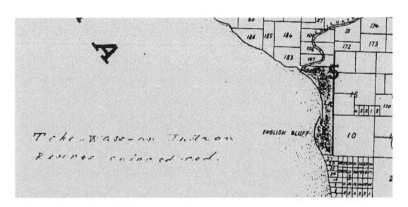

FIGURE 2.1. "Tche-wass-an Indian Reserve Confirmed" (1878). Source: Image courtesy of the Tsawwassen First Nation Archives.

2000s his great-granddaughter, Chief Kim Baird, would lead her community in a set of actions that would include adhesion to the Framework Agreement on First Nation Land Management (the Framework Agreement)[6] and culminate in the TFNFA,[7] which included a set of lands—the Tsawwassen Treaty Settlement Lands—totalling 724 hectares.

The land considerations within the treaty negotiations and the resulting treaty were complex, with several stakeholders and competing needs. Within the regional context, the land base is relatively small: land for economic development opportunities, including commercial uses, market housing, and housing for Tsawwassen community members was required. All of the lands are vital in terms of Tsawwassen heritage, with archaeological evidence dating occupancy to—depending on interpretation— between 4,000 and 9,000 years; heritage sites therefore required assessment and protection.[8] At the same time, approximately half of the pre-existing Agricultural Land Reserve (ALR) lands remained within the land use designation, and the other half removed. Adding to the complexities, public misconceptions around issues such as consideration for what was then the potential expansion of the neighbouring port cluttered the process.[9]

The end result was a "new" Tsawwassen land base that straddles two strategic road accesses: Highway 17, leading to the Tsawwassen Ferry Terminal, and Deltaport Way, leading to the Roberts Bank port and terminal; a railway corridor also links the lands to broader national and international transportation networks (Figure 2.2). All of the lands have been transferred in "fee simple" to the Tsawwassen First Nation, with Certificate of Possession (CP) lands registered within the provincial land title registry.[10] The Tsawwassen treaty lands together form an intricate set of parcels and parcel holdings that must consider traditional uses, economic growth, and the public-private realm within very limited cultural and geographical space.

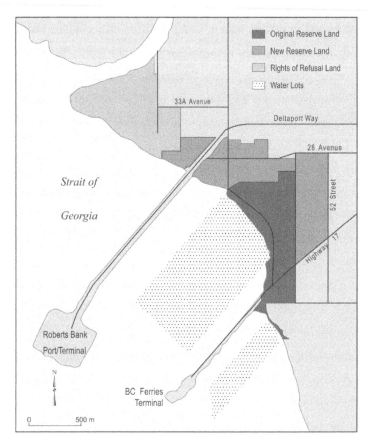

Map legend:
- Original Reserve Land
- New Reserve Land
- Rights of Refusal Land
- Water Lots

Labels on map: 33A Avenue, Deltaport Way, 28 Avenue, 52 Street, Highway 17, Strait of Georgia, Roberts Bank Port/Terminal, BC Ferries Terminal, N, 0 500 m

FIGURE 2.2. Tsawwassen Final Agreement Lands. *Source:* Author. Map by Weldon Hiebert.

The Challenge

As early as 2004, Chief Baird realized that regional-locational advantages would be central to her community's need to generate long-term
community sustainability. As treaty negotiations progressed, so too did
the frequency with which economic development opportunities
increased. Negotiations with the development of Deltaport's Roberts
Bank $47 million container terminal, for example, were well underway
during treaty negotiations, and the resultant agreement would have to
fit within any land use planning process. At the same time, other entities
competed against any potential economic development considerations:

the Agricultural Land Commission, for instance, highlighted the ALR designation over much of the proposed treaty settlement lands. Other groups, such as those protecting migratory bird corridors and nesting grounds, signalled their interests. Regionally, the Greater Vancouver Regional District (GVRD) was working on its own planning strategy— the "Liveable Region Strategy"—and initially hoped to include the Tsawwassen First Nation's lands as green space and farmland. The neighbouring Municipality of Delta was concerned over potential growth, given its stated limited servicing capacities.

Within the Tsawwassen First Nation community, several voices were making themselves heard: CP holders vied for development opportunities, while non-CP holders raised concerns over potentially rapid development. Both groups wanted community amenities included and cultural and traditional values to be at the core, while the same two groups wanted a planning process that would include all members. Land use planning was thus central to any treaty outcome, and it became clear that whatever the process, it would have to be inclusive of *all* interested parties, with Tsawwassen First Nation members guiding it.[11]

The community planning process that was ultimately devised was an incremental and cumulative one, beginning with the powers acquired by the First Nation as signatory to the Framework Agreement and, eventually, as a partner with Canada in the TFNFA.

The Tsawwassen Land Use Plan: The Framework Agreement on First Nation Land Management

In 2003, the Tsawwassen Chief and Council decided that while persistently negotiating within the British Columbia Treaty Process, the First Nation would become a signatory to the Framework Agreement, enabling a land code to be developed, complete with a set of community-specific laws that would help govern the nation's lands.[12] The Chief and her Council felt that the nation should broaden its jurisdiction in light of what the treaty had thus far accomplished. A key point is that the Framework Agreement is an innovative agreement offering the opportunity for First Nations jurisdiction and control (legal authority) over reserve lands and resources to First Nations who become signatories to it. At a minimum, this removes some 25 percent of the Indian Act provisions over the First Nation and thus provides the nation with much greater flexibility in terms of lands governance, including the efficient and immediate development of any type of land-related plan.[13] Signatory First Nations take the necessary steps to ratify the Framework Agreement through the drafting and enacting of a land code and by proceeding to reassume control over their lands and resources.[14]

For the Tsawwassen First Nation, this would represent a major step toward lands governance autonomy, all the while establishing a minimum threshold in terms of negotiating lands management and governance within the treaty. Nowhere, outside of a few modern treaties and self-governing agreements, do we find greater First Nations autonomy for the governance over reserve lands in Canada. First Nations operating under the Framework Agreement can define land use planning processes that can be managed internally and be completely controlled by the same community. This can include any planning process that the First Nation might choose. Such an approach might consider traditional Indigenous planning concepts blended with Western planning principles that together result in a land use plan that corresponds more closely to the First Nation's planning ideals.[15]

Operating under the Framework Agreement, community involvement in developing a land use plan is of key importance. For the Tsawwassen First Nation, while a significant amount of reserve lands were held by CPs, the nation's Chief and Council wanted as much community member involvement as possible. At the same time, treaty negotiating assessments were required: Would the proposed set of treaty lands be adequate for the Tsawwassen First Nation's community needs? Thus the land planning exercise consisted of actual planning, paralleled by hypothetical planning in order to test treaty possibilities. The resulting process is outlined in Figure 2.3.

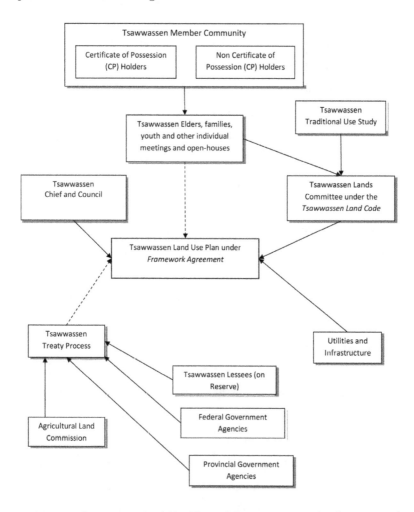

FIGURE 2.3. Tsawwassen Land Use Planning Process—Input under the Framework Agreement on First Nation Land Management (2005–6). *Source:* Image prepared by author.

Community input was inclusive, with several overlapping opportunities for Tsawwassen members, whether CP holders or not, to provide
comments or land use suggestions.[16] In this way, Tsawwassen Elders,
youth, Chief and Council, families, and individuals were invited to
participate.[17] Thus, the first level of opportunity for community input
took place at community meetings, open to all Tsawwassen members.
The information was generally channelled through a Lands Committee,
with the planner in attendance at meetings, recording community
member suggestions and comments.[18] The Lands Committee was made
up of representative community groups—families, Elders, youths,
Chief and Council members, CP holders and non-holders. The com-
position of the committee therefore made it relatively straightforward
to facilitate consultation meetings between the different community
components.

Family meetings, for example, were arranged by the corresponding
family members on the Lands Committee. Similarly, meetings with
individuals, who may or may not have wanted to be public with their
land use ideas, were facilitated by the Lands Committee. Chief and
Council, although directly providing input to the planner, were connected to the Lands Committee with one member of Chief and Council
being a member of the Lands Committee. A comprehensive Traditional
Use Study, undertaken earlier, also informed the process in terms of
Traditional Use Sites and heritage values.[19] Related to what were at
the time intense treaty negotiations, the planning process also included
a component whereby specific treaty land options were discussed and
tested. Options and considerations based on federal and provincial
government agencies were explored within the process; this included
what were reserve lands at the time as well as what were then "potential
treaty settlement lands." As the Agricultural Land Commission's
mandate applied to some of the lands under consideration for treaty,

commission staff were also provided with opportunity for comments. Finally, the planner, assisted by a community member, dealt directly with public utilities, servicing, and infrastructure.

The process therefore focused on inclusivity on as many levels as possible, while operating as a test site for the more expansive set of lands that might eventually come through treaty. In essence, the land use planning process developed under the Framework Agreement was devised in part to accommodate what were largely unknowns: CP holder agreements with third parties, port expansion details, potential commercial interests, and so on. The land use plan that was therefore generated was the first phase of the broader process (Figure 2.4). In recognition that there had never been a detailed land use plan,[20] one section of the reserve lands was grandfathered within what is referred to as the Tsawwassen village site. Fronting the same zone is the foreshore, designated as an "Environmentally Sensitive" zone. In effect, much of the area is a marsh that had cumulated over several decades, resulting from the two causeways leading to the coal/container port to the north and the British Columbia Ferries terminal to the south. Another zone was designated as "Environmentally and Culturally Sensitive," sited along the slope of the bluff (English Bluff). One slightly controversial zone was the "CP Uses" zone. This was a somewhat temporary compromise agreed to by the parties, given the economic development potential of the land coupled to the strategic realities of treaty negotiations. The precise types of land use for this zone were therefore undetermined at the time of the land use plan development, although it was agreed that specific uses would have to be approved on a case-by-case basis prior to any development taking place.

Along the highway leading to the British Columbia Ferries terminal, the land was zoned as "Commercial" (status quo and mid-density). The Tsawwassen member community felt that whether there would

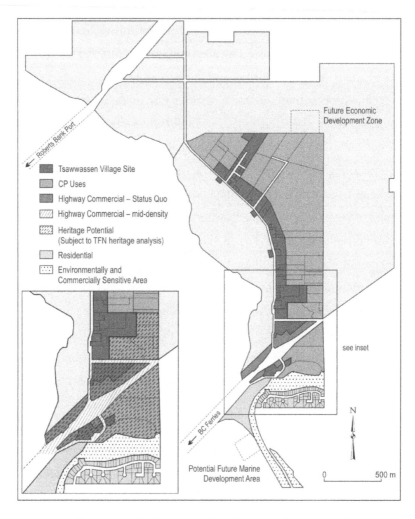

FIGURE 2.4. Tsawwassen First Nation Land Use Plan under the Framework Agreement on First Nation Land Management (2005–6). *Source:* Plan courtesy of the Tsawwassen First Nation (Land Use Plan by Daniel M. Millette, RPP, MCIP). Map by Weldon Hiebert.

be a treaty or not, any commercial development would stand a better chance of being successful if located along Highway 99. A "Future Economic Development" zone was designated on community land, relatively close to where any future inland port activities might occur. Given a shortage of community housing and a need for income-generating market housing, a substantial parcel was zoned as "Residential" (single family and medium density).

Finally, a significant area was designated as having "Heritage Potential," overlaying several zones simultaneously. Heritage impacts would be assessed as development took place. A "Potential Future Marine Development" area, along the foreshore to the south of the British Columbia Ferries causeway, was also identified as a specific zone. Beyond the reserve lands and, at the time, purely hypothetically, other zones were tentatively identified. In several ways, adhesion to the Framework Agreement and the subsequent Tsawwassen First Nation Land Code served as steps toward greater land governance autonomy, with several sets of policies and processes developed during the period immediately following the community's enactment of its land code. The first land use plan for the Tsawwassen First Nation reserve lands thus came to fruition at the end of 2005 and served as a guide for future plans and development considerations. Meanwhile, the TFNFA was being negotiated.

The Tsawwassen Land Planning Process: The Tsawwassen First Nation Final Agreement

Once the TFNFA was ratified by the Tsawwassen community in 2009, among the list of pressing governance matters was the development of a more detailed land use plan.[21] The process would be a complex one, with a multifarious stakeholder combination that included Tsawwassen members and a host of other important interest groups: leaseholders, the neighbouring Municipality of Delta, the regional government, public utilities, and several potential development partners. All wanted a transparent and engaging process that would focus on communication between stakeholders. The most challenging aspect of the process lay in the fact that these peri-urban lands had not been developed and therefore no substantial services or infrastructure were in place; on the one hand, the undeveloped lands were considered from a tabula rasa perspective, while on the other hand, the cost implications of bringing in services were considerable. Ultimately, the new land use plan would aim to reconcile the advantages of undeveloped lands with the costs of developing those lands. At the same time, the planning process would endeavour to integrate the needs and ambitions of individual land holders with those of the new Tsawwassen government, all the while providing a process for amending the same plan in the future. A key underlying tenet for Chief Baird was that whatever solution might arise from a land use planning process, the lands were to provide very long-term economic benefits to improve her community's quality of life.

Among the land-related laws that the Tsawwassen First Nation is empowered to legislate under the TFNFA, the Tsawwassen government can make laws relating to the management and use of Tsawwassen lands, including planning, zoning, and development,[22] the provision of services to the same lands,[23] and the approval of developments.[24] Within its treaty, the Tsawwassen First Nation also commits to providing a process through which residents of its lands who might be affected by a law regarding planning, zoning, and development are consulted, similar to a municipal process where such a law might be pondered.[25] Mechanisms and commitments were therefore put in place to ensure a planning process that is inclusive and familiar to residents.[26] As a further, unique feature, the TFNFA included a provision that recognized that the Tsawwassen community's land use plan would be deemed compatible with the GVRD's "Liveable Region Strategy." In spite of the complexities and competing needs, the planning process within the TFNFA was devised to accommodate all parties within a balanced approach (Figure 2.5).

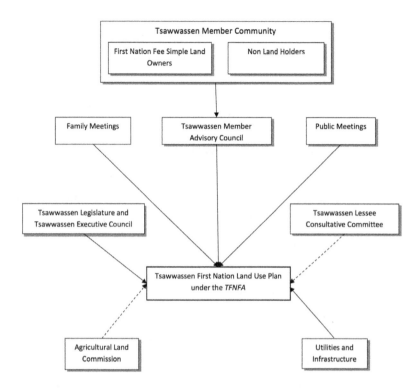

FIGURE 2.5. Tsawwassen First Nation Land Use Plan Input Process under the TFNFA. *Source:* Image prepared by author.

As with the process under the Framework Agreement, the community led the initiative. Several groups of families and individuals, including CP holders and non-holders, were organized to provide a first tier of input. The community's input flowed directly to the Tsawwassen Member Advisory Council, who in turn informed the planner. Family meetings and public meetings also provided input and worked as a way of communicating progress to the Tsawwassen and broader communities. Paralleling the community's input through the Tsawwassen Advisory Council, the Executive Council also provided direct input to the planner. With the new treaty commitments and the general will to provide an opportunity for non–Tsawwassen members (lessees) residing within the Treaty Settlement Lands to offer comments on potential land uses, the process accommodated the same group within an advisory role.[27] Finally, the planner dealt directly with the Agricultural Land Commission and service entities.

At the end of the initial meetings with the community and lessees, the plan's guiding principles were clear, including offering a wide range of economic development opportunities and housing options (for members), placing a strong emphasis on environmental sustainability, preserving and enhancing a strong village centre, maintaining a Tsawwassen First Nation cultural identity, and enabling and encouraging community members to work together in maximizing opportunities and economic returns. The first set of plans that flowed from the initial consultation meetings tended to reflect the plan devised under the Framework Agreement (Figure 2.6).

The Tsawwassen village site was left relatively unchanged, for the most part grandfathered, with a greenway separating it from most other land uses. Similarly, the area previously designated as "Environmentally Sensitive" was preserved, as well as portions of the "Commercial" zone along Highway 99. Within the new land parcels, an "Industrial" zone was, not surprisingly, set aside for inland port activities, as were areas for ALR consideration (including a potential "Managed Forest" zone) and a "Mixed Use" zone. Once these general zones were identified through the community input process, the same zones were (and continue to be) refined through further, continuous, and dynamic stakeholder input.

In Figure 2.7 we see the first example of the refined zoning process with the "Neighbourhood Plan" ("Preferred Land Use Concept"). The CP-held lands that were zones for "CP Uses" in the land use plan under the Framework Agreement have now been brought together within the preferred land use concept under the TFNFA. The zoning is detailed, complete with community preferences on housing types by area, and a

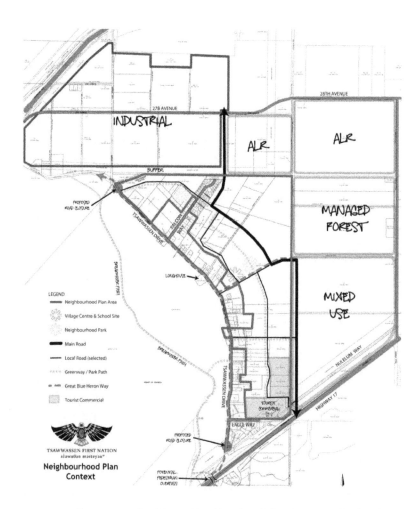

FIGURE 2.6. Tsawwassen First Nation Neighbourhood Plan Context under the TFNFA (2008–9). *Source:* Plan courtesy of the Tsawwassen First Nation (Neighborhood Plan Context by AECOM).

clearly defined central community amenity area. Housing development is being planned at predetermined intervals according to community wishes, third-party investor strategies, and market conditions. The other broad zones are similarly being refined by the community.

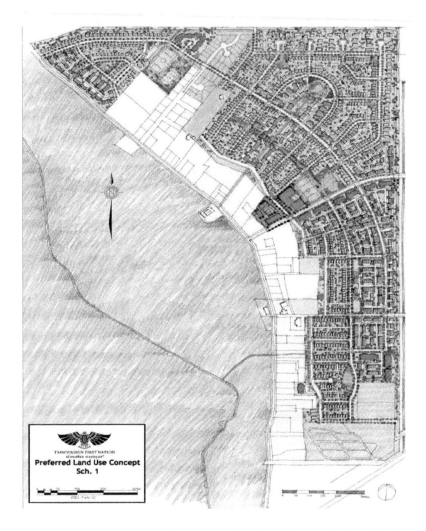

FIGURE 2.7. Tsawwassen First Nation Neighbourhood Plan (refined) under the TFNFA (2011). *Source:* Plan courtesy of the Tsawwassen First Nation, http://www. tsawwassenfirstnation.com/pdfs/TFN-About/Information-Centre/Strategic-Planning/Land_Use_Concept_2011.pdf (Neighbourhood Plan by AECOM).

Conclusion

The planning process of integrating the Tsawwassen lands within a peri-urban framework while maintaining a progressive, jurisdictional approach that places traditional values, First Nations culture, and community well-being at the forefront of several important and at times competing planning tenets has been challenging. In spite of some criticism, the Tsawwassen First Nation has had the opportunity to plan its lands in an incremental fashion that looks at the community in a holistic sense. For former Chief Baird, the journey has been a long one, having its roots in colonial times, with her great-grandfather's eventual address to the McKenna-McBride Commission, adhering to the British Columbia Treaty Commission's Treaty Process, becoming a signatory to the Framework Agreement, and culminating in what would be the first treaty concluded within the British Columbia Treaty Process. For the Tsawwassen First Nation community, the resulting land base and treaty commitments, while complicated in terms of expectations from the varied stakeholders, will go a long way toward reconciling the culturally important past with an economically viable future.

With its land use plan in place, the community can readily engage with potential investors and newcomers. In terms of community land use planning in Canada, the community has undergone (and continues to undergo) one of the most challenging processes in present-day planning practice. Since the signing of the TFNFA, several economic development activities have been negotiated, all within the comprehensive land use planning strategy that was initiated by former Chief Kim Baird. The community members appear fully satisfied, having voted 97 percent in favour of the latest commercial venture.

The land use planning process for this very special set of lands has not been straightforward, requiring cultural sensitivity and an incremental approach that is novel and worth consideration for other communities undergoing rapid change. Key lessons learned from the earlier planning processes include the need for extensive community and stakeholder input, the requirement for servicing negotiations from the initial planning stages, the prioritization of projects within the plan,

and the need for flexibility in implementation (reacting to broader
economic changes). Most of these lessons learned from the earlier
planning exercises formed part of the later planning process. There
remain challenges, including difficult political and technical issues,
particularly in wading through servicing agreements and resident
consultation processes requiring continued perseverance. However,
because the planning process is comprehensive, based on a common
community vision, and set out within an incremental approach, the
chances of success are high indeed.

NOTES

◆

1   Father L. Fouquet, letter sent to the Lands and Work Department in New
        Westminster, 15 August 1865, British Columbia Public Archives, Document File
        Number B1328.

2   Chief Baird was in office from 1999 to 2012.

3   R. Moody, Chief Commissioner of Lands and Works, letter sent to the Attorney
        General, 5 April 1860, British Columbia Public Archives, Document File Number
        F 920, 37A, B 1337. See also a related letter in which the settler undertakes to
        respect the same boundaries (undated document): British Columbia Public
        Archives, Document File Number F 920, 37A, B 1337.

4   The Tsawwassen Traditional Territory is vast. It is bordered on the northeast by
        the watersheds that feed into Pitt Lake and follows the course of the Pitt River to
        Pitt Meadows, where it empties into the Fraser River. It includes the portion of
        New Westminster along the Fraser River and follows the outflow of the Fraser just
        south of Sea Island. From Sea Island it cuts across the Strait of Georgia to
        Galiano Island. It includes all of Saltspring Island. The western border is
        Sampson Narrows. It runs between Saltspring Island and the Saanich Peninsula
        in Satellite Channel, then heads north to Swanson Channel and includes Pender
        and then Saturna islands, heading south to Boundary Pass. At the northern
        extremity of Boundary Pass, the boundary of the territory heads directly
        northeast to White Rock. It misses the watershed of the Campbell River as we
        move north to Aldergrove. From Aldergrove, the territory winds north, including
        the watersheds of the Serpentine and Nicomekl rivers, until reaching Pitt
        Meadows again. Much, although not all, of the territory has become urbanized.
        A great deal of it is now agricultural, while some areas around Pitt Lake remain

heavily forested. For a detailed analysis of the territory, see Daniel M. Millette, *Reconstructing Culture: A Traditional Use Study of the Tsawwassen First Nation* (Delta, BC: Tsawwassen First Nation and British Columbia Ministry of Forests, 1998).

5   *British Columbia Papers—Indian Land Question 1850–1875* (Victoria, BC: R. Wolfenden, 1875), 92.

6   The Tsawwassen First Nation became a signatory to the Framework Agreement on First Nation Land Management in 2003, enacting its land code in 2005.

7   The Tsawwassen First Nation Final Agreement was enacted in 2009.

8   See ARCAS Consulting Archaeologists, *Archaeological Investigations at Tsawwassen, BC*, vols. 1–4 (Delta, BC: ARCAS Consulting Archaeologists, 1992–96).

9   The Deltaport Roberts Bank Container Terminal was built in 1970, with expansions in 1983–84, 1997, and 2010. In 2004, outside of the treaty negotiation process, Chief Baird negotiated an agreement with the Vancouver Port Authority in its $1 billion plans to expand the port, for compensation and employment for her people.

10   A Certificate of Possession (CP) is documentary evidence of a First Nations member's lawful possession of reserve lands pursuant to the Indian Act. The Government of Canada retains legal title to the land. The CP holder is entitled to the use of the land, and rights are transferable by sale or bequeathal to another First Nations individual.

11   For an example of the complexities involved in planning municipal lands where Indian Act reserves have been surveyed, see Jordan Stanger-Ross, "Municipal Colonialism in Vancouver: City Planning and Conflict over Indian Reserves, 1928–1950s," *Canadian Historical Review* 89, no. 4 (2008): 541–80.

12   The Framework Agreement on First Nation Land Management was signed by thirteen First Nations and Canada on 12 February 1996. It is ratified by individual First Nations and brought into effect by Canada in the First Nations Land Management Act, assented to 17 June 1999. For the full text of the First Nations Lands Management Act, see https://laws-lois.justice.gc.ca/eng/acts/F-31.46/.

13   There are several (land) aspects that underlie the Framework Agreement, including the removal of reserve lands from the Indian Act and establishing community control over the First Nation's land management and governance; increased accountability to members of the First Nation; more efficient management of First Nations lands; the transfer by Canada of previous land revenues to the First Nation; the ability of the First Nation to protect the environment; the ability of the First Nation to address rules related to land during marriage breakdowns: the recognition of significant law-making powers respecting First Nations lands; the removal of the need to obtain ministerial approval for First Nations land-related laws; the recognition in Canadian courts of First Nations laws; the ability to create local dispute resolution processes; the establishment of a legal registry system; and the establishment of a First Nations–run Lands Advisory Board to provide technical assistance. The Framework Agreement applies to existing reserve lands, including natural resources (except for oil and gas, migratory birds, fish, and atomic energy).

14   As the First Nation's principal land law, the land code becomes the document that enables the same First Nation to pass further land laws, including land use–related laws and any associated policies and land governance processes.

15   For a discussion of a theoretical approach ("blended planning approach"), see Daniel M. Millette, "Land Use Planning on Aboriginal Lands—Towards a New Model for Planning on Reserve Lands," *Canadian Journal of Urban Research* 20, no. 2 (2012): 20–35.

16   For a discussion on the positive results of inclusive community participation, see Sheeri Torjmann and Ann Makhoul, *Community-Led Development* (Ottawa: Institute of Social Policy, 2012).

17   The pre-treaty lands of the Tsawwassen First Nation reserve were comprised of over 85 percent of lands held by Certificate of Possession.

18   Through its land code, the community had established a Lands Committee, which, for the development of this particular land use plan, served as a steering committee, with direct input to the planner.

19   See Millette, *Reconstructing Culture.*

20   A previous land use plan was developed in 2002 for a portion of the Tsawwassen reserve lands.

21   For a brief summary of the issues facing Chief Baird within the treaty process, see Mike Harcourt and Ken Cameron, with Sean Rossiter, *City Making in Paradise: Nine Decisions That Saved Vancouver* (Vancouver: Douglas and McIntyre, 2007), 198–203.

22   Tsawwassen First Nation Final Agreement, 6.1.d. https://tsawwassenfirstnation.com/wp-content/uploads/2019/07/1_Tsawwassen_First_Nation_Final_Agreement.pdf.

23   Ibid., 6.1.f.

24   Ibid., 6.1.h.

25   Ibid., 10.

26   There are several land-related chapters included in the Tsawwassen First Nation Final Agreement. These include Chapter 4, "Lands"; Chapter 5, "Land Title"; and Chapter 6, "Land Management." The latter reflects to some extent the legislative powers and commitments that affect planning and other land development activities on Tsawwassen Lands.

27   The same non-member population also has representation on the community's tax authority.

CHAPTER 3

✦

Fulfilling Treaty Promises: Treaty Land Entitlement and Muskeg Lake Cree Nation's First Urban Reserve in Saskatoon

✦

Charlotte Bezamat-Mantes

At the beginning of the 1980s, the leadership of Muskeg Lake Cree Nation was looking for a way to improve the community's economic self-sufficiency and enhance its members' socio-economic conditions. In an innovative solution, the First Nation capitalized on Canada's recognition of the community's land claim to create an economic development zone in Saskatoon, Saskatchewan's largest urban centre. Since this urban reserve was created in 1988, it has developed into a successful business park in the Sutherland Industrial neighbourhood of Saskatoon and has inspired dozens of other First Nations to follow the same strategy. Muskeg Lake's experience clearly demonstrates how an economic development strategy that is designed and implemented by the community itself—and not by external agents or governments—can help a community meet its needs in a capitalist economy. In the course of its unprecedented endeavour to create an urban reserve, the First Nation showed determination and resilience in the face of the challenges associated with the process: navigating an unclear legislative framework, overcoming departmental rivalries for the land, and creating an entirely new relationship with a municipal government.

The goal of this chapter is to provide an overview of Muskeg Lake's motivations for creating an urban reserve, and to highlight the innovative solutions the community implemented to overcome the difficulties in creating the reserve.[1] The chapter draws from the existing literature on Indigenous economic development zones and from interviews conducted with individuals directly involved in the creation and development of Muskeg Lake's urban reserve in the 1980s and '90s. The first part of the chapter presents the context for the creation of the urban reserve, based on the recognition of Muskeg Lake's land rights and the development of an original economic and territorial strategy. The second part focuses on the challenges the First Nation encountered at the federal level and how the community overcame those. The third part explores the relationship created between Muskeg Lake and the City of Saskatoon, identifying its characteristics and showing how it has positively influenced the First Nation's economic development strategy. The theme that emerges of mutual support between First Nations and municipalities also lies at the heart of the story told by Wanda Wuttunee in Chapter 11.

The Asimakaniseekan Askiy[2] Urban Reserve: A Tool to Rebuild a Self-Supporting Community

Muskeg Lake Cree Nation's economic and territorial strategy can be interpreted as a creative and locally led response to what were extremely difficult living conditions on the rural reserve, located roughly 100 kilometres north of Saskatoon. Harry Lafond, former Chief and Councillor for the First Nation,[3] explained: "We were a community of people who suffered from a perennial depression, depression that wouldn't go away. During the seventies, the community was racked with alcohol and violence and it was a scary place to live."[4] At the time, the First Nation's primary source of revenue was the federal government, which chronically underfunded the band government. Under these conditions, not only was Muskeg Lake unable to provide for all the needs of its members but there was also no available money for economic development opportunities. Thus, the First Nation was both dependent on insufficient federal dollars and lacking the means to create own-source revenue streams. In Harry Lafond's view, this situation fuelled a cycle of poverty from one generation to the next.

The 1982 election of a new Chief and Council was a watershed for Muskeg Lake. With the help of Muskeg Lake businessman Lester Lafond,[5] Chief Wallace Tawpisim and his Council developed a new vision, aimed at diversifying the band's revenue sources in order to achieve two goals. First, own-source revenues would help mitigate the chronic federal underfunding of the reserve and enable it to provide community members with a decent level of services and infrastructure, thus enhancing the well-being of the rural reserve residents. The urban reserve was meant as a tool to support the home community, which had limited economic development opportunities. Second, creating own-source revenue streams would decrease the First Nation's almost total financial dependency on the federal government, thus allowing the community to move toward economic self-sufficiency. As Lester Lafond explained, mitigating Muskeg Lake's reliance on federal monies would offer the First Nation greater autonomy through the ability to "make our own decisions on our own cash."[6] The urban reserve, creating new own-source revenues for the First Nation (as opposed to welfare or Indigenous Affairs–supported programs), was thus seen as the basis for recreating the strong, resilient, and self-supporting community that the leaders negotiating Treaty 6 had envisioned.

At the beginning of the 1980s, the leadership of Muskeg Lake Cree Nation thus had a clearly defined socio-economic vision for the community. The Treaty Land Entitlement settlement process provided the First Nation with the means to make this vision a reality.

Muskeg Lake Cree Nation is a signatory to Treaty 6, signed with representatives of the Crown on 23 August 1876. Treaty 6 contains the promise that the Crown will set apart as a reserve 128 acres of land for each member of a signatory First Nation. Many First Nations in Saskatchewan and elsewhere never received the full amount of reserve lands they were entitled to under treaty. This created a reserve land shortfall. The Crown thus has a land debt to those First Nations, known as Treaty Land Entitlement (TLE). Though Canada had been aware of its land debt since at least 1929,[7] no measures were taken to resolve it until the 1970s. In 1976, the Saskatchewan and federal governments came to an agreement with the Federation of Saskatchewan Indian Nations[8] in order to resolve the land shortfall. This agreement provided a formula to calculate the land entitlement for each First Nation affected by the federal government's breach of its treaty obligations.[9] This agreement, and the formula it contains, are referred to as the "Saskatchewan Formula." Though the agreement was actually never implemented,[10] it played a vital role in the implementation of Muskeg Lake's economic development agenda. Indeed, the Saskatchewan Formula contained provisions for a Treaty Land Entitlement Exchange Program (TLEEP) that survived the failed agreement. Through TLEEP, federal and provincial governments agreed to "place occupied and unoccupied Crown lands on the table for selection"[11] by Entitlement First Nations, which could then request to have them converted to reserve status in partial fulfillment of their Treaty Land Entitlement.[12]

Under the leadership of Chief Tawpisim, research was undertaken to prove that Muskeg Lake had a valid land claim.[13] In 1983, the federal government recognized that it owed 48,640 acres of reserve land to the community.[14] The First Nation was then able to select land and request to have it converted to reserve status under the conditions set out in the federal Additions to Reserve Policy.[15] In order to create its urban reserve, Muskeg Lake would have to deal with both the federal government and the City of Saskatoon.

There are several reasons why the federal government is implicated in the process of creating an urban reserve. First, as previously mentioned, the federal government has a land debt toward many First Nations flowing from the eleven Numbered Treaties (1871 to 1921). It is the responsibility for this land debt and the steps to resolve it—such as TLEEP—that partly explain the federal government's involvement in the creation of the Muskeg Lake's urban reserve in Saskatoon. Second, Section 91(24) of the Constitution Act of 1867, a section that remains in force, states that "Indians, and Lands reserved for the Indians" are considered to be under the exclusive legislative authority of the Parliament of Canada.[16] In addition, the Indian Act specifies that the legal title of reserve lands is "vested in Her Majesty" and administered by the minister responsible for Indigenous Affairs. Together, Section 91(24) and the Indian Act meant that the federal government would hold the title to Muskeg Lake's urban reserve, thus explaining why it participated in the creation of the new reserve in Saskatoon.

For a property to become an integral part of a First Nation's land base, it has to have reserve status. A reserve is "a tract of land, the legal title to which is vested in Her Majesty, that has been set apart by Her Majesty for the use and benefit of a band."[17] Two elements explain why the conversion of the Sutherland Industrial property to reserve status was a necessary step. First, the property needed to be acquired by Muskeg Lake through its Treaty Land Entitlement. For the land to be counted in the settlement of the federal government's land debt toward the First Nation, the property in question had to be converted to reserve status. Otherwise, the land would not be part of the First Nation's land base and Canada's legal obligations would remain. Second, under the current legal framework, the jurisdiction of a First Nations government, represented by the elected Chief and Council, only applies to its reserve lands.[18] When reserve status is obtained, "the First Nation which owns that reserve land becomes the local government on that land."[19] Moreover, as previously mentioned, reserve lands are governed by the Indian Act. This act guarantees, in accordance with provisions from the Numbered Treaties, that reserve lands may not be taxed by a government other than that of the First Nation.[20] Far from being a mere administrative detail, the taxation regime of reserve lands is significant for two interrelated reasons. First, taxes represent a source of revenue for any government, First Nations included. For Muskeg Lake, levying taxes on the products and services sold on its urban reserve would allow for the creation of a steady stream of revenues that the band would then be able to spend as it saw fit—much as provinces do with the revenues collected through the provincial sales tax (PST), or Canada does with the goods and services tax (GST). Second, some First Nations see taxation powers as inherent to their sovereignty. In Lester Lafond's view, "a true government has tax revenues."[21] Indeed, the revenue created through the collection of taxes on the urban reserve was seen by the Muskeg Lake leadership as a means for greater leeway in its decisions and projects than if the band government relied solely on federal government transfers. The Sutherland Industrial property's conversion to reserve status was thus a necessary step in the Muskeg Lake Cree Nation's economic development plan.

Muskeg Lake's Creative Responses to the Challenges of Urban Reserve Creation

When Lester Lafond approached the federal government in August 1984 to inform it of the Muskeg Lake Cree Nation's interest in acquiring the Sutherland Industrial property he had identified, the First Nation encountered its first challenge. The property was surplus federal Crown land, meaning Canada owned it. Divergent opinions between various federal departments emerged. The question arose as to whether the land was indeed "surplus" to begin with, meaning that its owner was ready to sell it. Then, if the land was indeed surplus, the issue was whether it should be used to satisfy a First Nation's land entitlement. While the Department of Indian Affairs supported the transfer of the land in partial fulfillment of Muskeg Lake's entitlement, the Department of Public Works, which owned the land, and the Treasury Board opposed it.[22] At a time when the Mulroney government had announced it would be selling federal surplus Crown lands and buildings to improve its financial situation, Public Works and the Treasury Board favoured the sale of the land to the City of Saskatoon, from which they expected a higher financial return than from the First Nation.[23]

This situation of interdepartmental rivalries for the Sutherland Industrial property was compounded by the unclear legal framework surrounding reserve creation at this time. Indeed, the Additions to Reserve Policy was "still in its fledgling state" and had seldom been used to create a reserve in a city or town before Muskeg Lake's project in Saskatoon.[24] Harry Lafond, then band Councillor, recalled that the federal government "had all kinds of policies, reserve-creation policies, that were very restrictive and antiquated, ancient" with which the First Nation was not familiar.[25] It was the involvement of several individuals and their capacity to work together that helped Muskeg Lake overcome the federal departments' competing interests and the lack of a clear federal policy regarding reserve creation.

Lester Lafond was one whose involvement positively influenced the outcome of the First Nation's urban reserve project. He was Muskeg Lake's TLE coordinator and chief negotiator for matters relating to the urban reserve. As a businessman, he had gained credibility and trust within the business community in Saskatoon.[26] His participation in the process may have acted as a guarantee that the development plan put forward by Muskeg Lake would be viable. He was also elected federal chairperson of the Progressive Conservative Party Aboriginal Caucus in 1986,[27] a time when that party was dominating the national political scene. As Lafond noted, this position allowed him to be "in meetings across Canada where [he]'d get one-on-one with the ministers"[28] and have access to individuals capable of supporting Muskeg Lake's project in higher circles.

Bill McKnight was another individual instrumental to the creation of Muskeg Lake's urban reserve. Minister for Indian Affairs between 1986 and 1989, McKnight was described by Harry Lafond as "a businessman who was not afraid to look beyond the boundaries of . . . status quo."[29] He supported the idea of creating an urban reserve designed to support Muskeg Lake's economic development strategy and favoured using the surplus Crown land property of Sutherland Industrial for this purpose. The interest he took in Muskeg Lake's project influenced the position of other federal departments.

Lester Lafond managed to secure the support of Deputy Prime Minister Don Mazankowski.[30] Through Mazankowski's and McKnight's efforts, a meeting was organized in the summer of 1987, where Lafond presented Muskeg Lake's project to representatives of the Department of Public Works. He was able to get them on board with the development plan for the land and prove to them that the First Nation had the support of Cliff Wright, the Mayor of Saskatoon, meaning there would be no conflict with the City. A few weeks after the meeting, Muskeg Lake received news that it would get the land.

The City of Saskatoon, a potential rival buyer, was satisfied with acquiring only part of the land for a roadway it needed to build, and Treasury Board approved the rate at which the property was to be sold to the First Nation.[31] McKnight's importance in the creation of the urban reserve was such that the Muskeg Lake Cree Nation made him Honorary Chief and named the first commercial centre on the reserve after him.[32]

Overcoming federal rivalries over the fate of the property was only a preliminary step in creating the urban reserve. During the many-staged process of converting the Sutherland property to reserve status, Muskeg Lake was able to count on McKnight's support. According to Harry Lafond, the minister "worked with Muskeg, he worked with the City [of Saskatoon], to allow the process to proceed through the federal government steps for reserve creation."[33] Indeed, obtaining the land was not enough to make it a reserve: the First Nation was required by the federal government to negotiate an agreement with the City of Saskatoon. Another representative of the federal government assisted Muskeg Lake: Rose Boyko, an Indigenous lawyer with the federal Department of Justice who had an office in Saskatoon, helped protect Muskeg Lake's interests in the agreement that would be signed with the City.[34]

When Muskeg Lake Cree Nation's claim was "validated" by Canada in 1983, living conditions on the home reserve were difficult.[35] Only a handful of farmers were able to make a living from their agricultural activities on the reserve, and "everybody else had to leave to go find work."[36] Although Saskatchewan was a very rural province then, the economy had started to urbanize: economic activities were strongly shifting toward urban centres. Harry Lafond explained that Muskeg Lake deliberately sought to get a foothold in an urban environment because this would be the most economically dynamic setting.[37] By acquiring land in an urban location, the band implemented an unprecedented economic and territorial strategy, thanks to its Treaty Land Entitlement rights: "instead of bringing the market to the reserve, the Muskeg Lake Cree Nation decided to bring the reserve to the market."[38]

Although they were originally thought of as places "reserved" for Indigenous peoples should they wish to take up farming—as treaty texts explicitly stipulate[39]—reserves became a means of containing Indigenous peoples, governments, and economies within the boundaries of these federal Crown lands. Economic initiatives on reserves were hindered or stifled by legislative and other means, as many scholars have documented.[40] In short, reserve lands have often failed to be the basis for First Nations peoples' sustenance that was envisioned by and agreed to in the treaties. In that light, Muskeg Lake's urban reserve should not be seen as a departure from the community's earlier efforts towards economic self-reliance and improved well-being for its members. Rather, the urban reserve represents a new means to attain an old goal the community has been pursuing with tenacity since the signing of Treaty 6 and through the lengthy land claim process: to adapt to a changing environment while retaining (or regaining) control over lands, a necessary basis for economic development aimed at providing the community members with the means to live a good life. Thus, though urban reserves are a fairly recent phenomenon in reserve lands history, the dynamic underlying their creation is not new. Rather, urban reserves are one tool that a growing number of First Nations have chosen to turn to in order to pursue economic self-sufficiency, a sine qua non condition for Indigenous communities to be able to govern themselves.

Harry Lafond emphasized that the Saskatoon urban reserve was "intended to be the economic arm of the Muskeg Lake community."[41] It would not be used for residential purposes by band members or others. Establishing a reserve in an urban environment would help the community achieve two sets of goals: first, to diversify the First Nation's land portfolio, which in turn would allow for the creation of various own-source revenue streams, with potential benefits much higher than could be generated on the home reserve; and second, to provide employment and economic opportunities to Muskeg Lake members,[42] through either band-owned or individual companies.[43] Harry Lafond noted that job creation and the economic success of the Saskatoon reserve not only impacted the financial and material situation of community members but also had deeper ramifications, instilling "a strong sense of pride" among them.[44]

Thus, in the context of the economic plan developed by Muskeg Lake Cree Nation under Chief Tawpisim at the beginning of the 1980s, the acquisition of raw land away from an urban centre, though a cheaper option, was not pertinent. Having an urban reserve close to or within a city would allow for an easier and cheaper connection to the municipal transportation, power, water, and sewer systems; the land's proximity to large customer markets and economic opportunities would also be vital to the development and success of the industrial park. Muskeg Lake's strategy had thus been devised long before the urban reserve was created in Saskatoon.

Before the 1992 Treaty Land Entitlement Framework Agreement,[45] some First Nations could already place claims on Crown lands through TLEEP; nevertheless, the federal and the provincial governments were not required to notify First Nations when Crown lands became surplus and available for potential additions to the reserve. This meant that First Nations had to look for potentially available Crown lands themselves.

As soon as Muskeg Lake's Treaty Land Entitlement rights were "validated by Canada," Lester Lafond was named TLE coordinator and tasked with finding surplus Crown lands available for selection within or near to Saskatoon. In August 1984, Lafond located the title of a piece of surplus federal Crown land located in Saskatoon. Since no one was required to notify First Nations when Crown lands became surplus, he relied on personal connections to identify parcels of land that would be available and relevant to Muskeg Lake's economic strategy.[46] Finding Crown lands located in urban areas was already difficult around that time period:[47] the scarcity of urban Crown lands, combined with the limited cooperation of the federal and provincial governments, made the likelihood of easily locating a suitable parcel of land quite remote, and thus Lester Lafond finding such a property was exceptional.

After Lester Lafond had identified the land, the community placed a claim on it. This would "put the right of refusal in Muskeg's hands"[48] and ensure that the federal government could not dispose of the land before the First Nation had had the opportunity to determine whether it actually wanted to acquire it. The First Nation commissioned a study to ensure that the land fit its established objectives. The study concluded that "the site could offer considerable economic benefit to the First Nation and that steps should be taken to negotiate its transfer to reserve status."[49] It is worth noting that Lester Lafond's optimism was the departure point for Muskeg Lake's vision becoming a reality. He recalled that "in my mind there was never a doubt . . . , I never thought that we couldn't get it."[50]

Less than a year after Muskeg Lake's Treaty Land Entitlement rights were recognized by Canada, the First Nation thus had devised an economic and territorial strategy and secured the means to achieve it. Its TLE coordinator had found a piece of land that matched the community's development plan and filed a claim with the federal government. This was, however, only the beginning of the process; the next step would be to create a relationship with the urban reserve's neighbour, the City of Saskatoon.

Theresa Dust, former City Solicitor for Saskatoon,[51] summarized well the stakes associated with the creation of an urban reserve: "For First Nations, it is the first opportunity to be a real player within the urban environment; and for cities it means that they need to adjust to having another jurisdiction within their midst."[52] She identified three challenges that arise from the creation of an urban reserve: land use planning, service provision, and the question of sovereignty on the land, especially in regards to issues of taxation.[53]

Canada's constitution stipulates that provinces have exclusive jurisdiction for land use planning; however, provincial governments usually delegate this responsibility to local urban and municipal governments,[54] who exercise this power through municipal bylaws. At the same time, "Indians and lands reserved for Indians" are an area under exclusive federal jurisdiction.[55] This means that provincial legislation regarding land use planning and municipal bylaws pertaining to it do not apply to reserve lands. Thus, the creation of a reserve within a municipality "takes place outside of the provincial structure of land use planning and land use conflict resolution."[56] This situation of intertwined jurisdictions has the potential to create problems for both the First Nation and the municipality.

First at stake is the issue of zoning. Municipalities, particularly urban ones, define what uses are permitted on each parcel of land within their boundaries: residential, commercial, light or heavy industrial, etc. Buildings and activities must comply with the zoning requirements of their area. When there is no convergence at all between the First Nation's zoning and the surrounding municipal area's zoning, issues may arise. For example, if a First Nation decided to use its urban reserve to build a waste treatment facility in the middle of a densely populated area, the municipality would have no means to oppose the project; the opposite situation—where a municipality authorizes land use directly in conflict with the activities on the urban reserve—can be imagined just as easily, and the First Nation may have no recourse to stop the unwanted municipal developments. The second issue arising from the intertwinement of jurisdictions pertains to building standards and health regulations. Provincial legislation in these areas may not apply to reserve lands.[57] This is a non-issue in rural areas, but can have important consequences in an urban environment, since "what happens in one jurisdiction is so likely to affect the other jurisdiction, simply because they are so close together."[58] This observation has led some municipalities to become concerned that when an urban reserve is created within their boundaries, the First Nation may not respect building standards and health regulations and thus endanger the neighbourhood—a fire starting on the reserve would evidently not stop at the reserve boundary. This fear may stem from the fact that many First Nations have little or no experience in planning for densely populated and highly developed areas, which is unsurprising since reserves are predominantly rural. Joseph Garcea observed that municipal distrust toward the planning capacities of First Nations governments was also fuelled by prejudice against Indigenous people, thinking that they would not be concerned about matters of safety and security and so would be willing to accept arrangements that do not meet provincial standards.[59] Land use planning was thus one of the issues that would have to be discussed by the City of Saskatoon and the Muskeg Lake Cree Nation.

Another matter that brought Muskeg Lake and Saskatoon to the negotiating table was the taxation regime on the urban reserve and its consequences on the provision of municipal services. First, since only the First Nation's government has the authority to tax its urban reserve, the municipality cannot finance the services it provides to the reserve by taxing people and activities there as it usually would.[60] This leaves the municipality and the First Nation with three options: (1) the First Nation does not resort to municipal services and there is no issue of paying for them; (2) the municipal government provides services to the reserve for free, and raises the level of taxation for other properties in order to compensate for the loss of revenues;[61] and (3) the municipality provides services and the First Nation pays for it, but not through taxes. The first option does not ensure cost efficiency and requires more logistics on the part of the First Nation; it has seldom been used.[62] The second option would be the surest way to alienate local residents and businesses and to feed the misconception that Indigenous people do not pay taxes. In the case of Muskeg Lake Cree Nation and the City of Saskatoon, the third option was felt to be the only viable one, but it required intense negotiations so that both the First Nation's interest (receiving services while protecting its exclusive taxation powers over the reserve) and the municipality's (receiving compensation for the services provided to the reserve) could be preserved. A further issue was that since companies based on the urban reserve do not have to include the cost of PST, GST, or business and property taxes, they can offer lower prices than those charged off-reserve.[63] Members from the Saskatoon business community voiced their concerns about what they viewed as an unfair competitive advantage for businesses located on the urban reserve.[64] Muskeg Lake Cree Nation and the City of Saskatoon thus included taxation issues in their negotiations preceding the creation of the Sutherland Industrial reserve.

The questions raised by the reserve's creation regarding land use planning, service provision, and taxation all relate, in the end, to the all-encompassing issue of sovereignty. First Nations and municipalities, in the current constitutional framework, exercise "much the same power to make local legislation."[65] Given that land use and development and taxation regimes on a First Nation's or municipality's territory can affect the other, and that these powers are at the heart of both governments' sovereignty over their respective jurisdictions, an important question emerges when an urban reserve is created: how can the First Nation's and the City's interests regarding their own lands be preserved while at the same time allowing for the full exercise of the other government's sovereignty over its own jurisdiction? This question arose early on in the process of creating Muskeg Lake's urban reserve in Saskatoon and was at the heart of the negotiations between the two governments.

Land use and development, taxation, and sovereignty issues were addressed in the negotiations held between 1985 and 1988 that led to the signing of the first First Nation–municipal formal agreement,[66] followed by two additional ones in 1992 and 1993.[67] Due to space constraints, analyzing the details of these agreements is not possible here. In the next section, I propose instead to explore the events that led to the 1988 agreement to try to understand the tensions that Muskeg Lake's project raised and the solutions that were found, as well as the intergovernmental relationship that was created and its positive impacts on the establishment of the urban reserve.

Muskeg Lake Cree Nation and the City of Saskatoon: Building a Constructive and Mutually Beneficial Relationship

After Muskeg Lake Cree Nation claimed the Sutherland Industrial property, it was required by the federal government to enter into a formal agreement with the City of Saskatoon. Chief negotiator Lester Lafond explained that while negotiating with the municipality, the band "was in uncharted waters."[68] At the time, neither the City nor the First Nation anticipated the aforementioned issues, as they would arise from the negotiations. The lack of a fully and clearly defined federal policy, previously mentioned, meant the two parties did not have any guidance about the "focus and extent of negotiations" required from them.[69] Three elements help understand how Muskeg Lake managed to overcome the difficulty posed by the unclear policy framework.

The first element relates to the economic dimension of the urban reserve. When Muskeg Lake first contacted Saskatoon, it chose to emphasize the economic aspect of its project and to stress that the future reserve represented an opportunity not only for the First Nation but also for the City.[70] When the negotiations started, the Sutherland Industrial property was raw land but basic services such as road maintenance or snow clearing were still required, which entailed costs for the municipality; since the land was undeveloped, the City did not derive any revenue from it. The development of Muskeg Lake's urban reserve into an industrial park would greatly enhance the level of activities on the land and, indirectly, the City's potential tax revenue.[71] In addition, the municipality would receive payment for services provided to the reserve. The way Muskeg Lake presented the urban reserve as a mutually beneficial economic enterprise was considered by both Lester Lafond and Marty Irwin, former Saskatoon City Commissioner, to have been a major factor in the positive response the First Nation received from the municipality.[72]

Muskeg Lake's strategy of emphasizing the economic purpose of its future urban reserve resonated with Saskatoon Mayor Cliff Wright. Wright has often been presented as a business-oriented person, and Harry Lafond noted that this made Wright "quite open to listen to the reserve and the ideas that the reserve was bringing forward about economic development."[73] Lester Lafond remembered that when he first met the Mayor to discuss the urban reserve, Wright was indeed very enthusiastic about the project and wanted to make it an example for the rest of the country to follow.[74] The City Commissioner, whom Lafond also met that day, supported the project, too: each time Lester Lafond had to deal with the legal department, the engineering department, or any other department, the Commissioner "told them 'deal with them [Muskeg Lake], make it work.'"[75] In the eyes of both Harry Lafond and Lester Lafond, the support Muskeg Lake managed to secure from the Mayor and the City Commissioner prevented resistance from lower levels of the administration and thus facilitated the administrative side of the negotiations.[76]

Convincing the Saskatoon municipal council was not as easy as obtaining the Mayor's and the City Commissioner's support. Both Lester Lafond and Harry Lafond pointed out that some Councillors opposed the urban reserve. This difficulty was resolved, in part thanks to the leadership of the Mayor and the attitude Muskeg Lake brought to the discussion. According to Lester Lafond, although Wright was not an autocrat he was deeply respected by his council, which gave him "undeclared authority to do things without their consultation."[77] This suggests that the Mayor's authority and political aura helped placate opposition from within.[78] For its part, Muskeg Lake's openness to dialogue, explored further below, also helped gain the municipal council's support. Toward the end of the negotiations, Muskeg Lake identified which individuals might jeopardize the agreement's adoption by City Council. Those individuals were contacted through informal channels and literally taken to dinner, where the First Nation's representatives offered them an opportunity to ask questions about the band, its economic projects, and the envisioned development of the urban reserve. In Harry Lafond's view, this approach helped dispel uneasiness and fears about the urban reserve: "We always did it in a friendly 'we want to trust you and we want you to trust us' approach, and it worked, it really toned down the pushback in the community."[79] When the agreement was submitted to the municipal council in 1988, it was approved by all Councillors. Right before the vote, one Councillor still intended to reject the agreement. This was where another detail played out in Muskeg Lake's favour. The band had hired a law firm to assist it in the legal aspect of the negotiations with Saskatoon. According to Lester Lafond, one of those lawyers working for Muskeg Lake turned out to be the son-in-law of the very Councillor still opposing the urban reserve; the First Nation tasked the lawyer with convincing the Councillor before the vote took place.[80] The strategy was successful, and the agreement was adopted unanimously.

The relationship that Muskeg Lake and Saskatoon created during the negotiations for the municipal agreement was first characterized by the pragmatic and goal-oriented approach of the two governments. As Irwin stated, their objective was "to create a reserve with maximum cooperation and minimum delay."[81] This approach stemmed from the idea, previously mentioned, that the urban reserve would be a mutually beneficial economic project.[82] The prospect of economic benefits prevailed over concerns about sovereignty, land use and development, and fiscal authority. The details of Muskeg Lake's plan for the land helped sustain this approach and created a convergence of interests between the two governments.

The First Nation planned to develop the property as an industrial and commercial park in order to maximize potential revenues for the band. The existing municipal zoning bylaw for that area perfectly fit Muskeg Lake's plans. This meant that the potential for land use conflict was less, and that the development of the urban reserve as an industrial park would generate revenues for the City as well. In addition, the economic nature of the urban reserve held back potential opposition from the area's residents based on prejudice against First Nations people. Since the project was presented as a "business reserve," fears associated with the creation of a residential urban reserve had no grounds on which to build;[83] the City thus did not have to spend time and energy convincing the residents that the urban reserve would not have adverse effects on their own interests.[84] As Garcea pointed out, an urban reserve geared toward economic activities is less likely to provoke opposition from the residents of the area because they do not expect First Nations people to live there.[85] The federal government had also insisted the urban reserve be developed for industrial and commercial activities.[86] The economic nature of the urban reserve thus allowed for a strong convergence of interests between the First Nation, the City and its residents, and the federal government. Irwin noted that the fact that the urban reserve was perceived as mutually beneficial allowed for constructive negotiations between Saskatoon and Muskeg Lake, focusing on "issues that had to be addressed and resolved, rather than whether or not the reserve should be created."[87] Instead of debating the context of the reserve's creation—treaty rights and Treaty Land Entitlement, or the loaded history of First Nations–municipal relations—negotiators deliberately focused on the means to achieve their common goal: obtaining reserve status for the land. This pragmatic approach allowed them to focus on "practical, day-to-day issues such as building construction, parking, roads,"[88] which, far from being mere practical details, are essential for the success of an economic endeavour such as Muskeg Lake's urban reserve.

A second element that characterized this intergovernmental relationship was the will of both parties to engage in dialogue and find compromises rather than categorically assert their (perceived or actual) rights over the urban reserve. For Harry Lafond, the fact that each party is convinced it is within its rights and working for the preservation of its own interests—especially protecting sovereignty over its jurisdiction—should not prevent dialogue in good faith with the other party. This approach was reflected in the attitude of the City of Saskatoon, which understood that the federal government had the right to grant reserve status to land within municipal boundaries even without the City's consent.[89] The municipal government understood from the start that it was in its interest to negotiate with the First Nation rather than risk seeing the establishment of an enclave of Indigenous jurisdiction within its midst with which it would have no relationship at all. Saskatoon's attitude of dialogue can be understood in light of events that had surrounded the creation of another urban reserve in Prince Albert a few years before.[90] As Irwin indicated, this case "provided a model that was more instructive on what not to do than on what to do" for Saskatoon and Muskeg Lake.[91] The Prince Albert Council had strongly and unwaveringly refused to negotiate with the Peter Ballantyne Cree Nation, so no agreement was reached. The federal government nevertheless granted reserve status to the land, and the City of Prince Albert found itself host to an urban reserve governed by a government with which it had no relations at all, and no agreement relating to land use and development, taxation issues, or provision of services. In other words, the existence of the Prince Albert precedent led Saskatoon and Muskeg Lake to favour a non-conflictual approach to the creation of their intergovernmental relationship, based on dialogue and compromise.

The last major element in Muskeg Lake's and Saskatoon's inter-governmental relationship was the understanding by both parties that the negotiations for the agreement were only the beginning of a long-term relationship. Indeed, once the land was granted reserve status, the two governments would still have to deal with each other in matters relating to municipal services, land use and development, and bylaw compatibility. The understanding that the two jurisdictions would become neighbours indefinitely had several consequences for both parties' perceptions of their relationship to one another.

Muskeg Lake and Saskatoon chose to resort to bilateral negotiations. Rather than appealing to another order of government to negotiate on their behalf, the First Nation and the City designated a small group of officials. Representatives from the federal and provincial governments were involved in the negotiations only when their participation was necessary.[92] The rationale was that having only a few individuals involved, and ones with a direct interest in the swift conclusion of the negotiations, would allow for a close working relationship. Furthermore, since the issues raised by the creation of the urban reserve were essentially local in nature, the parties considered that solutions to these issues should come from those potentially affected by them: the First Nation and municipal governments.[93]

The other consequence of the understanding that their relationship was a long-term one was the level of trust developed between Saskatoon and the Muskeg Lake Cree Nation. Both Harry Lafond and officials from the City of Saskatoon insisted that building trust between the two governments was one of the most important steps of creating an urban reserve.[94] Lafond explained that as a First Nation establishing contact with a municipality, "you have to converse, you have to dialogue, you have to trust"—an attitude even more constructive given that municipalities often fear that First Nations governments will not take them seriously or take time to discuss issues affecting them both.[95]

The new neighbours' perception of their mutual relationship was evidenced by an unprecedented practice that Saskatoon and Muskeg Lake developed. After the urban reserve was created in 1988, the two parties decided to continue to meet on a regular basis, not necessarily in order to discuss issues concerning the reserve but simply to sustain their relationship.[96] Since the creation of the Sutherland Industrial reserve, representatives from both councils have met for a yearly Christmas lunch, hosted alternately by each party.[97]

In addition to this traditional Christmas gathering, both parties wished that regular meetings be organized between their respective representatives in order to discuss matters of mutual interest. Irwin insisted that it was important to hold these meetings "when things are going well and not only when problems arise."[98] This would preserve the positive perception of their relationship, born out of the initial negotiations and of the arrangements included in the agreement; it would also help familiarize new officials of either government with the ins and outs of the intergovernmental relationship itself.

Conclusion

Thanks to its tenacious efforts to have its Treaty Land Entitlement rights recognized and implemented, the Muskeg Lake Cree Nation obtained the means to acquire Crown lands at the beginning of the 1980s and have them added to its reserve lands. In an unprecedented move, the First Nation set out in 1984 to use these rights to establish an economic development zone in the City of Saskatoon. This urban reserve is designed to strengthen Muskeg Lake's economic self-sufficiency and enhance its members' socio-economic conditions. It is the product of an innovative territorial and economic strategy. This strategy became a reality, thanks to the continuous efforts of some of Muskeg Lake's members despite the many challenges they experienced in the lengthy process of obtaining reserve status, and thanks to their optimism that what they were trying to do would succeed in the end and benefit their community.

The events surrounding the creation of the urban reserve that we have explored in this chapter reveal some of the many challenges Muskeg Lake faced after 1984: interdepartmental federal rivalries over the land it had set out to acquire, an unclear policy framework offering little guidance, opposition from within the Saskatoon municipal council, and an overall lack of experience in First Nations–municipal relations for both Muskeg Lake and Saskatoon.

Difficulties at the federal level were resolved, thanks to the support of successive Ministers for Indian Affairs for Muskeg Lake's economic development project, and because one of the First Nation's members was able to capitalize on his network to win the support of previously adversarial federal departments. The support of the municipality was gained notably because of a strong convergence of interests between the City and the First Nation: the economic nature of the planned urban reserve forestalled opposition rooted in prejudice against First Nations people, and the idea that it would be beneficial to Saskatoon and not just the First Nation helped convince the City that it should support this endeavour. Opposition to the urban reserve from within the municipal council was placated through Muskeg Lake's representatives' readiness to engage in dialogue and make compromises while still protecting their inherent and treaty rights. Finally, the intergovernmental relationship that Muskeg Lake and Saskatoon created in the course of the negotiations preceding the establishment of the urban reserve was characterized by pragmatism, a willingness to engage in dialogue and build trust, and the understanding that the relationship would be durable and would need to be sustained over time.

The Muskeg Lake Cree Nation's urban reserve has become a model for the creation and development of Indigenous economic zones through-out the country and has inspired many other First Nations to follow its path, both in terms of economic and territorial strategy and regarding intergovernmental relations with the host municipality. Saskatchewan now has more than fifty urban reserves, six of which are in Saskatoon. Beyond the material benefits that Muskeg Lake and the City have derived from it, the urban reserve also stands as a symbol that the peaceful coexistence of two governments is not only possible but can also have positive consequences for both their communities. As Harry Lafond put it, "This is Canada's story, this is Saskatchewan's story, it's not an Indian story. It's an 'us' story."[99]

NOTES

✦

1   Developing the reserve into an economically viable site represented another challenge. Because of space limitations, I cannot explore here the tenacity and creativity the Muskeg Lake Cree Nation's members demonstrated to ensure the economic success of their urban reserve.

2   Asimakaniseekan askiy: "the soldier's land," "the veteran's land" in Cree. This is the official name of the land, though it is often referred to as the Sutherland reserve.

3   Harry Lafond was a Muskeg Lake Cree Nation Councillor from 1988 to 1990, and Chief between 1990 and 2000. He was Executive Director of the Treaty Relations Commission of Saskatchewan for several years. He was re-elected Councillor in 2009, a position he still occupied in 2021.

4   Harry Lafond, interview, 19 April 2017.

5   Lester Lafond has been Muskeg Lake Cree Nation's Treaty Land Entitlement coordinator since 1984. He was also president of the Saskatoon Chamber of Commerce and a Commissioner with the First Nations Tax Commission.

6   Lester Lafond, interview, 7 April 2017.

7   In 1929, three Natural Resources Transfer Acts were passed to allow for the transfer of jurisdiction over natural resources from the federal to the provincial governments of Alberta, Saskatchewan, and Manitoba. In each act, a provision stipulates that the Superintendent General of Indian Affairs may request unoccupied provincial Crown lands "to enable Canada to fulfil its obligations under the treaties with the Indians of the Province." This is an explicit acknowledgement that in 1929 not all First Nations had received their quantum of reserve lands.

8   Renamed Federation of Sovereign Indigenous Nations in 2016.

9   The Saskatchewan Formula is as follows: (number of band members as of 31 December 1976 multiplied by the per-capita acreage specified in the applicable treaty) minus the acreage of reserve lands already received. For example, for a First Nation signatory to Treaty 6 with a population of 300 and an existing reserve of 15,000 acres, the calculation would be (300 x 128) − 15,000 = 23,400. The First Nation would be entitled to an additional 23,400 acres of reserve lands.

10   F. Laurie Barron and Joseph Garcea, "The Genesis of Urban Reserves and the Role of Governmental Self-Interest," in *Urban Indian Reserves: Forging New Relationships in Saskatchewan*, ed. F. Laurie Barron and Joseph Garcea (Saskatoon: Purich Publishing, 1999), 80.

11   "Crown land" is the term used to describe land owned by the federal or provincial governments (national and provincial parks and buildings, Indian reserves, Canadian Forces bases, etc.).

12   Barron and Garcea, "Genesis of Urban Reserves," 25.

13   "Muskeg Lake Cree Nation," n.d., Saskatchewan Archival Information Network, Saskatchewan Council for Archives and Archivists, http://sain.scaa.sk.ca/collections/muskeg-lake-cree-nation.

14   Lester Lafond, "Creation, Governance, and Management of the McKnight Commercial Centre in Saskatoon," in *Urban Indian Reserves: Forging New Relationships in Saskatchewan*, ed. F. Laurie Barron and Joseph Garcea (Saskatoon: Purich Publishing, 1999), 189.

15   Though the term "policy" is most commonly used in the context of reserve creation, it is a misnomer: the Additions to Reserve Policy is actually Chapter 10 of the *First Nations Land Management Manual*. See Indigenous Services Canada, 2016, https://www.sac-isc.gc.ca/eng/1465827292799/1611938828195.

16   Constitution Act, 1867, 30 & 31 Vict, c 3, https://www.canlii.org/en/ca/laws/stat/30---31-vict-c-3/latest/30---31-vict-c-3.html.

17   Indian Act, RSC, 1985, c I-5, 22 December 2017, https://laws-lois.justice.gc.ca/eng/acts/I-5/page-1.html.

18   Ibid.

19   Theresa Dust, "Urban Neighbours Land Entitlement and Urban Reserves," 10 February 1994. Speech presented at a Statistics Canada, Future Focus Conference on the First Nations Community at Regina, Saskatchewan.

20   Indian Act, RSC, 1985, c I-5.

21 Lester Lafond, interview, 7 April 2017.

22 Lafond, "Creation, Governance, and Management," 190.

23 Barron and Garcea, "Genesis of Urban Reserves," 41.

24 Lester Lafond, "Creation, Governance, and Management," 190.

25 Harry Lafond, interview, 19 April 2017.

26 Ibid.

27 Barron and Garcea, "Genesis of Urban Reserves," 41.

28 Lester Lafond, interview, 9 May 2019.

29 Harry Lafond, interview, 19 April 2017.

30 Lester Lafond, interview, 9 May 2019.

31 Muskeg Lake agreed to remit about 400 acres of rural land from its land claims compensation package, concluded in 1983, in exchange for the thirty-five-acre property in Sutherland Industrial. See Barron and Garcea, "Genesis of Urban Reserves," 41.

32 Phil Tank, "Longtime Cabinet Minister Bill McKnight Built Framework for Settling Land Claims," *Saskatoon StarPhoenix*, 2 April 2017, https://thestarphoenix.com/news/saskatchewan/longtime-cabinet-minister-bill-mcknight-built-framework-for-settling-land-claims. See also Muskeg Lake Cree Nation, "Business," accessed 5 February 2019, https://muskeglake.com/business/muskeg-lake-property-management/.

33 Harry Lafond, interview, 19 April 2017.

34 Lester Lafond, interview, 9 May 2019.

35 Harry Lafond, interview, 19 April 2017.

36 Ibid.

37 Harry Lafond, interview, 19 April 2017.

38 Lafond, "Creation, Governance, and Management," 188–89.

39 Crown-Indigenous Relations and Northern Affairs Canada, "Treaty Texts," 29 August 2013, https://www.rcaanc-cirnac.gc.ca/eng/1370373165583/1581292088522.

40 See, for example, Sarah Carter, "Controlling Indian Movement: The Pass System," *NeWest Review* 10, no. 9 (1985): 8–9; Sarah Carter, *Lost Harvests: Prairie Indian Reserve Farmers and Government Policy* (Montreal: McGill-Queen's University Press, 1993); James W. Daschuk, *Clearing the Plains: Disease, Politics of Starvation, and the Loss of Aboriginal Life* (Regina: University of Regina Press, 2013); Howard Adams, *Prison of Grass: Canada from a Native Point of View*, rev. ed (Saskatoon: Fifth House Publishers, 1989); F. Laurie Barron, "The Indian Pass System in the Canadian West, 1882–1935," *Prairie Forum* 13, no. 1 (1988): 25–42.

41 Harry Lafond, interview, 19 April 2017.

42 Lafond, "Creation, Governance, and Management," 200.

43 Harry Lafond, interview, 19 April 2017.

44 Ibid.

45 The Saskatchewan Treaty Land Entitlement Framework Agreement is a tripartite agreement signed in 1992 by Canada, Saskatchewan, and the Entitlement First Nations in order to resolve federal obligations to set apart the amount of reserve land promised under treaty.

46 Lester Lafond, interview, 17 April 2017.

47 Dust, "Urban Neighbours Land Entitlement," 4.

48 Harry Lafond, interview, 19 April 2017; Lafond, "Creation, Governance, and Management," 189.

49 Lafond, "Creation, Governance, and Management," 189.

50 Lester Lafond, interview, 9 May 2019.

51 As City Solicitor, Dust participated in the negotiations between the Muskeg Lake Cree Nation and the City of Saskatoon for the Sutherland Industrial urban reserve.

52 Dust, "Urban Neighbours Land Entitlement," 4.

53 Ibid.; Theresa Dust, "The Impact of Aboriginal Land Claims and Self-Government on Canadian Municipalities: The Local Government Perspective," Intergovernmental Committee on Urban and Regional Research, September 1995; Theresa Dust, "Economic Development on Aboriginal Lands and Land Use Compatibility," cited in *Land Use Coordination: Servicing and Dispute Resolution*, Union of British Columbia Municipalities, 1998; Theresa Dust, "Common Questions about Urban Development Centres in Saskatchewan," in *Guide to Service Agreements*, Unit 3, June 2006, accessed 13 September 2023, https://sarm.ca/wp-content/uploads/2022/03/first-nations-municipal-community-infrastructure-partnership-program-service-agreement-toolkit-unit-3-guide-to-service-agreements.pdf.

54 Dust, "Economic Development on Aboriginal Lands," 1.

55 Constitution Act, 1867, 30 & 31 Vict, c 3.

56 Dust, "Economic Development on Aboriginal Lands," 2.

57 Dust, "Impact of Aboriginal Land Claims," 6.

58 Ibid., 36.

59 Joseph Garcea, interview, 12 April 2017.

60 Dust, "Impact of Aboriginal Land Claims," 8.

61 Ibid.

62 Long Plain First Nation in Manitoba is such an example. When its first urban reserve was created in the 1980s in Portage la Prairie, the First Nation and the municipality had not entered into a formal agreement, and Long Plain operated the reserve for several years without resorting to municipal services.

63 Joseph Garcea, "The FSIN and FSIN/SUMA Task Force Reports: Purposes, Processes, and Provisions," in *Urban Indian Reserves: Forging New Relationships in Saskatchewan*, ed. F. Laurie Barron and Joseph Garcea (Saskatoon: Purich

Publishing, 1999), 137–38; Barron and Garcea, "Genesis of Urban Reserves," 88.

64 Dust, "Impact of Aboriginal Land Claims," 9.

65 Ibid., 6.

66 Muskeg Lake Indian Band, Her Majesty the Queen in Right of Canada, and City of Saskatoon, "Original Agreement," 18 October 1988.

67 City of Saskatoon and Aspen Developments Inc., "Development and Servicing Agreement," 2 October 1992; Muskeg Lake Indian Band and City of Saskatoon, "Municipal Services Agreement," 18 September 1993.

68 Lester Lafond, "Creation, Governance, and Management," 190.

69 Ibid.

70 Marty Irwin, "Municipal Perspectives from Saskatoon," in *Urban Indian Reserves: Forging New Relationships in Saskatchewan*, ed. F. Laurie Barron and Joseph Garcea (Saskatoon: Purich Publishing, 1999), 214; Harry Lafond, interview, 19 April 2017.

71 Lester Lafond, interview, 17 April 2017.

72 Irwin, "Municipal Perspectives from Saskatoon," 215; Lester Lafond, interview, 17 April 2017.

73 Harry Lafond, interview, 19 April 2017.

74 Lester Lafond, interview, 17 April 2017.

75 Ibid.

76 Ibid.; Harry Lafond, interview, 19 April 2017.

77 Lester Lafond, interview, 17 April 2017.

78 Ibid.; Harry Lafond, interview, 19 April 2017; Gilles Dorval, Laura Hartney, and Dana Kripki, interview, 11 April 2017.

79 Harry Lafond, interview, 19 April 2017.

80 Lester Lafond, interview, 17 April 2017.

81 Irwin, "Municipal Perspectives from Saskatoon," 215.

82 Barron and Garcea, "Genesis of Urban Reserves," 32; Irwin, "Municipal Perspectives from Saskatoon," 215.

83 Lester Lafond, interview, 17 April 2017; Garcea, interview, 12 April 2017.

84 Dorval, Hartney, and Kripki, interview, 11 April 2017.

85 Garcea, interview, 12 April 2017.

86 Lafond, "Creation, Governance, and Management," 191.

87 Irwin, "Municipal Perspectives from Saskatoon," 215.

88 Ibid.

89 Dust, "Common Questions," 2.

90 For more details, see the Peter Ballantyne Cree Nation, "The Opawakoscikan Reserve in Prince Albert," in *Urban Indian Reserves: Forging New Relationships in Saskatchewan*, ed. F. Laurie Barron and Joseph Garcea (Saskatoon: Purich

Publishing, 1999), 159–76; Denton Yeo, "Municipal Perspectives from Prince Albert," in *Urban Indian Reserves: Forging New Relationships in Saskatchewan* (Saskatoon: Purich Publishing, 1999), 177–87.

91 Irwin, "Municipal Perspectives from Saskatoon," 216.

92 Ibid., 215.

93 Dust, "Economic Development on Aboriginal Lands," 3.

94 Harry Lafond, interview, 19 April 2017; Dorval, Hartney, and Kripki, interview, 11 April 2017.

95 Dust, "Urban Neighbours Land Entitlement," 5.

96 Irwin, "Municipal Perspectives from Saskatoon," 227; Harry Lafond, interview, 19 April 2017.

97 Other urban reserves have been established in the City of Saskatoon since the creation of Muskeg Lake's in 1988; those meetings now include representatives from all the First Nations that have an urban reserve in Saskatoon (Mike Icton, interview, 18 April 2017).

98 Irwin, "Municipal Perspectives from Saskatoon," 227.

99 Harry Lafond, interview, 19 April 2017.

PART TWO

◆

Culturally on Point

R e-centring Indigenous ways of being lies close to the heart of the chapters in this part, as each author shines a light on instructive stories of rebirthing culture and tradition in ways that make sense in meeting the challenges of the day.

The efforts of the Northern Saskatchewan Trappers Association to meet its mandate of supporting the trapping lifestyle, which was almost destroyed in the name of animal rights, are vigorously portrayed in Isobel Findlay's article. Banding together in a cooperative, this association works to rebuild a resilient lifestyle that honours culture meaningfully, with a special focus on the youth who have encountered the legal system. The association's mandate also includes making a space to be heard in policy circles for their vision of a healthy economy based on traditional lifeways and guiding those who want a life on the land to the teachers who have the needed skills. As Findlay notes, this discourse has much to offer the current dialogue around sustainability, climate change, and much-needed innovation to address pervasive global issues from a place of experience that has been neglected but is rich in wise practices and cultural integrity.

What does it mean to bring capitalism into an Indigenous context? Clifford Gordon Atleo tackles this question and others in his chapter.

Economic justice or imperialism at work is addressed by evaluating four approaches to these questions using a Western, academic approach that is unique in this book and used here to best advantage. After an extensive critique, Atleo concludes that in fact the cost is too high to Indigenous world views, values, and principles for Indigenous peoples engaging in capitalism. He concludes that alternative strategies embracing the "good life" are much more meaningful in honouring the tenacity of past leaders in protecting the integrity of their communities.

Based on her leadership experiences, Judith Sayers offers her personal perspectives on the complex issues surrounding sustainable development of British Columbia First Nations communities in ways that align with community-held cultural values. Clean energy options are prized while non-renewable energy options are scrutinized. Referring to international agreements such as the United Nations Declaration on the Rights of Indigenous Peoples, the provincial legislation that supports this declaration, and the duty to consult, Sayers addresses many critical issues, including the ways in which policy has aggravated the situation around sustainable development. The tenacity of First Nations in protecting their communities has not ceased and will continue for ensuing generations.

CHAPTER 4

✦

Trading on Tradition:
Innovative Indigenous Enterprise

✦

Isobel M. Findlay

I would like to talk about the land use studies. [We] had to do a planning study. [It's] a big book and very detailed. It tells you about the bush economy and about how people survive and how much money and how much food. And that was done for four or five years and the government said we are going to use it and honour that. Now they used it for their own use.

—*trapper*

When they get in trouble, when they break the law, well of course they send them to jail or give them a sentence. But send them to a camp where they can learn about their culture—how to trap, how to hunt, and all that was done in the old days. If they start learning about the Indian people's ways, maybe they can learn about who they are.

—*trapper*

We are not looking for handouts;
we would like to be self-sustainable.
—*trapper*[1]

In the global context of environmental crisis, growing inequality, and fraying social fabric,[2] the entrenched habits of those with access to levers of power (media, government, and resources) threaten to highjack the agenda. These corporate and political elites characterize climate change and ecological interests as impediments to prosperity, as luxuries we can no longer afford. They even go so far as to propose a "war room" to counter critique,[3] while reducing the plurality of economies and entrepreneurial models to a single, ruthlessly reductive logic. In resisting the inevitabilities of such neocolonial logics, knowledge monopolies, and a unilingual market in ways suggested by Clifford Gordon Atleo (see Chapter 5), Indigenous communities are demonstrating their remarkable economic tenacity (see also Wanda Wuttunee and Fred Wien's Preface). They are bridging traditional and social economies to achieve a common vision of a healthy, sustainable community and planet. This is the philosophy (of food security, healthy living, and sustainability) that drove Winnipeg's Neechi Commons (see Chapter 9). This chapter—based on a long-term research relationship[4]—discusses how one Indigenous organization, the Northern Saskatchewan Trappers Association (NSTA), reconstituted itself as a non-profit community development cooperative in order to reinvent itself and engage youth to retrieve and redefine trapping and cooperative enterprise in its own terms (much as David Newhouse argues in his introduction).

The words of the trappers from northern Saskatchewan with which I begin offer an important context and motivation for the research partnership between the Community-University Institute for Social Research at the University of Saskatchewan and the then Northern Saskatchewan Trappers Association Co-operative (NSTAC). The partnership, which began in 2007, was developed under the auspices of a project entitled "Linking, Learning, Leveraging: Social Enterprises, Knowledgeable Economies and Sustainable Development," funded by the Social Sciences and Humanities Research Council of Canada. The community-driven research both documented and drove activities within the NSTAC in response to government interventions that were as misguided as they were paternalistic and to systemic injustices that further undermined cultural identities, as the trappers suggest. These activities were designed to regain legitimacy and voice in policy and other decision making,[5] engage Indigenous youth, reconnect the generations, and contribute to environmental sustainability, socio-economic development, and cultural revitalization of northern communities. In the current context there are opportunities as well as obligations to educate the public and policy makers on the meanings of trapping, to link with, learn from, and leverage trapping teachings in social enterprises for knowledgeable economies and sustainable communities.

The NSTA represents about 2,400 registered trappers in eighty fur blocks covering 500,000 square kilometres of Treaty 6, 8, and 10 territories in northern Saskatchewan. It is mandated to monitor and guide major developments in trapping, develop policy, deliver training, and lobby government. Nearly forty years after being established, on the recommendation of the provincial government, the NSTA in 2007 transformed its organizational structure, becoming legally incorporated as a non-profit community development cooperative. It did so to gain legitimacy it did not have as an unincorporated association and to pursue a vision of self-determination and sustainability. As one of the trappers made clear, the NSTA was not interested in handouts but in retrieving its self-determining and self-sustaining ways. From the stand-point of the government—the organization's primary funder—the restructuring enhanced and formalized the NSTA's operational account-ability and transparency. But the meanings and benefits of becoming legally incorporated as a cooperative—from ownership and control to borrowing capacity and security from liability for debt for individual members—needed to be clear to its predominantly Métis, Cree, and Dene members while effectively addressing their needs and concerns, respecting their values and traditions, and engaging their wisdom and energy.

This chapter traces the history of trapping and the economic marginalization and underdevelopment caused by globalization and colonial law, policy, and regulation. It tells the story of the trappers' economic tenacity in efforts to resist bureaucratic and economic ration-alities and costly misconstructions of trapping. They did so in order to reposition trapping as an invaluable activity expressing the values of both the ongoing and revitalizing traditional economy and the social economy. It was about putting people before profits, promoting inclusion and democratic participation, and sustainable environments and live-lihoods. If the cooperative form has helped Indigenous communities revitalize entrepreneurship and resist neocolonial incursions, as was the case with Neechi Commons (Chapter 9), Indigenous communities have brought new energies and understandings to cooperatives, a renewed respect for Indigenous knowledge with a capacity to combine governance and enterprise in fashioning sustainable futures.[6] The trapper story is an important source of understanding Indigenous economic resilience in responding to the tests of dominant discourses and globalizing forces. The trapper story is especially important in the context of the Truth and Reconciliation Commission (TRC) of Canada's Calls to Action and Ten Principles of Reconciliation grounded in the

United Nations Declaration on the Rights of Indigenous Peoples, recognition and respect for treaty, constitutional, and human rights, and "public truth sharing" to "acknowledge and redress past harms" and to "create a more equitable and inclusive society."[7]

Context and Background

Globalization and ongoing colonial legacies continue to impact Indigenous communities disproportionately. A growing, young Indigenous population[8] continues to experience higher rates of unemployment, lower earnings, and lower labour participation rates when compared with the non-Indigenous population in Canada.[9] Although Indigenous people contribute importantly to Canadian society and economy, the 2019 National Indigenous Economic Development Board progress report documents persistent disparities in income, education, and employment, despite the board's determination to reach parity with non-Indigenous people by 2022 (adding in the process an estimated $27.7 billion annually to the Canadian economy). The median income gap was reduced by 9.3 percentage points between 2005 and 2015 but remains at 26.2 percentage points (from 64.5 percent to 73.8 percent of the non-Indigenous rate); median income for on-reserve First Nations ($14,580) is just over 35 percent of the median non-Indigenous rate of $41,230. High school completion rates similarly show improvement (by 4.5 percentage points between 2006 and 2016), but a 14.8 percentage point gap remains. The Indigenous college/ trades completion, however, exceeded the non-Indigenous rate by 2.6 percentage points in 2016. The gap in unemployment rates remained stagnant at 8.4 percentage points, while the university completion rate gap increased by 1.7 percent to 18.8 percentage points. Results were most positive for Métis and least for First Nations individuals on-reserve.[10]

In northern Saskatchewan, a region where the population is 80 percent Indigenous (only Nunavut and Nunavik, QC, have larger Indigenous populations) and education levels remain lower than in the rest of Saskatchewan, few opportunities for employment are available in an underdeveloped employment sector (with the exception of mining, health, and education).[11] In 2016, the employment rate in northern Saskatchewan at 38.4 percent (Indigenous employment is 32.4 percent and declining) was substantially lower than that in the rest of the province (65.1 percent).[12] Youth are particularly disadvantaged in a province where First Nations employment rates for those aged twenty-five to sixty-four has ranged from 31.1 percent for First Nations and 50.2 percent for Métis, among those who had no certificate,[13] and northern Saskatchewan is especially vulnerable to "the drain of money to other regions."[14]

Northern regions represent rich territory worth an estimated $84.8 billion in real GDP (gross domestic product) in 2009 ($16.2 billion in primary industries of forestry, mining, fishing, and hunting), marking a decline over the previous decade.[15] Still, northern Saskatchewan has experienced low capital investment and a legacy of overreliance on uranium mining at the expense of a diversified economy. So-called subsistence activities are not even tracked by Statistics Canada or other databases despite their important economic contribution. Yet fishing, trapping, hunting, and gathering remain "integral to the economies of many, if not most Aboriginal communities"; these pursuits are estimated to meet 50 percent of dietary intake in 78 percent of Inuit households in Nunavik, 73 percent in Nunavut, 70 percent in Inuvialuit, and 56 percent in Nunatsiavut, and to be worth $60 million annually in Nunavut alone (in 2001) in addition to contributing to health, well-being, and cultural value, including norms of reciprocity.[16] And a 2016 study found that 96.3 percent of Indigenous people in the forty-five northern

Saskatchewan communities want "to protect their traditional northern ways of life (hunting, trapping, fishing, gathering) and the distributive values associated with it." Of those surveyed, 50.6 percent believe that "too many decisions" are made by Regina and Ottawa, and that constitutionally protected Aboriginal and treaty rights and the duty to consult can and should constrain development on traditional lands and resources.[17]

Against this context and background, many for whom "the natural environment is at the heart of their economies and their very existence" resist the ways in which the "dominant socio-economic system marginalizes and fails Indigenous communities." In fact they "are no longer satisfied to watch while their communities are turned into vast tracts of wasteland."[18] Like the Royal Commission on Aboriginal Peoples, they know that economic development is "much more than individuals striving to maximize incomes and prestige. . . . It is about maintaining and developing culture and identity; supporting self-governing institutions; and sustaining traditional ways of making a living. It is about giving people choice in their lives."[19] Such thinking lies behind NSTAC initiatives to offer important opportunities for alternative livelihoods. As one trapper put it, "Not everybody can teach or go into the health training aspect. Yes, it is good to have those people, but those that cannot follow this path must have an alternative. And that is what I am looking at. I feel sorry for people that can't get a job. You need to train them in a different field. Maybe they are more comfortable in fishing or trapping. If that is what they are comfortable in, then that is what they like to do. Then give them an opportunity to make a living."[20] In the context of unequal employment and other opportunities, the key roles of the NSTAC in the traditional as well as the social economies need to be broadly understood and communicated. This involves the sort of cultural revitalization and historical reclamation projects from layers of colonial presumption (including anti-fur lobbies) that the NSTAC, like many Indigenous organizations, has been promoting in the interest of health and sustainability.[21]

Colonial History and Cultural Memory

It has long been known that poverty is a major reason for Indigenous overrepresentation in the criminal justice system in Canada,[22] though it has been less obvious that the law has itself impoverished Indigenous peoples by constraining their use of land, labour, and resources and criminalizing behaviours in attempts to "civilize" them.[23] From the Royal Proclamation of 1763 through the Constitution (British North America) Act, 1867, Indian Acts and Indian Advancement Act, 1884, to the Constitution Act, 1982, the regimes of ownership, development, and regulation have cut far deeper than "the depth of the plough blade" specified in the treaties.[24] The legacy was "poverty and power-lessness" for "a people who once governed their own affairs in full self-sufficiency."[25] The law enforced policies and bureaucratic and other controls (with significant discretionary powers) on everything from residence and movement, timing and mode of hunting, to definitions of leadership and governance and provision of electoral instruments, specifying how and when leaders could be removed, imposing involuntary enfranchisement (at expense of status), proscribing religious ceremony and cultural activities, and imposing residential schools.[26] The transfer of land in the Hudson's Bay Company sale to Canada in 1870, the transfer from federal to provincial jurisdiction in the 1930 Natural Resources Transfer Agreement, and the 1946 Saskatchewan government division of the province into two wildlife management zones were completed without consultation and with no regard to natural and traditional boundaries.

The effect of these unilateral decisions, compounded by provincial conservation law, policy, and regulation, has been to severely curtail traditional livelihoods and Aboriginal and treaty rights ("commercial and subsistence hunting and trapping" were the "usual vocation" at treaty making).[27] The result effectively reduced trapping from its unique relationship with the land and its resources to a "commercial activity" subject to the "same regulatory regime that applies to all trappers, without concern for the Aboriginality of the trapping activity."[28] Trade was always more than "economic exchange: for Indigenous communities . . . [it] strengthened security through alliances and relationships of 'equality and reciprocity.'"[29] The imposed wildlife management system "displaced the Aboriginal community-based wildlife management paradigm" and cooperative rules that had guided Indigenous trappers in favour of "white trappers who ignored those rules," with "devastating effects on fur-bearing animal populations and on Aboriginal economies."[30]

Overzealous conservation officers, encouraged by government and court decisions, continue the "over-criminalization" of those engaged in traditional livelihoods. One recent case witnessed a protracted and expensive surveillance exercise ending in charges for one First Nations fisherman in northern Saskatchewan caught selling $90 worth of fish without a licence, adding to resentments about enforcement that ignores larger environmental protection issues and corporate wrongdoing as well as important co-management opportunities while disrespecting land-based cultures.[31] Such actions underline the "double jeopardy" of marginalized groups who "are over policed and under protected."[32]

Similar policy interventions sustain to this day something like legislated poverty in terms of the "moderate livelihood" allowed for the exercise of Aboriginal treaty rights (*R. v. Marshall* [1999]). The effect has been to burden Indigenous communities with costly investments in court and other actions in order to resist and respond to the violence of dominant frames.[33] The effect has also been to undermine thriving social economies—long before the mainstream had invented the term— governed by *pimâcihowin* (making a living) grounded in *pimâtisiwin* (life) and *askiy* (land), as promised in the treaties as a continuing right, while guiding respectful relations with nature and all that it supports.[34] As Grand Chief Sheila North Wilson, Manitoba Keewatinowi Okimakanak, has said of the unequal playing field that creates barriers to health and self-sufficiency: "Our people are ready. But right now the rules are stacked against us. . . . Our food has to compete against federally sub-sidized monopoly retailers whose businesses are making us sick." Most importantly, she underlines how governments "were *also* 'taking the Indian out of the economy.'"[35] Policy and regulatory interventions, including damming, flooding, and water level regulation, funding biases favouring mainstream agriculture (but not fishing, hunting, trapping, or gathering), public health regulations, and licensing have moved communities from food security and sovereignty to insecurity—and to food-based community economic development initiatives to restore healthy, sustainable ways.[36]

Retelling the Trapping Story

It is this history and the current realities of ongoing encroachment and deteriorating land, water, and other conditions, together with their hopes for the youth and for sustainability, that motivate trappers to right the record, remap the territory, and retell their story. The trappers do so in order to build on trapping's role in the social, cultural, environ-mental, and economic development of the North. Their vision is to strengthen the multiple dimensions of trapping as a whole way of life, encompassing stewardship of the land and wildlife; preservation of culture, values, and a unique way of life; food sovereignty and security;

and support for just relationships, traditional medicines and healthy lifestyles, and community development. Passing on traditional knowledge and practices to youth, they believe, can preserve the cultural wisdom so necessary to the welfare and spirit of Indigenous communities. Though youth have always been welcome, since 2016, the annual NSTA convention and annual general meeting has included youth events, so that they "carry on the organization and make the industry strong," according to Robin McLeod.[37] Trapper memory of the treaty promises remains an important incentive ("They need to live up to treaty promises," said one trapper). As a trapper put it at a recent NSTA annual convention, "When the mace and beaded pillow (made by Florence Highway) help open the Saskatchewan legislature, they are a reminder from the Elders that we have treaties—living, breathing documents—that are part of who we are."[38] At the same convention, another trapper spoke to the frustration felt by many about the need "to beg for our own monies" in a province that "can't put up dollars for their trappers. . . . This is Creator's land. Revenue sharing should be half and half. How many millions come from the north?" And government should have an interest in trapping as "the healthiest lifestyle you can have here. . . . You have to do all these activities and you're physically active and you're eating good food that is healthy that doesn't have herbicides, pesticides, or any other 'cide.' The government, we have told them, it will save them twenty years from now." The government thinks it is saving money by not investing in trapping, but they "are not."[39]

In addition to considering developing their own "buying company" and renewing gardening practices for healthy food, trappers have also been exploring fur tanning and other value-added processing, as well as "a production centre based in the central part of the province in La Ronge. So we can have employment there. A lot of people know how to sew mukluks and jackets and stuff like that, but they don't have any place to sell them." This project, as well as eco-tourism opportunities, has been explored with the support of federal Co-operative Development Initiative grants, which were invaluable resources until their termination in 2013.[40] The trappers find strength in the networks developed through these initiatives and also in "the tenacity of local commercial fishing cooperatives," which, despite transportation and market pressures, "remain viable with about 700 licensed commercial fishers employing an estimated 1500 seasonal helpers."[41] They also find strength in "the resilience of [member] trappers. They work together. At the end of the day they have consensus . . . for the best interest of all."[42]

The government could also save lives and reduce justice and corrections costs if it invested in land-based learning, engaging traditional Indigenous law and justice principles. A "tough on crime" agenda that dominated criminal justice policy for some years has resulted in "poor policy choices grounded more in ideology than in evidence" and increasing prison populations and sentence lengths, reducing parole, and deteriorating conditions.[43] As of 2018, Indigenous overrepresentation was at "historic highs," increasing 42.8 percent in ten years and involving 38.4 percent Indigenous youth who report joining gangs "as a (misguided) way of obtaining personal protection against abuse, bullying, and violence."[44] Saskatchewan has had the worst record of the provinces on the incarceration of Indigenous youth, at 92 percent for males and 98 percent for female youth in 2018.[45]

A 2004 report for the Commission on First Nations and Métis Peoples and Justice Reform sent a strong message of decolonization, calling for institutional powers to relinquish their control of Indigenous justice and open doors for more cost-effective, holistic, and, most importantly, traditional alternatives. Although this theme has been present to a lesser or greater extent in the literature on Indigenous overrepresentation in the criminal justice system, the report states that "recognizing Aboriginal and treaty rights is not a privilege but a constitutional fact to be defended by all Canadians because all our freedoms and privileges depend on such recognition." The report concludes in this way: "We can with proactive and preventative measures, investments in collective, community solutions and alternative measures move beyond the adversarial and punitive to recognize and act on the value of education, community capacity building, or programs for youth and inmates in making policy decisions. . . . The seventh generation cannot afford the social or financial consequences of the status quo."[46] Specifically to address these shocking statistics, the TRC Calls to Action 30–32 address the overrepresentation, the need for community sanctions, and an end to mandatory minimum sentences and limited use of conditional sentences.[47]

Alternative justice programs that place Indigenous youth in traditional settings address these principles and allow offenders to reconnect with their histories, identities, and traditional culture. They have opportunities to hear the stories and learn the lessons of Indigenous knowledge and the holistic way of life—*pimâcihowin*, or making a living—that teach traditional law and justice principles about responsibility to Creator, the land, and "all my relations." In short, providing such alternative education to Indigenous offenders in a positive setting can help them rebuild their cultural awareness of sustainable, responsible, respectful stewardship, learn codes of behaviour, and provide an opportunity to rebuild their lives as meaningful community members.

The trappers had high hopes for the 2007 pilot Justice Trapline program (funded by Northern Affairs of First Nations and Métis Relations, Government of Saskatchewan). One trapper was motivated by his belief that "Sask Justice, the court system, and the RCMP" are the only beneficiaries of high incarceration rates for what are largely "petty crimes," adding, "So this is what we hope to offset also as we train these young offenders to become something, to be proud of something knowing that they have a title."[48]

Justice Trapline takes at-risk youth out on the trapline to give them a holistic education experience, renewing traditional values, learning across generations, and celebrating the diverse traditional meanings of trapping as world view. The trapline becomes a site of learning one's place in the world, one's roles and responsibilities, and the meaning of justice, and a place to develop one's land-based knowledge for health, healing, and hope. It offers an education where "in the bush you don't have to use a pencil. You have to use your brain because that is your gift, to use your brain and your heart."[49] It offers an education that tells youth who they are and can be if they take the opportunity to choose their own paths and rewrite their life stories.

The project targets Indigenous youth (ages twelve through twenty-four) residing in northeastern Saskatchewan communities. These youth, living in the five northernmost census divisions of the province, are subjected to a disproportionately high number of detractors from resilience and are particularly at risk for gang membership. In addition to educational and employment barriers discussed earlier, barriers to resilience faced by northern Indigenous youth include drug and alcohol dependencies, dysfunctional households, high levels of homelessness, and high levels of suicide.[50] The funnelling of resources to major urban centres has created a gap in culturally relevant programming and further aggravates challenges to resilience. This initiative seeks to address these gaps by implementing a justice trapline program in northern communities that offers participants the opportunity to experience traditional livelihood with experiential guidance from Elders and professional trappers. It takes inspiration from a history of justice trapline success in a number of predominantly Indigenous jurisdictions, including the Yukon, Northwest Territories, and Manitoba.[51]

The Justice Trapline pilot paired at-risk youth with trappers in a year-long program designed to strengthen organizational legitimacy, reshape social and legal relations, and increase economic opportunities, while providing youth with education and skills to sustain livelihoods at home. The pilot provided eight youth in conflict with the law with an alternative to remanded custody as they awaited trial. They were referred through court services and community justice, subject to an interview selection process, matched by the coordinator with trapper trainers, and trained in a range of traditional/life skills. Program objectives were to develop self-reliance, leadership, judgement, team-work, respect, and confidence, while acquiring certified training and developing complex skills through experiential learning and land-based methods.

This program was well-received by participants, schools, police, courts, and probation services and operated with cooperation from the NSTAC, the Sandy Bay RCMP detachment, local Crown prosecutors, judges, and probation services. The participants were diverted from exposure to the negative effects of incarceration and received training in a sustainable lifestyle. Clifford Ray, then president of the NSTAC, reported that the youth left the program feeling very connected to traditional lifestyles, which they found to be an excellent way of dealing with their problems. They learned that respecting nature, living a healthy lifestyle, and sustaining the land are hallmarks of trapper culture and the foundation of educational, cultural, and economic opportunities as well as human, social, and cultural capacity. The youth recovered a sense of voice and choice—of self-determination—as a key part of relearning positive selfhood and making a life narrative from a restorative episode. The initiative (which remains in great need and the trappers would like to renew) sent a strong message about the need to decolonize our institutions and thinking, a need for education, justice, and other institutions to relinquish their control and open doors for more cost-effective, holistic, and, most importantly, traditional alternatives.

Conclusion

The ongoing commitment of the NSTA and its executive members to their traditional livelihood is a measure of their tenacity and resistance to the alienating individualism required and rewarded by mainstream economies. In encouraging new appreciation for trapping as a holistic way of life that has typically been obscured, reduced, and distorted in public discourse, the NSTA has importantly solidified and sustained relationships within and beyond its membership. Pluralizing the economy as it does has enriched thinking and practice, underlining change through inventiveness and reimagined community, recognizing "all our relations."

Although the NSTA continues to struggle with resources and infrastructure ill-designed for the vast territory it represents, the initiatives it has undertaken in the last ten and more years have renewed its sense of legitimacy and developed new solidarities within and beyond the cooperative community, confirming the importance of cultural foundations and critical relationships to economic development (see Wuttunee and Wien's Conclusion). These initiatives have underlined the trappers' shared history of principled practice and brought home the proud history of a cooperative, knowledgeable, and sustainable economy long before the mainstream popularized the concepts. The NSTA has extended the cooperative movement's sense of its own history and underlined that neither cooperatives nor Indigenous communities are frozen in time. They can be powerful meeting places for intergenerational and intercultural dialogue, for coming together to critique dominant and exclusionary socio-economic narratives and to rewrite histories and ongoing realities, imagining and organizing otherwise for mutually beneficial futures. The northern trappers adapted the cooperative model in mutually enriching ways, enhancing appreciation of and accountability to Creator, community, land, and all that it sustains and is sustained by. Refusing to be "idle no more," they promote economic, cultural, eco-logical, and educational democracy. One such initiative was the Justice Trapline pilot project that diverted youth from the justice system while introducing the youth to a range of traditional (and transferable) life skills that opened up new opportunities and capacities. The project entailed partnerships with RCMP, Crown prosecutors, judges, and probation services while increasing a sense of self-determination for NSTAC and the youth. The NSTA continues to partner and share with provincial government, Indigenous government and organizations, schools, and postsecondary institutions, valuing culture as the foundation of participation and prosperity on their own terms. As we face climate change, and financial, economic, and other crises, the trappers' finding innovative Indigenous enterprise in tradition has much to teach us about who and what count, which knowledges and practices can be sustained, and how we might answer the TRC's call to "create a more equitable and inclusive society."[52]

NOTES

◆

1   Dwayne Pattison and Isobel M. Findlay, *Self Determination in Action: The Entrepreneurship of the Northern Saskatchewan Trappers Association Co-operative*, research report prepared for the Northern Ontario, Manitoba, and Saskatchewan Regional Node of the Social Economy Suite (Saskatoon: Centre for the Study of

Co-operatives and Community-University Institute for Social Research, 2010),
25–34, https://cuisr.usask.ca/documents/publications/2010-2014/Self%20
Determination%20in%20Action-%20NSTAC%202010.pdf.

2   World Economic Forum, *The Global Risks Report 2019*, 14th ed. (Geneva: World
       Economic Forum, 2019), http://www3.weforum.org/docs/WEF_Global_Risks_
       Report_2019.pdf.

3   James Keller, "Kenney Building 'War Room' to Counter Environmental Groups,
       Negative Media Coverage of Alberta's Oil Industry," *Globe and Mail*, 18 April
       2019,https://www.theglobeandmail.com/canada/alberta/
       article-kenney-building-war-room-to-counter-environmental-groups-negative/.

4   Isobel M. Findlay, Clifford Ray, and Maria Basualdo, "Research as Engagement:
       Rebuilding the Knowledge Economy of the Northern Saskatchewan Trappers
       Association Co-operative," in *Community-University Research Partnerships: Reflections on
       the Canadian Social Economy Experience*, ed. Peter V. Hall and Ian MacPherson
       (Victoria: University of Victoria Press, 2011), 141–58; Isobel M. Findlay, Clifford
       Ray, and Maria Basualdo, "The Ethics of Engagement: Learning with an
       Aboriginal Cooperative in Saskatchewan," in *Journeys in Community-Based Research*,
       ed. Bonnie Jeffery, Isobel M. Findlay, Diane Martz, and Louise Clarke (Regina:
       University of Regina Press, 2014), 29–49.

5   On the need for more meaningful policy and other relationships with Indigenous
       peoples, see Bonita Beatty, "Beyond Advising: Aboriginal Peoples and Social
       Policy-Making in Saskatchewan," in *New Directions in Saskatchewan Public Policy*, ed.
       David P. McGrane (Regina: Canadian Plains Research Center, 2011), 201–23.

6   See, for example, Isobel M. Findlay and Len Findlay, "Co-operatives: After the
       Crisis and Beyond the Binaries," in *Genossenschaften im Fokus einer neuen
       Wirtschaftspolitik* [Cooperatives in the Focus of a New Economic Policy], 2012
       XVII International Conference on Cooperative Studies, Association of
       Cooperative Research Institutes, University of Vienna, ed. Johann Brazda,
       Markus Dellinger, and Dietmar Rößl (Vienna: LIT Verlag AG, 2013), 809–20.

7   For Calls to Action, see Truth and Reconciliation Commission of Canada,
       *Honouring the Truth, Reconciling for the Future: Summary of the Final Report of the Truth and
       Reconciliation Commission of Canada* (Ottawa: Truth and Reconciliation Commission,
       2015), 319–38; for the Ten Principles, see Truth and Reconciliation Commission
       of Canada, *Canada's Residential Schools: Reconciliation*, vol. 6 of *Final Report of the Truth
       and Reconciliation Commission of Canada* (Montreal: McGill-Queen's University Press
       for the Truth and Reconciliation Commission of Canada, 2015), 16.

8   Statistics Canada, *First Nations People, Métis and Inuit in Canada: Diverse and Growing
       Populations*, catalogue no. 89-659-x2018001, 20 March 2018 (Ottawa: Minister of
       Industry, 2018). https://www150.statcan.gc.ca/n1/en/pub/89-659-x/89-659-
       x2018001-eng.pdf?st=B9cnxlDd.

9   Employment and Social Development Canada (EDSC), *Indicators of Well-Being in
       Canada: Canadians in Context—Aboriginal Population* (Ottawa: EDSC, 2014), http://
       www4.hrsdc.gc.ca/.3ndic.1t.4r@-eng.jsp?iid=36; Kar-Fai Gee and Andrew
       Sharpe, *Aboriginal Labour Market Performance in Canada: 2007–2011* (Ottawa: Centre
       for the Study of Living Standards, 2012), http://www.csls.ca/reports/

csls2012-04.pdf; National Indigenous Economic Development Board (NIEDB), *The Indigenous Economic Progress Report 2019* (Gatineau, QC: NIEDB, 2019), Statistics Canada, *National Household Survey*, 2011, https://www12.statcan.gc.ca/nhs-enm/index-eng.cfm.

10   NIEDB, *Indigenous Economic Progress Report*.

11   Keewatin Career Development Corporation, *Northern Economic and Labour Market Trends Report*, November 2016, http://www.kcdc.ca/economicandlabourmarkettrendsreport.pdf.

12   Ibid., 14.

13   Karen Kelly-Scott, *Aboriginal Peoples: Fact Sheet for Saskatchewan*, Aboriginal Peoples: Fact Sheets, Statistics Canada Catalogue no. 89-656-X2016009, released 14 March 2016, https://www150.statcan.gc.ca/n1/en/pub/89-656-x/89-656-x2016009-eng.pdf?st=lyyakbFt.

14   Keewatin Career Development Corporation, *Northern Economic and Labour Market Trends*, 7.

15   Conference Board of Canada, *Estimating Economic Activity in Canada's Northern Regions*, briefing, February 2011, https://www.conferenceboard.caproduct/estimating-economic-activity-in-canada's-northern-regions/.

16   David Natcher, "Subsistence and the Social Economy of Canada's Aboriginal North," *Northern Review* 30 (Spring 2009): 83–98, https://thenorthernreview.ca/index.php/nr/article/view/6/5.

17   Bonita Beatty, "A Distributive Aboriginal Political Culture Is Alive and Well in Northern Saskatchewan," *Journal of Aboriginal Economic Development* 10, no. 1 (2016): 38–53.

18   Priscilla Settee, "Indigenous Perspectives on Building the Social Economy of Saskatchewan," in *New Directions in Saskatchewan Public Policy*, ed. David P. McGrane (Regina: Canadian Plains Research Center, 2011), 73–74.

19   Royal Commission on Aboriginal Peoples, *Report of the Royal Commission on Aboriginal Peoples*, vol. 2, *Restructuring the Relationship* (Ottawa: Minister of Supply and Services Canada, 1996), 780.

20   Pattison and Findlay, *Self-Determination in Action*, 31–32.

21   Katie Big-Canoe and Chantelle A.M. Richmond, "Anishinabe Youth Perceptions about Community Health: Toward Environmental Repossession," *Health Place* 26 (2014): 127–35; Natalie Clark, Cu7Me7 q'wele'Wu-kt, "'Come On, Let's Go Berry-Picking': Revival of Secwepemc Wellness Approaches for Healing Child and Youth Experiences of Violence" (PhD diss., Simon Fraser University, 2018). For discussion of trapping within the fur trade, see, for example, Arthur J. Ray, *Indians in the Fur Trade*, with new introduction (Toronto: University of Toronto Press, 2005). On the cultural politics of fur, see Julia V. Emberley, *The Cultural Politics of Fur* (Ithaca: Cornell University Press, 1997).

22   Michael Jackson, *Locking Up Natives in Canada: A Report of the Committee of the Canadian Bar Association on Imprisonment and Release* (Vancouver: University of British Columbia, 1988).

23   Isobel M. Findlay and Warren Weir, "Aboriginal Justice in Saskatchewan
     2002–2021: The Benefits of Change," in *Legacy of Hope: An Agenda for Change*, vol.
     1 of the *Final Report from the Commission on First Nations and Métis Peoples and Justice
     Reform* (Saskatoon: Commission on First Nations and Métis Peoples and Justice
     Reform, 2004), 9-1–9-161.

24   See the words of Elder Peter Waskahat quoted in Harold Cardinal and Walter
     Hildebrandt, *Treaty Elders of Saskatchewan: Our Dream Is That Our People Will One Day
     Be Clearly Recognized as Nations* (Calgary: University of Calgary Press, 2000), 31.

25   Manitoba, Aboriginal Justice Inquiry of Manitoba, *Report of the Aboriginal Justice
     Inquiry of Manitoba*, vol. 1 (Winnipeg: Province of Manitoba, 1991), 1.

26   See Findlay and Weir, "Aboriginal Justice in Saskatchewan"; J. Miller, "The
     Historical Context," in *Continuing Poundmaker and Riel's Quest*, ed. R. Gosse, J. Y.
     Henderson, and R. Carter (Saskatoon: Purich Publishing; Saskatoon: College of
     Law, University of Saskatchewan, 1994), 41–51. See also Truth and
     Reconciliation Commission of Canada, *Honouring the Truth*.

27   Monique M. Passelac-Ross, *The Trapping Rights of Aboriginal Peoples in Northern
     Alberta*, Canadian Institute of Resource Law Occasional Paper 5 (Calgary:
     University of Calgary, April 2005), 7, 37, https://prism.ucalgary.ca/server/api/
     core/bitstreams/d09abcf8-cc8b-455e-9e40-1c217e7fc171/content. See also
     Beatty, "Distributive Aboriginal Political Culture"; Findlay, Ray, and Basualdo,
     "Research as Engagement"; Natcher, "Subsistence and the Social Economy."

28   Passelac-Ross, *Trapping Rights of Aboriginal Peoples*, 37.

29   Ibid., 31.

30   Ibid., 13.

31   Bonita Beatty, *Straining a Gnat but Swallowing a Camel: Policing First Nation Fishers in
     Northern Saskatchewan*, Yellowhead Institute Policy Brief 22, 13 February 2019,
     https://yellowheadinstitute.org/2019/02/13/policing-first-nation-fishers/.

32   Mary Corcoran, "'Be Careful What You Ask For': Findings from the Seminar
     Series on the 'Third Sector in Criminal Justice,'" *Prison Service Journal* 204
     (November 2012): 19.

33   Isobel M. Findlay, "Weaving the Interdisciplinary Basket: Building Resilient and
     Knowledgeable Communities and Economies," in *Visioning a Mi'kmaw Humanities:
     Indigenizing the Academy*, ed. Marie Battiste (Sydney, NS: Cape Breton University
     Press, 2016), 107–22.

34   Cardinal and Hildebrandt, *Treaty Elders of Saskatchewan*, 43–47.

35   Grand Chief Sheila North Wilson, preface to Shaun Loney with Will Braun, *An
     Army of Problem Solvers: Reconciliation and the Solutions Economy* (Winnipeg: Friesens,
     2016).

36   Shirley Thompson, Asfia Gulrukh, Myrle Ballard, Byron Beardy, Durdana Islam,
     Vanessa Lozeznik, and Kimlee Wong, "Is Community Economic Development
     Putting Healthy Food on the Table? Food Sovereignty in Northern Manitoba's
     Aboriginal Communities," *Journal of Aboriginal Economic Development* 7, no. 2 (2011):
     14–39.

37 Quoted in Linda Mikolayenko, "Trappers Engage Youth at Annual Convention," *EagleFeather News,* 26 April 2016, https://www.eaglefeathernews.com/arts/index.php?detail=2068.

38 Trapper words that are not documented in Pattison and Findlay, *Self-Determination in Action*, or cited elsewhere are derived from unpublished transcripts of discussions and also from public statements made by trappers at their lively, engaging annual conventions in Prince Albert or LaRonge.

39 Pattison and Findlay, *Self-Determination in Action*, 35.

40 Ibid., 32.

41 Beatty, "Distributive Aboriginal Political Culture," 44.

42 Pattison and Findlay, *Self-Determination in Action*, 28. See also Beatty, "Distributive Aboriginal Political Culture," 46–47, on the high levels of community engagement and volunteer care and support for community events and activities and the production of "resilient community 'builders.'"

43 Office of the Correctional Investigator, *Annual Report 2017–2018* (Ottawa: Correctional Investigator Canada, 2018), accessed 13 September 2023, https://oci-bec.gc.ca/index.php/en/content/office-correctional-investigator-annual-report-2017-2018.

44 Ibid., 61, 75.

45 Statistics Canada, "Adult and Youth Correctional Statistics in Canada, 2016/2017," *Juristat,* 19 June 2018, https://www150.statcan.gc.ca/n1/pub/85-002-x/2018001/article/54972-eng.htm. See especially Table 13.

46 Findlay and Weir, "Aboriginal Justice in Saskatchewan," 12, 149.

47 Truth and Reconciliation Commission of Canada, *Honouring the Truth*, 324.

48 Pattison and Findlay, *Self-Determination in Action*, 34.

49 Ibid., 33.

50 Bryan Hogeveen, "Toward 'Safer' and 'Better' Communities? Canada's Youth Criminal Justice Act, Aboriginal Youth and the Processes of Exclusion," *Critical Criminology* 15, no. 3 (2005): 287–305.

51 Fur Institute of Canada, *Reconnecting with the Land: Beaufort-Delta Region Youth Trapper Training Program, 2005. Final Report: Evaluation and Recommendations,* https://www.enr.gov.nt.ca/sites/enr/files/reports/sitidgi_lake_2005.pdf.

52 Truth and Reconciliation Commission of Canada, *Canada's Residential Schools*, 16.

CHAPTER 5

✦

Capitalism: Can It Be Indigenized?

✦

Clifford Gordon Atleo

M any would argue that studying economic development—with the purpose of practical and relevant analysis for Indigenous communities—requires a thorough understanding of the mainstream economies that we must interact with and/or resist. Without a doubt, capitalism is *the* dominant economic system and possibly the number one threat to Indigenous community health. Capitalism has been one of the primary means by which settler society has assaulted Indigenous lands and peoples. Since contact, Indigenous peoples have had complex and evolving economic relationships with European settlers. For a significant portion of the twentieth century, many Indigenous peoples resisted colonial efforts to exploit and extract resources, but in recent years, more Indigenous communities have begun to partner with resource extraction companies. Is this a form of economic justice or a nuanced form of imperialism that coopts the resistance of Indigenous peoples who have been effectively starved into submission?

In this chapter, I explore how Indigenous communities have attempted to navigate capitalist economies and markets. I am also interested in how Indigenous people contend with capitalism to mitigate its more harmful effects while at the same time exhibiting tenacity by trying to protect and promote their cultures, assert self-determination, and provide economic opportunities. Specifically, I want to know whether capitalism can be Aboriginalized, that is, adapted or engaged with in a way that is consistent with Indigenous world views and values. In this chapter I look at four forms of Aboriginal capitalism: "reservation capitalism," as defined by Robert Miller; "tribal capitalism," identified by Duane Champagne; "capitalism with a red face," described by David Newhouse; and "community capitalism," advocated by Wanda Wuttunee. It is my contention that capitalism cannot be Indigenized without radically altering it into something else, and that Indigenous people cannot act as capitalists without radically altering their own community-derived world views and principles. This issue of whether capitalism can be Aboriginalized is fundamental to any discussion of Aboriginal economic development, and indeed it is a theme in many of the chapters in this book. Several of the case studies, for example, describe community-based economic developments that have been quite successful according to (capitalist) economic criteria while also showing how important Indigenous values and practices have been maintained, although there is always a struggle. While this chapter primarily looks at Aboriginal capitalism, I conclude with a few ideas and examples of potential Indigenous alternatives in a contemporary context.

Understanding Capitalism and the Challenges in Indigenous Communities

"Capitalism is not a monolithic form of economic organization but rather . . . it takes many forms,"[1] but I do want to begin with *my* understanding of capitalism, as it exists in our daily lives and communities. Capitalism emphasizes the importance of the individual rather than the collective, although many capitalist proponents going back to Adam Smith have argued that individual self-interest ultimately improves the collective.[2] This leads to massive inequality, however, as the freedom of individuals to accumulate wealth is not only protected, it is encouraged and celebrated. Competition between individuals and corporations is favoured over cooperation and consensus decision making. Capitalism prioritizes the protection of private property for profit and the commodification of all things, even life forms.[3] Capitalist economies require incessant growth and profit maximization, which depletes finite resources and, in resource-intensive economies like Canada's, is harmful to ecosystems. Connected to this is the prioritization of exchange value over use value, which requires a radical reorientation of Indigenous world views. Capitalism has proven to be fluid and adaptive, but I believe that its core tenets remain consistent. It is with these commonly held views in mind that I critique the following attempts to Aboriginalize capitalism.

After years of ongoing colonial domination, many Indigenous people are struggling to survive, in many cases simply trying to meet basic human needs while still fighting to retain their unique cultures and identities. Robert Miller believes that the problem in "Indian Country" is one of extreme poverty, writing, "American Indians are today the poorest of the poor in the United States."[4] Of course, Miller is not alone in focusing on poverty, but he does draw some different conclusions. In *Reservation "Capitalism,"* he writes, "American Indians and tribal governments have the right to enjoy the same prosperity and security as other Americans."[5] Miller's conception of Native American poverty is relative to the broader American population. He also believes that there are several social pathologies that accompany poverty. Miller quotes a tribal chairman from Oregon, stating, "We need to make it acceptable in Indian country to be in business."[6] Miller believes that there is a stigma against Native American participation in capitalist enterprises, and that this has led to rampant poverty. He offers "reservation capitalism" as the solution. Miller writes, "Expanding and creating new forms of economic development and activities in Indian Country is probably the most important political, social, community, and financial concern that Indian nations, tribal leaders, and Indian peoples face today."[7] My concern is that if we uncritically accept narrow settler ideas of wealth and poverty, we may also accept conditions that potentially limit our own Indigenous world views and solutions.

From Duane Champagne's perspective, the key problem is one of Indigenous autonomy or the lack thereof, and tribal engagement with capitalism is just one aspect of a broader community development approach. He writes, "The indigenous self-determination movement is about maintaining land, culture, institutional relations, government, and self-sufficiency *under terms compatible with indigenous cultures and beliefs.*"[8] This is where it gets tricky, because he later adds that many traditional Indigenous beliefs and values are *incompatible with capitalism*. Champagne writes, "Tribal leadership often argues that sovereignty is not possible without freedom from economic dependence on government programs and funding. High rates of poverty and unemployment on reservations, with their attendant problems and issues, are a major stimulus for tribal governments to promote economic development."[9] Like the others, Champagne conflates economic development with capitalism, but must this inevitably and always be the case? Are non-capitalist economies possible currently? He remains optimistic that not "all nations and communities will converge toward a common market-based institutional order."[10] Champagne's solution is "tribal capitalism," which includes some key distinctions that he believes protect tribal autonomy and culture.

David Newhouse writes that "one of the most persistent problems facing Aboriginal people throughout Canada has been low incomes and low participation in the labor force."[11] Although he seems to take participation in the mainstream economy for granted, Newhouse also warns of the "Borg of capitalism," an irresistible and consuming force. Instead of shunning it altogether, however, he calls for "capitalism with a red face." He acknowledges that engagement with capitalism is transformative, but feels that Indigenous people have no other choice, hence the assimilative Borg analogy. Like Miller, Newhouse believes that one of the biggest obstacles standing in the way of successful Aboriginal economic development is Aboriginal people themselves, writing, "It is important to develop within the community a sense of legitimacy for economic development and its related activities."[12] Newhouse also at times conflates economic development and capitalism, which I believe inhibits the possibility of Indigenous alternatives. In this volume, Newhouse offers an insightful understanding of Indigenous economic history as a history of tenacity, where leaders have struggled in a variety of ways to engage with capitalism differently, attending to Indigenous world views and cultural values. I agree with his general assertion that Indigenous communities have worked hard to take an Indigenous-centric and Indigenous-led approach to economic development, but I also agree with his earlier astute assessment of the overwhelming assimilative power of capitalism. I believe that Borg capitalism is alive and well.

Unlike the others, Wanda Wuttunee does not really begin with an urgent rationale for Aboriginal economic development. In her book *Living Rhythms*, she writes, "This is not a story of dysfunction and despair. I do not ignore these aspects, for they are woven into the fabric of community life; they are also the subject of extensive debate elsewhere."[13] Wuttunee chooses to emphasize "success stories" and takes an approach that accepts that economic development is happening in Aboriginal communities, seeking to reveal "best practices" that attempt to counteract the toxicity of capitalism with "community capitalism" based on Indigenous values and priorities. At the same time, she writes, "Capitalism is seductive in its all pervasiveness and in what it promises to deliver."[14] This differs slightly from Newhouse's Borg analogy, as it captures the fact that some Indigenous people are attracted to capitalism's promises rather than simply trying to make the best of it. Wuttunee certainly understands Indigenous ambivalence with respect to capitalist engagement. She writes, "As Aboriginal peoples, we may not want to mirror mainstream business choices."[15] Wuttunee is careful to withhold judgement in her case studies, writing, "Each community must walk its own path and live its own truth."[16] Indigenous peoples in Canada have long struggled for self-determination in many ways, and recently this has come in the form of economic independence. Of the Tsuu T'ina Nation, Wuttunee writes that "the goal . . . was to move away from dependence on government. The main strategy was to heal community members and develop economically viable projects that earned revenue and provided employment."[17] She also echoes a common refrain regarding Canadian taxpayer concerns. Given the opportunity to participate economically, Wuttunee writes, "Aboriginal peoples will impact the country positively as their potential is developed. They will be a drain on resources if social and economic issues are not dealt with effectively."[18] This appeal certainly resonates with many people, Indigenous and non-Indigenous alike, but I fear it lacks legitimate criticism of some of capitalism's fundamental tenets and mainstream perceptions about wealth and poverty.

Reservation Capitalism

There is nothing traditional about having the federal
government take care of us. There is nothing cultural about
that. . . . My idea of tribal economic development is that
sovereignty is economic independence. Until we get there,
we are not independent.

—*Clifford Lyle Marshall, Chairman, Hoopa Valley Tribe*[19]

Despite the title of his book, Miller does not offer a succinct definition
of "reservation capitalism." He does not suggest how capitalism might
be adjusted or tweaked to better suit Native communities. Miller is an
unapologetic capitalist who lacks the ambivalence of his peers and
simply advocates for increased mainstream capitalism on Native
American reservations. And while he acknowledges that some are
concerned over the negative impacts of capitalism on Native cultures,
he counters these concerns with the argument that cultural integrity
is in greater danger when Native communities are in poverty. Going
further, Miller makes the case that Native Americans are not culturally
opposed to capitalist principles in the first place, writing, "Native peoples
understood, appreciated, and lived by principles that today we call
private property rights, entrepreneurship, and free market economics
in which individuals voluntarily participate in the manufacture of excess
crops and goods and engage in trade mostly without governmental
direction or control."[20] He does not believe that Native Americans lived
in "socialistic societies where everything was jointly owned and shared
by the community."[21] Just as I agree that it is incorrect to impose
socialism on our understanding of historical Indigenous communities,
it is equally incorrect to make assumptions that lean in the liberal
capitalist direction. Miller suggests the Pacific Northwest potlatch as
an example of wealth accumulation and redistribution, writing that it

is similar to "how U.S. society today chooses to spend money on activities we desire, which includes giving extra wealth to social and charitable organizations for tax deductions and because our society values that kind of generosity."[22] This is a horribly simplistic view of the potlatch, and his equating it with contemporary American capitalism and charitable activity is utterly wrong. Many potlatch hosts gave until they had nothing left to give. Like many coastal Indigenous understandings of the interconnected and cyclical nature of life, potlatch economies depended on communal reciprocity, which is not how settler society currently governs itself.

According to Miller, tribal governments need to create "business-friendly environments where other tribes, Indian and non-Indian companies, and individuals will invest money and human capital in economic endeavors."[23] This falls in line with the findings of the Harvard Project on American Indian Economic Development, which also includes the creation of stable governing institutions and bureaucracies, fair dispute-resolution processes, attractive tax regimes, and clear distinctions between tribal politics and economics. A major concern I have with this approach is that when tribal communities have supposedly freed themselves from poverty and government dependency, they may then be burdened with a new dependency: the capitalist market. In an age where efficiency is paramount and neoliberal "comparative advantage" is dictated by the market, Indigenous nations are likely to find themselves vulnerable to the uncaring whims of those markets. This dynamic has already played itself out around the world in countries that have officially "decolonized" but maintain asymmetrical neocolonial relations with their former imperial masters.

Miller also calls for increased entrepreneurship, pointing out that Native American private business ownership is at the lowest per capita rate for any group in the United States.[24] He writes, "Increasing entrepreneurship and economic development on reservations in a careful and respectful manner will support tribal cultures, not injure them."[25] I have to ask whether entrepreneurship *must* be practised within a capitalist framework, and what is meant by "a careful and respectful manner"? Miller does not approach capitalism with any degree of criticism, especially with respect to profit maximization or resource depletion, and he does not consider the broader implications of increased Native American participation in capitalist economies. Instead, he writes, "You do not have to be poor to be Indian or to be a cultural person, you do not stop being an Indian or a cultural person if you become materially well off."[26] Again, economic development may be acted out as a form of capitalism, but does it have to be? There are alternatives, as well as Indigenous challenges to the presumed universalism of what it means to be materially well off. I agree that the poverty that Indigenous people endure today is something that must be addressed, but I do not believe that reservation capitalism is the only, or the appropriate, solution.

Tribal Capitalism

For Champagne, the term "tribal capitalism" reflects its "predominantly collective" nature.[27] He believes the primary goal of tribal communities is the preservation and perpetuation of Native American political and cultural autonomy. Champagne writes of Native American tenacity, "Despite five hundred years of colonialism, Native people are loath to give up the primary aspects of Native life and community."[28] Paramount among these is a unique understanding of people's place in creation. He writes, "Cosmic harmony and order were preserved by maintaining respectful relations with all spirit beings, including human groups and individuals."[29] This is a different orientation from one that places humanity at the top of earthly creation with the

God-given right to dominate all other life on earth. For Champagne, there are many key differences between Indigenous and settler world views, and for Native people to engage with capitalism is an endeavour fraught with complications.

The first of these complications is what Max Weber called an "Iron Cage." Once the forces of capitalism "are unleashed, other economic actors must follow suit or be forced out of business."[30] This is a straightforward argument. Market competitiveness demands decision making that often goes against other community interests. One example of this would be a decline in hunting, trapping, gathering, and fishing in favour of wage labour or entrepreneurship. Indigenous peoples then risk losing a vital connection with the lands and waters that sustained their communities for millennia. Additionally, when business ventures run their course, as in the case with intensive resource extraction, communities are often left with generations who no longer know how to live with the land. My people, the Nuu-chah-nulth-aht, along with many other coastal peoples, have experienced this with respect to fishing. I am not saying that choosing one economic activity over another can only have these outcomes, or even that it is always a choice in the first place. Many Indigenous peoples have been forced to abandon their traditional ways of living. Thus, the Iron Cage argument is at least partially true, but Champagne is not thoroughly convinced, writing, "Communities can take on capitalist elements and participate in capitalist markets and still retain core aspects of identity, tradition, institutional relations—the close interconnectedness of polity, culture, economy, and community—and cultural values."[31] To be clear, Champagne is saying something quite different from Miller. Champagne acknowledges the potentially toxic effects of capitalism, whereas Miller sees nothing inherently wrong with capitalism.

Champagne believes that Native nations, as collectives, are resilient enough to survive the engagement intact, hence the term "tribal capitalism." While I recognize the significance of the tribal collectivity as a repository and protector of Indigenous ways, I am not as optimistic. Champagne argues that "for most Native communities, economic development is a means to an end. Even the most strongly market-oriented tribal economic planners see economic development as a way to support the reservation community, retain tribal members on reservations, and promote self-supporting Native communities."[32] Unlike Miller, Champagne believes that traditional Native values are not compatible with modern capitalist values. He writes, "Most Native nations believe in maintaining respectful relations among humans and other entities of the universe such as places, water, air, fire, earth, animals, birds, heavenly bodies, and the rest of the cosmos."[33] In contrast, Champagne states, "Capitalist philosophies see the earth as a natural resource, where exploitation of raw materials through labor transforms raw materials into useful objects for further economic production or consumption and the creation of additional wealth."[34] How then do we explain the slide of Native communities toward capitalism? Again, Newhouse does a great job of explaining this in the Canadian context in the introductory chapter.

Native American entrepreneurship has increased dramatically since the 1970s. Despite this growth, Champagne writes, "Business ownership has not obliterated Native identity, [which] reflects the continuity of Native cultural values [and] political relations."[35] He believes that Native American communities discourage individual capitalist values and instead favour "generosity, redistribution, and egalitarianism."[36] And differing from Miller, Champagne writes, "Most reservation communities prefer relatively holistic institutional relations among economy, community, polity, and culture.[37] He writes, "Natives are opting for a collective

capitalism rather than individual capitalism."[38] Champagne believes
that tribal capitalism is different from American capitalism. Regarding
the Iron Cage, he concedes that the outcomes are mixed, writing,
"Market competition forces the Indian communities to consider and
engage in market enterprise, but they wish to do so under their own
terms, which means subordinating capitalist accumulation to collective
goals of community and cultural and political enhancement and preservation."[39] He acknowledges the power of capitalism to consume and
discipline, but Champagne is optimistic that Native American communities will continue to survive. He considers the changes in Native
communities and culture evidence of "social change" rather than
outright assimilation.[40] I too am confident about the resilience and
tenacity of Indigenous communities, but not because of our ability to
navigate capitalism but rather our ability to innovate alternatives to it.

Capitalism with a Red Face

In his earlier writings on capitalism, David Newhouse began by citing
the final report of the Royal Commission on Aboriginal Peoples (RCAP),
which "reflected the conventional and accepted wisdom that a major
part of the solution to the problems facing Aboriginal peoples is
economic development."[41] He also points out that Aboriginal economic
development, regardless of form, must exist within the broader national
and global economies. Newhouse writes, "In the search for a better life
within the context of contemporary North America, we encounter
capitalism. We simply have no choice."[42] And thus, Newhouse offers
us his Borg of capitalism analogy.[43] He writes, "I think of our encounter
as Aboriginal peoples meeting the Borg of capitalism. . . . They absorb
peoples at will . . . they broadcast the following message: 'Your existence
as you know it has come to an end. Resistance is futile.'"[44] Like
Champagne and unlike Miller, Newhouse believes that traditional

Indigenous world views are quite distinct from the values of Western capitalism. He writes rather gravely, "We have participated at the edges of capitalism, as labourers, as small business people, as debtors. Now we seek to enter its heart. We will be transformed by it . . . capitalism will absorb Aboriginal cultures. And the moral order of Aboriginal societies will be changed."[45] Newhouse's rather blunt but astute assessment of Indigenous encounters with capitalism seems to differ from Champagne's optimism, but as we shall see, they may be closer than first appearances indicate. According to Newhouse, "The idea that we can somehow participate in capitalism without being changed by it is in my view wrongheaded."[46] This does not incline Newhouse to shy away from capitalism, however. Again, he begins with the assertion that we have no choice. Of his own role, he writes, "I can describe much of my own work as making capitalism work better for Aboriginal communities, developing, as it were, capitalism with a red face."[47]

Newhouse asks, "What unique perspectives do aboriginal people bring to the ongoing debate about the practice of capitalism? . . . Can aboriginal peoples find a way to adapt capitalism to their own particular world views?"[48] He recognizes that these questions are complicated and suggests that the challenge is to develop "contemporary interpretations of traditional ideas."[49] Newhouse draws on his experience with the RCAP and on the testimony of James Dumont, who offered seven primary Native values: kindness, honesty, sharing, strength, bravery, wisdom, and humility.[50] Newhouse adds that Aboriginal societies are collectivist in orientation, and that efforts to "re-traditionalize" or "reinterpret traditional values within a contemporary (and communal context) . . . offer some hope for the development of aboriginal economies."[51] In this respect, he is in agreement with Champagne.

Newhouse recognizes that capitalism has a difficult problem to overcome, especially if it is to be adapted by Aboriginal societies, and that is the problem of inequity. Despite this, he believes that "there is no fear that capitalism cannot be adapted to aboriginal realities."[52] Newhouse offers ten points that distinguish capitalism with a red face:[53]

1. Development will take a holistic approach including four dimensions similar to the Cree Medicine Wheel: physical, mental, emotional, and spiritual.

2. Development will be a process or a journey and not a product, with an emphasis on long-term over short-term results.

3. Development will be collaborative rather than competitive and a joint effort between individuals and the collective.

4. Individual actions will respect the interconnectivity of the world and affirm that humanity is but one small part.

5. Development will prioritize "human capital investment rather than individual capital accumulation" and respect quality of life, including the environment.

6. Traditional knowledge, with Elder guidance, will inform planning and decision making.

7. Aboriginal values of kindness and sharing will guide how communities deal with wealth distribution, and individuals with a lot of accumulated wealth will be expected to share.[54]

8. Native economic institutions will be "primarily western in nature with adaptations to ensure that they operate in a manner which is appropriate to the local aboriginal community."

9. Decisions will be made by consensus, and in particular, large development projects will require broad community consensus.

10. "The notions of honesty and respect will result in a heightened sense of accountability for economic institutions and decision makers."

This list is consistent with the tone of the RCAP recommendations and interesting insofar as it all seems highly improbable given Newhouse's

Borg of capitalism analogy. Despite the relative strength of these ten points, Newhouse concludes with an ominous warning: "The process of modernization and the adoption of capitalism as a dominant political-economic system within aboriginal society is well underway. It would be sheer folly to attempt to reverse the process or to attempt dramatic shifts in direction. I would argue that the forces of modernization are much too great to resist."[55]

Newhouse wrote two more articles on the Borg of capitalism, shifting his tone slightly. In 2002, he wrote, "Canadians, and I would dare say Aboriginal people, have come to see market society and capitalism as offering the best option for improving human welfare."[56] But Newhouse also notes growing resistance in Native communities, and commenting on the nature of that resistance, he writes, "I believe that we resist through stating and restating our own objectives as Aboriginal peoples for cultural distinctiveness, for societies based upon traditional ideas, values and customs, for sustainable development, for equitable distribution of wealth, for the idea of progress that is broad and multi-faceted, for communities that are more than markets, among other things."[57] In 2004, Newhouse shifts even further, challenging people to think critically and ask the right questions, "so that we begin to be able to engage the Borg in a way that will allow us to come out of it with our own selves intact."[58] Ultimately, he does not think capitalism can be replaced, but he does think there is a possibility of developing a "compassionate capitalism . . . that begins to operate under a set of values that balances market and community."[59] A tall order to be sure, and I am not convinced that it is possible, but I am encouraged to see Newhouse at least acknowledge the possibility of resisting the more destructive parts of capitalism.

Community Capitalism

Wuttunee's co-authored (with Stelios Loizides) paper, "Creating Wealth and Employment in Aboriginal Communities," was published in 2005, one year after her book *Living Rhythms* came out.[60] In this paper she explicitly introduces the idea of "community capitalism," but before getting into it, I want to back up to *Living Rhythms* to engage some of her theoretical groundwork, including her critiques of capitalism. Wuttunee writes, "The statistics regarding stress, addiction, failing families, and youth at risk in western society indicate that we [are] not happier and healthier as a result of this philosophy of maximum growth for maximum profits."[61] She suggests a shift: "In my view, a shift must occur away from an approach to economic development that is secular in nature [what the Harvard Project recommends], that is, considers a limited number of issues such as readily quantifiable costs in reaching decisions. We must move instead towards an economic development approach that includes these costs but also attempts to quantify all the costs of development decisions on environment, people, communities, and future generations."[62] I have a number of concerns. First, this approach might require that we apply mainstream metrics to Indigenous understandings of our environments, peoples, communities, and commitments to future generations. I am not convinced that this can be done without losing context in the process. Second, we are still dealing with an "add Aboriginal and stir" approach that *does not centre* Indigenous perspectives but rather attempts to make them fit within a capitalist framework. I appreciate the practicality of this approach, but I still believe that caution is warranted. Further, Wuttunee calls for "reasonable profit" instead of maximum profit.[63] She elaborates, "Basic elements of earning a reasonable return on investment may be learned and practiced by anyone regardless of ethnicity. The way in which Aboriginal society defines 'good business practices and standards,' for example, is a function of currently held values and traditions. These may be *any* blend on a spectrum of traditional and capitalist values."[64] Wuttunee's conception of an Aboriginalized community capitalism rests upon her understanding of values as a blending process, existing on a spectrum, rather than as a collision of incompatibility. This is something that is very difficult to measure, and Wuttunee acknowledges that these are complex matters in a constant state of flux. She recognizes that in many cases, First Nations communities are forced to make difficult decisions for short-term survival at the expense of long-term responsibilities.[65] Throughout Wuttunee's writings she indicates that unrestrained capitalism is dangerous, but she remains optimistic that it may *be* restrained through Aboriginal input, writing, "In the mainstream business world, traditions such as ceremonies or honouring the collective nature of Aboriginal communities oftentimes are seen as burdensome or meaningless. Acknowledging that the single-minded focus on profit as the norm, to the exclusion of balance and respect, has significantly marred the quality of life for future generations is a giant step towards realizing that capitalism in its present form does not have all the answers."[66] What she proposes is community capitalism, which shares some traits with Champagne's tribal capitalism as well as with the Harvard Project.

Wuttunee and Loizides write, "There is a general consensus among leaders in traditional Aboriginal communities that economic self-sufficiency must come about through the establishment and growth of business enterprises within the communities."[67] Referencing the National Aboriginal Financing Task Force, they argue, "The most effective way (and probably the only way) for Aboriginal communities to address their current socio-economic challenges is to create wealth through business activity."[68] They also cite Stephen Kakfwi, former Premier of the Northwest Territories, who states, "We have two choices. We can hide away in our communities and live simple little lives, but there will still be huge social problems. Or we can embrace development and build a better future. It's a double-edged sword—but that's true of anything. So you focus on the good and deal with the bad."[69] If we take Wuttunee's original assertion that Western society is not healthier or happier, then it follows that social problems are likely to persist after economic development as well. Several prominent Indigenous economic development advocates have taken similar positions, including Clarence Louie, Calvin Helin, and Ray Halbritter.[70] The rhetoric of economic self-reliance is compelling, but it is often simplified as an either/or proposition, which can lack the nuance necessary to address our complex contemporary realities.

Wuttunee and Loizides write, "Aboriginal people want to become self-sufficient while preserving their traditional values in the process. . . . The values of respect, pride, dignity, sharing, hospitality and mutual aid are at the root of Aboriginal culture in all its expressions."[71] Wuttunee has written at length on many of the problems with capitalism, but not enough to compel her to disregard it entirely. She clarifies, "Differences exist between the key tenets of capitalism—such as individualism, profit maximization, accumulation of wealth and the market economy—and the Aboriginal values of harmony, balance and reciprocity."[72] According to Loizides and Wuttunee, the concept of community capitalism originated with Ted DeJong, the CEO of the Prince Albert Development Corporation. They write, "Inherent in the concept of community capitalism is the nurturing of a business culture that incorporates the best of capitalism *and* Aboriginal values. It incorporates effective business principles and focuses on profits and jobs while giving weight to socio-cultural factors in the business planning and implementation phases."[73] It is not hard to see in this statement that the "focus" is on profits and jobs, while "weight" is given to Aboriginal socio-cultural factors. Again, this is far from centring Indigenous values, but instead an attempt to augment the relatively unchallenged tenets of capitalism with Aboriginal perspectives. I do not believe that this goes far enough to actually mitigate the toxicity of capitalism.

Loizides and Wuttunee offer six factors that "contribute to the success of Aboriginal community-owned enterprises" and community capitalism. They are

1. strong leadership and vision;
2. a strategic community economic development plan;
3. access to capital, markets, and management expertise;
4. good governance and management;
5. transparency and accountability; and
6. the positive interplay of business and politics.[74]

Interestingly, there is nothing explicitly *Indigenous* about these factors. They are also quite consistent with the findings of the Harvard Project. It is not that I do not appreciate these studies; it is that the conclusions too often lack a critical analysis of how mainstream markets and business protocols thoroughly dominate. I appreciate the earnest desire to make the best of challenging circumstances, but not the rhetoric that obfuscates the specific aspects of capitalism that in practice represent existential threats to Indigenous cultures, peoples, waters, and lands.

Wuttunee and Loizides write, "All of the Aboriginal communities documented in this study had dedicated leaders who were committed to economic self-reliance. These leaders are searching for business opportunities to create wealth, and are determined to join forces with corporations and governments to build better futures for their communities."[75] Strong leadership and vision in this context is understood to be displayed by those who would join forces with corporations, even when those corporations often lack the respect that should be afforded to Indigenous territories and people. In general, I do not oppose any of these key factors as they are written, but I cannot ignore that they necessarily operate within the veritable straightjacket of neoliberal capitalism.

Before moving on I want to address the final factor regarding the positive interplay between business and politics. Citing the work of Miriam Jorgensen and Jonathan B. Taylor, Loizides and Wuttunee write, "American research has found that Aboriginal community-owned business enterprises in the United States that are subject to undue political influence frequently fail to thrive. This finding suggests that separating business and politics leads to more effective business operations."[76] This is entirely consistent with the Harvard Project findings and current neoliberal paradigms. I have also seen how political interference has hampered business operations first-hand, but that may not always be a bad thing. I am not talking about corruption but about the need for political and cultural safeguards that ensure Indigenous priorities are respected and not automatically subsumed to merciless market efficiencies. None of this is simple or straightforward. Community, tribal, or compassionate capitalism may be better than unrestrained neoliberal capitalism, but I maintain that we should not limit ourselves to economic solutions that must fit within the strict confines of foreign economic systems. Increasing numbers of people around the world, Indigenous and non-Indigenous, are looking for alternatives to capitalism.[77]

Conclusion

> For Indigenous nations to live, capitalism must die. And for capitalism to die, we must actively participate in the construction of Indigenous alternatives to it.
> —*Glen Coulthard*[78]

Can capitalism be Aboriginalized? Can it be apprehended and adapted in ways that are consistent with Indigenous world views and principles? I do not believe it can without radical changes to either capitalism or Indigenous world views that might render either unrecognizable. First, it is important to remember that capitalism happened to Indigenous peoples, manifested initially as European imperial ambitions for riches, the transformation of Indigenous lands into private property and all of creation into commodities to be bought and sold. Capitalism was a means by which colonists assaulted Turtle Island. Throughout the centuries of settler colonial expansion, Indigenous peoples and world views stood in the way of development. As Indigenous populations decreased, they were herded onto reserves, and the settler governments of Canada and the United States awkwardly and shamefully struggled with what to do about the persistent "Indian Problem." These legacies continue today. Governments still try to manage their political, legal, and economic relations with Indigenous peoples, but what are Indigenous people doing? In Canada, as many as 60 to 70 percent of Indigenous people live away from home in settler towns and cities. Our lands and waters are under constant threat and poverty remains rampant in Indigenous communities; however, I suggest we expand beyond the typical Human Development Index indicators and re-embrace Indigenous conceptions of health and well-being. The Anishinaabe concept of *mino-bimaadziwin*, meaning the "good life" or "continuous rebirth," is a great example of this.[79] I am not saying that we discard socio-economic indicators altogether, but there is a danger in uncritically accepting the narrow focus of these measurement tools without appropriate regard for Indigenous conceptions of health, wealth, and well-being. We cannot ignore the acute needs of the present, but we must not act in ways that disregard the neocolonial context within which we find ourselves or in ways that threaten the viability of long-term solutions that respect

Indigenous world views and values. Mitigation and harm reduction cannot completely displace fundamental change rooted in Indigenous world views and principles of respect and reciprocity.

We need to re-centre Indigenous values and principles in our analysis and planning. In doing so, we must ask critical questions, as Newhouse suggests, about the basic tenets of capitalism. In a revival and assertion of Indigenous principles, we might begin to see where the dominant economic system should be vigorously resisted. We must also explore and create alternatives. People are already attempting to live alternatively, amongst both Indigenous and non-Indigenous peoples. We must acknowledge the tenacious efforts of previous generations who fought to survive under difficult circumstances, often making hard decisions so that our communities would endure—including engagements with mainstream markets. Indigenous populations are rebounding, and many of our stories and ways of living have survived and/or been revived. Many of us are still able to access time-tested traditional teachings, critically interpret them, and apply them to our contemporary challenges without creating new dependencies on settler-centric institutions and economies.

When I make these criticisms of capitalism, I am often pressed to offer viable alternatives or find examples of Indigenous people doing capitalism right. The more I research it, the more I realize the frightening accuracy of Newhouse's Borg analogy. Capitalism may be adaptable, but its core tenets are so dominant that they suffocate true alternatives. As for Indigenous people making capitalism work for them, I think Newhouse, Champagne, and Wuttunee will agree that it cannot happen without compromise and consequences. How Indigenous people and peoples will endure is not something I can predict, but there are some encouraging signs of tenacity, resilience, and resurgence. In my father's community of Ahousaht, the Hereditary Chiefs have worked hard to regain control of the economic activities in their territories. This has not happened without compromise or controversy, but they continually try to reassert their jurisdiction in economic and political matters. After more than a decade of legal wrangling, Ahousaht and four other Nuu-chah-nulth communities won the right to re-establish themselves in the coastal commercial fisheries. Negotiations on implementation continue, but many of our people have hope of making a living on the water again. Another small but important example is a community garden that began several years ago with some modest financial assistance from the First Nations Agricultural Association. I am told that the garden is still being tended by community volunteers and thrives as a promising alternative, which might become increasingly necessary as warming ocean and river waters threaten our traditional food security. Of course, I would prefer it if we were able to always eat fresh fish *and* vegetables, nourishing our families and re-creating a strong foundation for protecting our homelands and waters. I believe that the grounds and waters of Indigenous resistance and resurgence are fertile.

NOTES

✦

1   William J. Baumol, Robert E. Litan, and Carl J. Schramm, eds., *Good Capitalism, Bad Capitalism, and the Economics of Growth and Prosperity* (New Haven, CN: Yale University Press, 2007), vii.

2   Adam Smith, *The Wealth of Nations.* Books I–III (Markham, ON: Penguin Books Canada, 1986).

3   Rachel Durkee Walker and Jill Doerfler, "Wild Rice: The Minnesota Legislature, a Distinctive Crop, GMOs, and Ojibwe Perspectives." *Hamline Law Review* 32, no. 2 (2009): 499–527.

4   Robert J. Miller, *Reservation "Capitalism": Economic Development in Indian Country* (Lincoln: University of Nebraska Press, 2013), 1.

5   Ibid.

6   Ibid., 5.

7   Ibid., 3.

8   Duane Champagne, *Social Change and Cultural Continuity among Native Nations* (Lanham, MD: Altamira Press, 2007), 2; emphasis added.

9   Ibid., 57.

10 Ibid., 46.

11 David R. Newhouse, "Resistance Is Futile: Aboriginal Peoples Meet the Borg of Capitalism," in *Ethics and Capitalism*, ed. John Douglas Bishop (Toronto: University of Toronto Press, 2000), 145.

12 David Newhouse, "The Development of the Aboriginal Economy over the Next 20 Years," *Journal of Aboriginal Economic Development* 1, no.1 (1999): 75.

13 Wanda Wuttunee, *Living Rhythms: Lessons in Aboriginal Economic Resilience and Vision* (Montreal: McGill-Queen's University Press, 2004), 16.

14 Ibid., xiii.

15 Ibid.

16 Ibid., 186.

17 Ibid., 32.

18 Ibid., 54.

19 Miller, *Reservation "Capitalism,"* 157.

20 Ibid., 11.

21 Ibid., 11–12.

22 Ibid., 17–18.

23 Ibid., 93.

24 Ibid., 113.

25 Ibid., 133.

26 Ibid., 161.

27 Champagne, *Social Change and Cultural Continuity*, 6.

28 Ibid., 10.

29 Ibid., 15.

30 Ibid., 46.

31 Ibid.

32 Ibid., 47.

33 Ibid., 48.

34 Ibid., 49.

35 Ibid., 56.

36 Ibid.

37 Ibid., 57.

38   Ibid., 58.

39   Ibid., 62.

40   Ibid., 144–66.

41   Newhouse, "Resistance Is Futile," 145.

42   Ibid., 147.

43   For those unfamiliar with the television series *Star Trek*, "The Borg is a collection of species that have been turned into cybernetic organisms functioning as drones of the collective, or the hive." "Borg (Star Trek)," *Wikipedia*, accessed 1 February 2015, http://en.wikipedia.org/wiki/Borg_(Star_Trek).

44   Newhouse, "Resistance Is Futile," 152.

45   Ibid., 153–54.

46   Ibid., 152.

47   Ibid., 149.

48   David Newhouse, "Modern Aboriginal Economies: Capitalism with a Red Face," *Journal of Aboriginal Economic Development* 1, no. 2 (2000): 56.

49   Ibid.

50   Ibid., 58.

51   Ibid.

52   Ibid., 57.

53   Ibid., 59–60.

54   Newhouse adds that over time, social hierarchies may change as material wealth gains in prominence over other factors like the knowledge of the Elders.

55   Newhouse, "Modern Aboriginal Economies," 60.

56   David Newhouse, "Aboriginal Economic Development in the Shadow of the Borg," *Journal of Aboriginal Economic Development* 3, no. 1 (2002): 110.

57   Ibid., 112.

58   David Newhouse, "The Challenges of Aboriginal Economic Development in the Shadow of the Borg," *Journal of Aboriginal Economic Development* 4, no. 1 (2004): 40.

59   Ibid., 41.

60   Stelios Loizides and Wanda Wuttunee, *Creating Wealth and Employment in Aboriginal Communities* (Ottawa: Conference Board of Canada, 2005). This paper was written for the Conference Board of Canada with funding from the Government of Canada as well as a number of energy companies, including BC Hydro, Syncrude, Suncor, Petro-Canada, and Transcanada Pipelines.

61   Wuttunee, *Living Rhythms*, 7.

62   Ibid.

63   Ibid.

64   Ibid., 12; emphasis added.

65   Ibid., 13–14.

66 Ibid., 187.

67 Loizides and Wuttunee, *Creating Wealth and Employment*, i.

68 Ibid., 2. Original quote from National Aboriginal Financing Task Force, *The Promise of the Future: Achieving Economic Self-Sufficiency through Access to Capital* (Ottawa: Government of Canada, 1996), 14; parentheses in original.

69 Andrea Mandel-Campbell, "Rough Trade: How Canada's Diamond Bonanza Is Turning a Secretive Industry Inside Out," *Walrus*, accessed 28 August 2015, http://thewalrus.ca/2004-04-society/.

70 For details on economic positions of Oneida leader Ray Halbritter, see Taiaiake Alfred, *Wasáse: Indigenous Pathways of Action and Freedom* (Peterborough: Broadview Press, 2005), 212–17.

71 Loizides and Wuttunee, "Creating Wealth and Employment," 2.

72 Ibid.

73 Ibid., 2; emphasis added.

74 Ibid., 4.

75 Ibid.

76 Ibid., 7.

77 See the works of Isabel Altamirano-Jiménez and Rauna Kuokkanen, as well as Maria Bargh, "A Blue Economy for Aotearoa New Zealand?" *Environment, Development and Sustainability* 16, no. 3 (2014): 459–70; and Maria Bargh, Sarsha-Leigh Douglas, and Annie Te One, "Fostering Sustainable Tribal Economies in a Time of Climate Change," *New Zealand Geographer* 70, no. 2 (2014): 103–15.

78 Glen Sean Coulthard, *Red Skin, White Masks: Rejecting the Colonial Politics of Recognition* (Minneapolis: University of Minnesota Press, 2014), 173.

79 Leanne Simpson, ed., *Lighting the Eighth Fire: The Liberation, Resurgence, and Protection of Indigenous Nations* (Winnipeg: Arbeiter Ring Press, 2008), 73–74.

CHAPTER 6

◆

The Challenges and Opportunities
for First Nations Economic Self-Determination
within British Columbia

◆

Judith Sayers

British Columbia (BC) is a complex place for First Nations sustainable development: some First Nations have Aboriginal title to lands and resources, while others have modern or historical treaties, self-government agreements, or land codes. Taking advantage of governments' intentions for reconciliation can be the opportunity for First Nations to advance their own economic development. The ability of First Nations to set up sustainable economic development includes creating mechanisms such as agreements, codes, and treaties to support economic tenacity and to provide opportunities, jobs, and revenue for their members. Indeed, the passing of acts by both the BC and federal governments to recognize the United Nations Declaration on the Rights of Indigenous Peoples (UNDRIP)[1] has added other mechanisms for tenacity, allowing for the changing laws and policies in Canada to foster sustainable economic development.

In this era of rapid climate change, the need for sustainable development with minimal greenhouse gas (GHG) emissions leading to net zero emissions is key to the future. Yet some First Nations are embracing liquid natural gas (LNG) and oil development, which in my opinion will be detrimental to their members and their lands and resources, now and into the future. This, of course, is their choice, but it must be commented upon. Other First Nations are looking into sustainable forestry, clean energy, manufacturing, and tourism. The challenges and opportunities in such a diverse province as BC will be explored in the following sections. The general context for BC Indigenous communities presented here also serves as a backdrop for the Tsawwassen Nation (Daniel Millette, Chapter 2) and Tahltan Nation experience (Jerry Asp, Chapter 10).

History of Our Ancestors

No First Nations Word for Sustainability

It is important to set the historical context of where First Nations have come from in their own development before determining where they can go. This history has set the stage for current situations and is the reason why First Nations can be so far behind mainstream society in economic development.

First Nations ancestors did not have to decide on the kinds of development they wanted in their territories as they do today. They had complete jurisdiction and management within their territories and managed the resources in any way they wanted. They did not have to decide on or fight against oil and gas development, liquid natural gas, mega-dams, clear-cut logging, or tailings from mines. First Nations stewardship over the lands and resources was how First Nations peoples lived historically, and they had high standards for ensuring the lands and resources would be there for many generations to come.

First Nations territories were rich in natural resources, land, water, fish, wildlife, and foodstuffs. In return for such richness, there was a great stewardship responsibility to ensure their sustainability. There may have been a few bad years because of drought or other natural phenomena, but normally there was more than enough to eat and harvest for the year, especially for the winter. We often hear stories of how our ancestors could walk across the backs of salmon in streams and rivers, as they were that plentiful. Cedar and other trees were readily available to use for shelter and tools, and the bark was used for cultural objects, clothing, baskets, and mats.

When needed, First Nations would trade with one another for resources not readily available in their own territories. This could include whale or seal oil, animal hides, and all types of fish, including herring eggs. When the first settler colonizers arrived, our nations also traded with them. There was always an entrepreneurial spirit amongst our people, as evidenced by the use of various currencies such as dentalium shells, obsidian stones, and blue beads. Obsidian stones found in First Nations territories have been located in many faraway places, so it is well known that trade happened with distant sources.[2] First Nations people in BC had great knowledge of the lands, resources, animals, and birds, and this knowledge guided them in the use and management of their resources. One such principle was to take only as much of a resource as needed, to prevent excess from going to waste. Another was to allow the first run of salmon to go through without catching them, as they were the leaders for the rest of the run to follow. Another principle was to take only small amounts of medicine from one place and move on to the next, so there would always be some left behind. First Nations people always knew how to retain enough resources so that there would always be more for the next generations. These teachings were ignored when the settlers arrived and started taking all the resources in a way that disturbed the ecological systems of trees and plants. Pollution was also a killer of many trees, plants, fish, and other species.[3]

The ancestors of BC First Nations never ceded or surrendered their lands. They never entered into treaties (with the exception of northeastern BC, where Treaty 8 applies), and they never went to war, nor were they defeated. By international law, land could only be acquired by war or treaty.[4] First Nations lands in BC were never discovered by the settlers, as they were already here. The concept of *terra nullius*, which means that the land is barren or unoccupied, has been used to justify taking of lands from Indigenous peoples. In a court case involving Western Sahara,[5] the notion of *terra nullius* was discredited by the International Court of Justice as a valid way to acquire lands from Indigenous peoples. BC/Canada was claimed by the now Canadian government using assertion, as opposed to getting it by legal means.[6] This is why First Nations in BC without treaties have retained title to their lands.

Sustainability is not a word you will find in most First Nations languages. Ask a First Nations person what the word in their language for sustainability is, and they would be hard pressed to find such a word, because all First Nations laws were about careful management and respect of resources as a way of life. In Nuu-chah-nulth, there is one word that comes close to sustainability, and that is the word *hi-shuk-ish-tswalk*. This word means everything is one, everything is connected. If an area was overfished in one year, there would not be a good return four years later. If old growth was destroyed by taking too much of it, their needed medicines would not be sustained. There would be less wildlife, which needs the old growth to winter in.

Today if you ask a First Nation person what sustainability is, they would say it is making sure there is enough for seven generations. In the Tsilhqot'in case that went before the Supreme Court of Canada, the court clearly said that "Aboriginal title, however, comes with an important restriction—it is a collective title held not only for the present generations but for all succeeding generations."[7] Clearly, the First Nations view of their responsibilities was conveyed to the court and accepted.

The BC First Nations Economic Action Plan states that the guiding principle on economic sustainability means all economic opportunities must be assessed in light of the needs of future generations.[8] As First Nations through history have used their lands and resources to sustain themselves through changing conditions, they have also had to change using their laws and values as the basis for economic tenacity.

Effects of Colonization

The colonization of First Nations peoples has had a huge impact on the ability to be self-determining with respect to economic development. First Nations find themselves trying to "catch up" to greater society in order to become economically independent.

When the white settler colonizers arrived and asserted themselves on First Nations lands, they took First Nations lands and resources, imposed their laws and values on First Nations, and did not allow First Nations peoples to manage their lands or territories in the way they had been doing since time immemorial. First Nations were put on small land bases called reserves and denied access to the resources within their territories that had sustained them. This did not allow for developing resources for any kind of livelihood that would sustain them. Settlers developed First Nations territories in ways that changed the landscape and destroyed many ecosystems that had sustained our way of life. This continues today.

Historically, First Nations had their own way of life, making a living from the land by hunting, fishing, trapping, and trading. When the white men arrived, they started trading with them. The colonizer tried to change who they were and make them farmers when they weren't farmers: in many coastal First Nations communities, being a fisher and getting a livelihood from the fisheries resources was their life. Throughout the colonial period, First Nations peoples struggled to overcome poverty, let alone create sustainable development, which in many ways still exists today. It is this history of making changes to First Nations' ways of life through colonization that has made the need for economic tenacity and resilience necessary in order to survive as a First Nation people.

Development On- and Off-Reserve

Home to 203 Diverse First Nations
BC is home to 203 First Nations, many with complex situations. There are First Nations that have unceded territories and possess Aboriginal title. There are historic treaties in the northeastern portion of the province (Treaty 8), and southern Vancouver Island has the Douglas Treaties. There are now modern treaties with the Tsawwassen, Maa-nulth (five First Nations), Tla'amin, and Nisga'a. These modern-day treaties have lands set aside under Final Agreements, and those First Nations are able to pass laws to direct economic and resource develop-ment on their lands. There are First Nations who have self-government agreements, like Westbank[9] and Sechelt,[10] and these agreements govern economic development and land use. Land codes created under the First Nations Land Management Act also allow First Nations to zone their lands, issue permits and leases, and create opportunities for economic development.[11]

Those First Nations that do not have a treaty and retain their title try to work with governments in economic development, obtaining lands through purchase or obtaining permits, licences, and leases to allow them to get involved in development within their territories. This is sometimes possible through accommodation agreements with governments and third parties that grant lands, leases, or permits, or equity through impact benefit agreements. First Nations will use all possible avenues to create sustainable economic development, another example of the exercise of economic tenacity.

Consent versus Consultation

Other third parties that try to develop resources within First Nations territories must follow processes established by law. The government must consult and accommodate First Nations if there is to be any impact to their rights by a proposed development. Consultation is a process where the concerns of the First Nations are to be substantially addressed. The duty to consult is grounded in the honour of the Crown. This process was confirmed in the Haida case by the Supreme Court of Canada.[12] When consultation and accommodation arise, it could be an opportunity for a First Nation to be involved in a proposed development. If it is a development the First Nation is opposed to, it can create uncertainty for projects by working against the development. Unfortunately, the Haida case allowed government to approve developments over the objections of First Nations if it is in the "public interest" to do so.

Third parties are not required to consult with First Nations, but governments are. As governments do not do consultations well, it is incumbent upon third parties to try to provide information and answer the First Nations' concerns if the party is serious about developing their project. If a First Nation goes to court (and many have) to prove the government did not properly consult them,[13] developments are put on hold at great expense to the developer.[14]

The issue of consent versus consultation is a matter of great discussion across Canada, as First Nations and governments clash over decisions made about developments. In the Delgamuukw decision, the

Supreme Court stated that in some instances of confirmed rights, consent would be required:[15] "Some cases may even *require the full consent of an aboriginal nation, particularly when provinces enact hunting and fishing regulations in relation to aboriginal lands.*"[16] The Haida case softened this ruling somewhat by stating: "This process does not give Aboriginal groups a veto over what can be done with land pending final proof of the claim. The Aboriginal consent referred to in *Delgamuukw is appropriate in cases of established rights, and then by no means in every case.* Rather what is required is a process of balancing interests of give and take."[17] Unfortunately, it is government that does the balancing, and its balance is always in favour of the government, corporations, and the public. The Tsilhqot'in ruling now says that First Nations must also be asked to balance interests, but the government gives that little if any weight.

The Chief Justice of BC provided his advice on whether to go for consultation or consent by stating in the Tsilhqot'in decision: "I add this. Governments and individuals proposing to use or exploit land, whether before or after a declaration of Aboriginal title, can avoid a charge of infringement or failure to adequately consult by obtaining the consent of the interested Aboriginal group."[18]

First Nations rights are collective in nature and are not individual. The Tsilhqot'in ruling talks about how rights are collective. When rights will be affected, there must be a vote of the membership on such a development, with full information about what the impacts on the Nation's rights and land are. There must be free, prior, and informed consent within the First Nation as well. If a First Nation proceeds with consent to a project by signing an agreement without the consent of its members, it would be open to a court challenge on the basis that rights will be affected and that the Chief and Council did not have the right to commit to such an agreement. When First Nations say they are going to buy a pipeline or participate in an LNG project, I often wonder if they have gone to their members for their consent. I know, for instance, that Huu-ay-aht First Nation went through an information process and then asked its members to vote on their proposed Kwispaa LNG project.[19] This project has now been placed on hold by the company that was to develop the project.

Add to the current legal landscape in Canada the fact that the governments of BC and Canada have now passed into law the implementation of UNDRIP and the need to align their laws with UNDRIP. One article has particular importance:

Article 32

1. Indigenous peoples have the right to determine and develop priorities and strategies for the development or use of their lands or territories and other resources.

2. States shall consult and cooperate in good faith with the indigenous peoples concerned through their own representative institutions in order to obtain their free and informed consent prior to the approval of any project affecting their lands or territories and other resources, particularly in connection with the development, utilization or exploitation of mineral, water or other resources.[20]

Article 32 makes it clear that First Nations have the right to free, prior, and informed consent on any development in their territories and the right to develop their lands and resources. This article can be used by First Nations to underpin their determination to ensure only sustainable development occurs in their territories.

Reserve Lands for Development

All First Nations were provided with reserves as defined by the Indian Act. Reserves vary in size, and the ability of a First Nation to do any developments on-reserve will depend on the size of the reserve, its location, and available infrastructure.

Coastal First Nations typically have small reserves that were created under the Indian Act. The treaty commissioners stopped making treaties when they reached the BC border, with the exception of northeastern BC. Instead, reserve commissioners were sent out to establish reserves. Many coastal First Nations were given small land bases because they did not use land for agricultural purposes. Their livelihoods were from the ocean and rivers in their territories, and the reserve commissioners promised continued access to sea resources when they allocated the land. This of course did not happen, and those First Nations have had limited opportunities to create economic development in their reserves due to their small land lots. First Nations like Osoyoos Indian Band and Kamloops Indian Band have large tracts of land (32,000 acres and 33,000 acres, respectively[21]) and have been able to create many businesses on their lands despite the limitations of the Indian Act. Compare this, for example, with the Esquimalt and Songhees Nation, having around forty-four acres and sixty acres of land, respectively, and are thus severely limited in their economic base. Some First Nations reserves were not quality lands and could not be developed, or were lands where services could not be developed due to the poor kinds of soils found.

First Nations could apply for more lands for housing and domestic purposes only through the Department of Indian Affairs (now Indigenous Services Canada [ISC]).[22] However, adding land for economic development was not a given and difficult to get the Department of Indian Affairs to agree to, as they felt they could not justify the cost of buying land for those purposes. Processes to get additions to the reserve also used to take many years. ISC has tried to streamline that process, and it is a lot easier to achieve now than it used to be.[23]

Other First Nations have developed land codes under the First Nations Land Management Act,[24] which allows them the ability to manage their lands and enter into permits and licences without having to wait until the Department of Justice negotiates and approves agreements that allow for developments on-reserve. Even a smaller First Nation like Lake Cowichan, with thirty members living on-reserve, has taken advantage of a land code.[25] First Nations with land codes have found them helpful for economic development on their own timeline and not the government's.

First Nations may also develop comprehensive community plans, which provide for the development of their lands and infrastructure for five years and are constantly updated.[26] Those that want to integrate clean energy also prepare a Community Energy Plan, either before or during a project. [27]

First Nations are trying to find ways to create revenue and jobs for their members. Funding from ISC has not kept up with inflation and population growth. The federal government has kept a 2 percent cap on flowing funding to First Nations for more than twenty years. The funding cap was put in place in 1996, with Prime Minister Justin Trudeau promising to lift it in 2015.[28] In reality, he maintained the 2 percent cap and added money for specific initiatives like clean drinking water and infrastructure funding for First Nations in housing, education, health, and other services.[29] It is never enough, and First Nations would like to create more revenue from sustainable businesses. This is not as easy for remote First Nations whose communities may only be accessed by boats or planes. Shipping supplies to these communities adds costs that can make a business development not feasible.

Due to the federal status of Indian reserves, federal laws like the Species at Risk Act and the Canadian Environmental Assessment Act can be applicable.[30] These laws can also make it even more difficult to develop reserve lands, as they may require setting aside various lands for species at risk that developers on provincial lands are not required to.

A common theme among First Nations is the desire for sustainable development and the ability to conserve, manage, and protect what is important to them. They want to continue their way of life and continue to exercise their rights. They want to be economically self-reliant and provide meaningful jobs for their youth up to their seniors. They also want a diversified economy that is not reliant on one industry. First Nations begin to do economic development when they can overcome some of the common issues that stand in their way, like archaic laws on-reserve such as the Indian Act,[31] obtaining equity and capital for businesses on- and off-reserve, and finding access to natural resources such as forestry in order to do business.[32] As a reflection of their economic tenacity, First Nations have been working to create new legislative regimes like the First Nations Land Management Act, streamlining the Additions to Reserve Policy, developing comprehensive community plans, and overcoming barriers like the Species at Risk Act and Canadian Environmental Assessment Act.

Economic Opportunities—or Not?

Within BC there are many unsustainable businesses that use non-renewable resources, create GHGs, negatively impact the land and water, and put at risk the ecosystems that support First Nations' abilities to exercise their rights. Businesses that are controversial within BC include LNG, pipelines for oil and gas, and tankers to ship the oil and LNG. Also controversial are mega-dams like Site C and mines like the Prosperity Mine.

The Site C project will be a third dam and hydroelectric generating station on the Peace River in northeast BC.[33] It will provide 1,100 megawatts (MW) of capacity and produce about 5,100 gigawatt hours (GWh) of electricity each year. It will flood 2,601 hectares of land, which includes critical habitat that sustains wildlife, historical, and cultural sites, including burial sites and carbon sinks. First Nations rights will be abrogated with the construction of this dam. Some First Nations are opposed to Site C and have been doing what they can stop it.[34]

Prosperity Mine is a proposed gold-copper mine by Taseko Mines Ltd.[35] First Nations have been opposed to it since mine tailings would be put into a lake they rely on for fish. The federal government turned the project down three times but the company still wants to proceed.[36] Tsilhqot'in Nation has been opposed to the Prosperity Mine from the beginning.[37]

First Nations fight against those businesses they do not want in their territories. They go through consultations with government, but the governments approve projects such as Site C and LNG.[38]

The Trans Mountain Pipeline (TMX) is another business that many First Nations oppose. Despite opposition on the land and in the courts, the federal government approved TMX. The court struck down the first approval of the project. The federal government had to begin their consultations again and made the second decision to proceed. The Tsleil-Waututh, Coldwater, Squamish, and other First Nations challenged this decision all the way to the Supreme Court of Canada, only to have the court agree to the project's going ahead.[39] The opposing Nations have vowed to stop the project despite the court ruling.[40]

Since the first court case, things have changed considerably. The federal government bought TMX from Kinder Morgan.[41] Kinder Morgan knew that getting the pipeline approved would be almost impossible and exited while they could get a sale price that covered the money they had invested. The federal government had hoped to sell the pipeline project but so far has not done so. Most people realize the difficulties of getting a pipeline approved in BC with unresolved title and consultations. In my opinion, it is a complete conflict of interest for the federal government to approve a project and to be the owners of the pipeline. After the project was bought by the federal government, the project was approved again and work has begun. Another approval of the project followed the decision to strike down the initial finding of the National Energy Board.

The Canadian government tried to convince people in BC that they were putting in place a "world class" marine safety system that would be able to clean up any oil spill in response to the TMX. This recovery system was called the Oceans Protection Plan and has a fund of $1.5 billion.[42] Some projects have commenced under the Oceans Protection Plan but there is much to do to protect all three of Canada's coastlines. Those who know the waters off the coast of BC know that at times the seas are so rough that nothing can be done for days and even weeks, and by then the oil would be spread everywhere. Crude oil sinks to the bottom of the ocean and it is difficult, if not impossible, to clean up.

Some First Nations joined together to attempt to buy the TMX in whole or in part. They believe that they can convince those First Nations who are now opposed to the project to approve it because it is owned by First Nations. There is nothing further from the truth. Those First Nations that oppose the projects, especially in key communities like the Tsleil-Waututh and Squamish Nations, are not changing their minds. The risks of environmental degradation to the land and water remain the same no matter who owns the pipelines, tankers, and facilities. These First Nations do not want to put their ability to exercise their rights at risk for further potential damage. Tsleil-Waututh did its own environmental assessment to prove the damage to their territory,[43] but the National Energy Board accepted it as evidence only.

It is hard from my perspective to understand why some First Nations would want to get involved in businesses that would be such a risk to Mother Earth. Some Elders have called this pipeline the black snake and have warned how it must be stopped. Building pipelines and using tankers to transport oil have many risks and run contrary to the values of many First Nations.

The TMX is not the only project that some First Nations have agreed to. Some have signed agreements with respect to LNG, Site C, and other types of projects. There are several reasons cited for these acceptances. One is jobs and money. Most First Nations are in dire need of more money for their governance, infrastructure, and other services. Those Chiefs who approve the projects explain in the media that they need to pull their people out of poverty and that they need jobs and training. That is why they are pursuing environmentally risky projects in their territory.[44] In my experience, jobs and money will never replace their sacred sites, their ability to hunt moose or fish in their lakes and rivers. No amount of money can ever compensate for the loss of such important rights. It is recognized that a First Nation has a say over its own territory, but when it agrees to projects that go beyond its territorial lines, it is up to other First Nations to say yes or no on behalf of their own territories.

Another reason Chiefs give for approving these projects is that the governments will approve them anyway, and they might as well get some benefits up front. If they wait until after the project is approved, governments or companies have no duty to provide compensation or accommodation. This is what the Chiefs and Councils tell their members to convince them that they must sign agreements up front or lose out on any money at all. It places these communities in a catch-22 situation because if leaders talk about benefits, it is assumed that they have agreed to the development. If they oppose and refuse to talk benefits, and the government approves the development, the communities are not entitled to compensation. This forces the First Nation into an untenable situation. This whole process needs to be changed so that a First Nation has every right to raise its concerns and have them addressed, and if the project goes through anyway, these concerns should be accommodated. This is why free, prior, and informed consent is key to approving developments and then there will not be issues on accommodation in this way.[45]

Governments and media sources try to create harmful public perceptions.[46] They will say, for example, that fifteen out of twenty First Nations are in favour of a project. Consultations do not work that way. Each First Nation must determine what sort of impacts the development will have on its territory and its ability to exercise its rights. A pipeline might go through an important fishery area, or a sacred site, or an area where medicinal plants can only be found. The degree of impact may vary from one First Nation to another. In the case of Tsleil-Waututh and Squamish First Nations, it means that their rights to the ocean are at high risk because the facility will be in their territory, subjecting them to the shipping of crude oil with the risks of spills and the destruction of beaches that are rich in shellfish. It is not possible to compare with another First Nation that may have a pipeline run through a small part of their territory, or a benign part of their territory where no rights are at risk. It does not matter how many First Nations say yes, it is the significance of the impact on those First Nations that are saying no that matters most, in my opinion, as has been stated by court cases like Haida.[47]

Some First Nations believe that there is no risk and have agreed to LNG facilities in their territories where GHG emissions are a big issue to watch for. When the BC Liberal government was in power, it told First Nations they could produce electricity in any way they wanted. They would, of course, burn natural gas to produce electricity and not build clean energy to power their facilities. Some who have embraced LNG have insisted on clean energy to power the facilities, but that does not address all the risks to the environment that sustains rights, such as fracking and its effects on clean water and activating earthquakes.

Who Decides? Hereditary Chiefs versus Elected Chiefs and Councils

One of the questions that keeps arising in BC for governments and third parties is who in a First Nation has the power to approve or reject a project. There are different forms of governments in place in First Nations, and sometimes there are two within one nation. One of the most common issues is the role of Hereditary Chiefs versus that of Chiefs elected under the Indian Act. If a company like Coastal GasLink has reached agreement with elected Chiefs while the Hereditary Chiefs of the Wet'suwet'en say no and that they are the only decision makers, the company and government have a problem.[48]

The Wet'suwet'en Hereditary Chiefs and people stood their ground against the construction of a pipeline, and fourteen were arrested. They were willing to face jail or large fines in order to protect their land. These charges were eventually withdrawn, but their actions show the extent to which First Nations people are willing to go to protect and defend their lands.[49] At the same time, the elected Chief and Council of Wet'suwet'en territory signed an agreement with Coastal GasLink over its proposed development.

At times like this, it is confusing as to who the authority is that a company must work with to secure agreement for a particular project. In the case of the Wet'suwet'en, the Hereditary Chiefs were the ones who brought the lawsuit on Aboriginal title based on their chieftainships and territories, following the Delgamuukw case.[50] The elected Chief and Council are the authority under the Indian Act and their powers are defined in the Indian Act. The Wet'suwet'en Hereditary Chiefs challenged the authority of the elected Chiefs on their ability to sign any agreements on their behalf. The BC government is now talking with the Hereditary Chiefs about this project, something that should have been done from the beginning, given that Hereditary Chiefs were the ones who brought the title case for Wet'suwet'en and have been defenders in land camps for over ten years.

The Lax Kw'alaams have territory on the northern west coast of BC that encompasses the city of Prince Rupert and are part of the Tsimshian First Nation. They are west of the Wet'suwet'en territory, and the pipeline will go through their territory to the Pacific Ocean. Lax Kw'alaams Hereditary Chiefs and their people took to the land to stop the laying of a pipeline and the building of an LNG facility on an island at the mouth of the Skeena River, close to Prince Rupert, where they believe the facility would affect the salmon runs that go up the Skeena. Salmon are the main staple food of the Lax Kw'alaams.[51] Pipelines face many challenges in seeking approvals for the many First Nations territories they run through.

It would be my advice, when committing to a multi-billion-dollar project, to ensure all leaders are consulted by the government and third parties, as community leaders can stop a project while waiting for court decisions to be rendered or required consultations concluded. While in some First Nations communities, it is the Hereditary Chiefs who have the responsibility to look after the land and the people under their laws, other communities have elected Chiefs and Councils, empowered under the Indian Act. Still other communities have both Hereditary and elected Chiefs; some work together and some do not. Obtaining consent relies on understanding who the authorities are in each community. Without this, the consent can be baseless.

Regardless, everyone who is making decisions on developments within their territories that will impact their rights should be fully informed before any decision is made and should be able to vote on it. It cannot be a vote of just Chief and Council alone, because that decision can be challenged by members, who collectively own the rights.

For most of the coastal First Nations from the Haida down to Coast Salish and Nuu-chah-nulth, it is about protecting the fishery and sea resources. Oil spills would be devastating to the fisheries run that migrates from Alaska and down the coast into Nuu-chah-nulth and Coast Salish territories. Some First Nations oppose the TMX pipeline based on the impact it would have on the sustainability of the fish, sea resources, and all living things in the ocean. Sustainability means different things to different First Nations, but they will always protect what is important to them and to continuing their way of life.

Governance structures in First Nations communities can be different, and it is incumbent upon governments and third parties to do their research and work with the right authorities.

The Impact on Development of the United Nations Declaration on the Rights of Indigenous Peoples

When the General Assembly of the United Nations adopted UNDRIP in September 2007,[52] First Nations in Canada thought that the declaration would make a difference in many areas, particularly in economic development. Articles set out the right to self-determination to freely pursue economic development; the right to development; the right to own, use, and manage lands and resources; the right to decision making; and the right to have financing for their institutions—all this gave hope for a new way of doing business.

When the federal Liberals were campaigning, they promised that they would implement UNDRIP if elected. Justin Trudeau said he would seek the consent of First Nations regarding developments in their territories, but he was not long in government when he started saying that consent did not mean the right to say no, or to veto a proposed development. I am not sure what he thinks consent is; usually it means yes or no, and veto does not come into it. Now some experts are trying to distinguish consent from the right to veto, but as noted above, Article 32 of UNDRIP talks of free prior and informed consent, as do Articles 19, 10, 11, 28, and 29. This will have to be worked out between Canada and First Nations. First Nations will have to be tenacious and fight for their right of consent in order to protect and manage their territories in sustainable fashion.

Bill C-262 was tabled in the House of Commons in January 2019 to implement UNDRIP through legislation.[53] It started as a private member's bill introduced by Romeo Saganash, a New Democratic Party (NDP) Member of Parliament. Interestingly enough, the bill talks of consultation and cooperation with Indigenous peoples, of taking measures to ensure the laws of Canada are consistent with UNDRIP, and of putting in place a national action plan to achieve the objectives of the Declaration. It did not mention the free, prior, and informed consent of Indigenous peoples. Bill C-262 was passed in Parliament but failed in the Senate in June 2019 and did not become law.

After being in power for five years, Prime Minister Trudeau's government tabled Bill C-15, the United Nations Declaration on Indigenous Rights of Indigenous Peoples Act, in the House of Commons on 3 December 2020.[54] This bill received mixed reviews from Indigenous peoples in Canada, and many felt there was little consultation. The bill introduces an action plan to "address injustices, combat prejudice and eliminate all forms of violence and discrimination, including systemic discrimination, against Indigenous peoples and Indigenous Elders, youth, children, women, men, persons with disabilities and gender-diverse persons and two-spirit persons." It is an encouraging step to combat systemic racism, a need recognized by the prime minister.[55] Bill C-15, the United Nations Declaration on the Rights of Indigenous Peoples Act, finally became law on 21 June 2021,[56] and now the federal government must begin implementing this law. First Nations must be assertive to ensure the true spirit and intent of UNDRIP are followed and within a reasonable time frame.

Meanwhile, BC's NDP government passed its Declaration on the Rights of Indigenous Peoples Act (DRIPA), which received royal assent on 28 November 2019.[57] DRIPA offers only two mechanisms to implement UNDRIP: one to change legislation to make all laws consistent with UNDRIP; the other to enter into shared decision-making agreements or agreements that allow for First Nations consent before statutory decision making. It has been more than two years since DRIPA was passed, and no laws have yet been changed to align with UNDRIP, nor have any joint decision-making agreements been concluded. The lack of progress has been frustrating, and Indigenous peoples really want more action under this new law.

Self-determination is the foundation of UNDRIP, but what does it mean? Article 3 of UNDRIP adopts the United Nations' definition of self-determination, whereby Indigenous peoples can freely determine their political status and pursue economic, social, and cultural development. BC must recognize the political status of Indigenous peoples as nations in whatever way they want to define themselves. It is not up to governments to determine what status a First Nation has, or who the rights and title holders are, or if they can be an Indigenous governing body as defined in DRIPA.

In order to implement UNDRIP, BC will need to remove from legislation any systemic barriers that stop First Nations from determining their economic, social, and cultural development in their own way and in their own time. First Nations must identify these barriers and have them removed from law. There must be recognition of First Nations' ownership of their lands and resources and guarantee of access to those resources. The government must recognize First Nations laws. DRIPA is another tool First Nations will be able to use for promoting their own economic development and make changes to laws, polices, and regulations in their favour. It is another way to get the government of BC to live up to its commitments to improve its relationship with First Nations.

It is not surprising that First Nations understand Article 32 of UNDRIP to mean they have the right of free, prior, and informed consent over any developments in their territories, and they will continue to promote their right of consent under any international, federal, or provincial law. Premier John Horgan and Minister of Indigenous Relations and Reconciliation Scott Fraser have repeatedly stated that the right to consent is not the same as the right to veto.

The right of free, prior, and informed consent applies to all Indigenous peoples, as set out in UNDRIP, including a project such as a pipeline or an LNG facility. Fracking is a part of the process for LNG and takes place at the source of the natural gas, with sometimes devastating effects on the land and water. I have heard LNG industry leaders say that they do not need to ask permission from the First Nation whose land is being fracked. This should be a basic requirement for every project that impacts First Nations territories and rights, as First Nations honour the law they want to protect them.

The federal and provincial governments still insist on consultation and on their ability to override First Nations rights in favour of public interest. This is evident in all of their decisions. A classic case that illustrates this is that of Taseko's proposed gold-copper Prosperity Mine. Governments turned down the permits twice but approved exploratory permits on the third attempt, despite an environmental assessment report that details the devastation the mine would cause to Tsilhqot'in rights. The Tsilhqot'in have now challenged the permits in court again and will continue to oppose this. The Tsilhqot'in have shown real tenacity in stopping a project they know will not be good for their lands and resources and will interfere with their own sustainable development.

Whether consultation or consent is used, First Nations that want to get involved in what they think will be a sustainable development/ business can use either process to negotiate an equity share in the business as part of their consent to the development. They can negotiate their equity if they can convince the proponent/developer that their consent is worth the value of the equity. There are many other benefits First Nations can negotiate during the consultation/consent process. First Nations in BC have negotiated many different benefits through impact benefit agreements.

Consent versus consultation will continue to be an issue that pits First Nations against governments. This is why governments work so hard to get First Nations involved in businesses they do not agree with, in order to provide certainty to businesses. Governments try to make this attractive by promoting revenue sharing or getting companies to provide profit sharing or even an equity share in the company.

A complaint was made by the United Nations' Office of the High Commissioner of Human Rights to the Committee on the Elimination of Racial Discrimination (CERD) about the projects of TMX, Site C, and Coastal GasLink (LNG). A decision on 13 December 2019 confirmed that Canada had not sought the free, informed, and prior consent of Indigenous peoples and ordered it to do so. Another letter was issued on 24 November 2020, asking for further information from Canada as to progress on seeking consent. Notably, the Chair of CERD stated: "The Committee regrets the State party interprets the free, prior and informed consent principle as well as the duty to consult as a duty to engage in a meaningful and good faith dialogue with indigenous peoples and to guarantee a process, but not a particular result. In this regard, the Committee would like to draw its attention to the Committee's general recommendation No. 23 (1997) on the rights of indigenous peoples, in which it calls upon State parties to ensure that no decisions directly relating to the rights or interests of indigenous peoples is taken without their informed consent."

Canada and BC cannot ignore CERD and its directives when they are signatories to the Convention on the Elimination of Racial Discrimination. Canada is being scrutinized by the United Nations and must change its way of business. It is to be hoped that this will help First Nations that are seeking to participate in the consent process on major developments happening in their territories.

What Are Sustainable Businesses for First Nations?

BC First Nations Working in Clean Energy?
One industry that First Nations in BC have embraced is the clean energy industry. More than 125 out of the 203 First Nations are involved in clean energy projects, from revenue sharing to equity ownership.

A survey conducted in 2016 with 105 First Nations respondents found that 98 percent of those surveyed were or wanted to be involved in clean energy.[58] First Nations surveyed were prepared to invest $3.4 billion dollars in new clean energy projects in the province, and if those First Nations that did not take part in the survey also were to agree then there would be approximately $7 billion they would invest.

The survey of the 105 First Nations respondents found that there were seventy-eight First Nations operating projects, forty-nine First Nations were involved in developing projects, and there were an additional 249 projects that First Nations wanted to build. This clearly sends a message to the BC government to find ways to continue the development and expansion of this sector for First Nations.

Through the years, BC First Nations have been building capacity in the industry, including in the following ways:

- preparing a toolkit to assist with building a project;
- developing Aboriginal Skills, Employment Training Strategy (ASETS) projects for jobs like powerhouse operators;
- training members on solar panel installation and other types of renewable energy projects, and developing businesses that employ their trained members to install solar panels in neighbouring communities;
- partnering with a renewable energy company one or more times, learning how to build a project, and then building a project on their own (e.g., Tla-o-qui-aht First Nation);
- designing renewable energy projects to ensure a lot of community buy-in and involvement (e.g., Haida Heritage Centre project);
- establishing several funds from which First Nations could borrow for equity in a project (one project has been stopped due to the lack of such a fund); and
- helping establish the BC Indigenous Clean Energy Initiative (BCICEI), which provides funds to First Nations in various categories for developing clean energy projects.[59]

A 2016 report by Clean Energy BC highlights the growth of the clean power industry:

- British Columbia's clean power industry has attracted more than $8.6 billion in investment, and the money is spent in local economies, including the province's northern and interior regions.

- The sector has to date supported 15,970 direct, full-time equivalent (FTE) person years of construction employment in every region of the province—with another 4,543 FTE person years of employment in the works on forthcoming projects.
- Renewable power companies now employ 641 people in operational roles around the province. Projects now under construction will support an additional 165 such positions once online.
- Independent Power producers produce 25 percent of BC Hydro's energy supply.[60]

The BC government has suspended any calls for clean energy for purchase by BC Hydro. Again showing their economic tenacity, First Nations have been building clean energy projects in their own communities like solar, run-of-the-river, wind, and geothermal power generation. While First Nations cannot use this to bring in revenue, it builds capacity for when there may be another call for power, takes them off diesel, and reduces their own power bills so they can use their money for other things.

BC First Nations Success Stories in Clean Energy

Clean or renewable energy is an important industry for First Nations. It has been an industry First Nations have embraced because projects can be developed with minimal impacts to their rights and to the environment that sustains those rights. It is also an industry consistent with their values and is considered very sustainable. There are opportunities to compete in the industry that have made it easier for First Nations to become an important part. There are First Nations that have led and developed their own projects and those that have partnered with companies. These independent power producers believe that it is important to work with First Nations in their territories, and there are many viable and valuable partnerships.

There are many clean energy success stories involving First Nations in BC, and a few will be highlighted here. One project that began a series of many was the Hupačasath Upnit Power Corporation run-of-the-river project located on China Creek.[61] This project is owned 72.5 percent by Hupačasath First Nation, 10 percent by Ucluelet First Nation, 12.5 percent by Synex, and 5 percent by the City of Port Alberni. The project produces 6.5 MW of power at full capacity. Two Hupačasath members operate and manage this project, which was led and developed by the Hupačasath.[62]

Hupačasath's electricity purchase agreement (EPA) with BC Hydro ends in 2025, a year after the Site C hydroelectric dam is set to come online. There are indications the province will not buy any more power from Hupačasath. The province has not been renewing other project EPAs that are ending, stating they have no need to buy power any more. It is likely Hupačasath will be told the same thing, even though there is an 82.5 percent ownership by First Nations. The debt of the Upnit project will be paid out a year or two before the end of the EPA, leaving very little time to make the profit that was envisioned. After an almost $14 million investment, Hupačasth had counted on having many years to make profit after paying off the debt acquired to build this project.

T'Sou-ke First Nation is renowned for its solar developments throughout its community and is a leader in the innovative use of clean energy.[63] T'Sou-ke First Nation is located on Vancouver Island, about sixty-four kilometres from Victoria. Within the community, solar arrays power community buildings, homes, and a charging station for electric vehicles. Each home has solar hot water components that can produce all of a family's hot water needs. There is a 6-kilowatt system for the fisheries office and a 7-kilowatt system for the band hall that sells excess power back to BC Hydro under their net metering program. T'Sou-ke also has a 62-kilowatt array on top of the First Nation's canoe shed that is used for the community and for sale to BC Hydro.

While building these projects, T'Sou-ke took opportunities to train its members on how to install solar panels. Eventually they made themselves available as a business installing solar panels for other communities. T'Sou-ke is a leader in solar energy in BC, and Chief Gordon Planes travels internationally to share the First Nation's expertise. T'Sou-ke also offers tours of its solar projects that explain their objectives, what has been learned, and what is envisioned going forward.

Tla-o-qui-aht First Nation is located in the Tofino area on Vancouver Island. In the first two clean energy projects the First Nation partnered with the Barkley Project Group, but the third one was developed independently, based on the capacity built from the first two projects. Tla-o-qui-aht was in the process of building a fourth project when the government of BC refused to buy from any more projects. Tla-o-qui-aht has invested money in developing this project, which may not be well used if energy sales cannot be realized. Tla-o-qui-aht wants to develop an additional eight projects if the opportunity arises. Current projects include Canoe Creek Hydro (6 MW), Haa-ak-suuk (6 MW), and Winchie Creek (4.1 MW), all wholly owned by Tla-o-qui-aht.[64] Clean energy is one of the main economic developments pursued by the First Nation, which has been working hard to get the province to create further opportunities for them.

Kanaka Bar has an incredible story of taking twenty-four years to develop a 50-MW run-of-the-river project on Kwoiek Creek, with the powerhouse on their reserve.[65] The band owns 50 percent and Innergex owns 50 percent. In forty years, the project will be owned wholly by Kanaka Bar. It is a good source of revenue and employment. Following the success of Kwoiek Creek, Kanaka Bar also installed 10 MW of solar power within its lands.[66] Once the community found clean energy, it embraced the industry and looked at all possibilities to create power. Kanaka Bar is one of five First Nations that were given an EPA after the Standing Offer Program was suspended. Kanaka Bar wanted to build a 1-MW run-of-the-river project, but the BC government and BC Hydro only provided an EPA for half that amount.

Skidegate First Nation on Haida Gwaii has installed 100-kilowatt generating solar panels at the cultural heritage centre and installed heat pumps in the community's homes.[67] Skidegate also plans to put solar panels on every house in the community. Being diesel-dependent, the community has been looking for ways to be on clean energy and will continue to find ways to get off diesel.

Hesquiaht First Nation, located on a remote island off the west coast of Vancouver Island, has now transitioned off diesel and has a run-of-the-river project as well as solar. It no longer needs to ship diesel over rough seas and create greenhouse gases. Empowering themselves through clean energy, leaders of the Huu-ay-aht First Nation embedded in their Final Agreement the right to develop Sarita River as a run-of-the-river project.[68]

There are so many success stories with First Nations, from those trying to get off diesel to those developing projects to sell to the grids and now to become energy independent. It is a real shame that the BC government has stopped the momentum of these projects and stymied First Nations development in clean energy, an industry that is sustainable and aligned with the values of First Nations. Clean energy is one industry First Nations have excelled in, and the BC government should be working with them so they can continue to provide clean energy to the grid.

Impact of Site C Decision on First Nations' Ability to Develop Clean Energy

In December 2017, the BC NDP government decided it would continue with Site C, a mega-dam on the Peace River that would supply 5,100 GWh of power that would serve 450,000 homes per year.

The power from Site C is to come online in 2024, assuming no delays, and will create more power than BC needs or has yet to find a market for. The province has also suspended the Standing Offer Program whereby First Nations could sell power to BC Hydro at any time up to 15 MWh.

The BC NDP government made this decision knowing that it would deprive First Nations of the opportunity to develop their approximately $7 billion investments in clean energy. They were well aware that First Nations have embraced the industry as falling within their environmental values and standards and that the program had been beneficial to First Nations in creating revenue, jobs, and capacity in the clean energy industry.

BC Hydro has now suspended indefinitely all calls for power, including its Standing Offer and Micro Standing Offer programs to which most First Nations were applying for clean energy opportunities.[69] The BC Clean Energy Act requires the BC government to provide for a Standing Offer Program except in prescribed circumstances.[70] Its objectives are to get First Nations and rural communities to use and develop clean energy. Clearly the decision to proceed with Site C dam runs contrary to the government's own law.

The value of clean energy projects is that they can be built as power is needed. All that is needed is to put out a call, and independent power producers will bid on the calls for proposals. Clean energy also provides for jobs, capacity building, and revenue generation, and contributes to the province-wide economy. It brings regional benefits, as opposed to Site C, which will only add to jobs in the northeast of the province and creates just twenty-five jobs in the long term. Contrast this with a map produced in 2014 by the Pembina Institute showing that small clean energy projects had produced 8,300 jobs.[71]

Premier John Horgan promised to provide opportunities to First Nations when he announced the continuation of the Site C project. The government has introduced a new plan called CleanBC in which clean energy is mentioned, but the amount of energy talked about equals the energy beyond that sold from Site C. The government has promised to meet with First Nations on clean energy opportunities but has not yet set a date.

To rationalize suspending indefinitely the production of clean energy, the BC government hired independent consultant Ken Davidson, who prepared a report called *Zapped*.[72] Davidson's experience is as a mathematician and accountant. He is a commercial banker by trade and specializes in restructuring and asset-realization transactions. He has no expertise in clean energy. The BC government has always inflated the cost of independent power and tries to compare it to power generated by large dams, which is like comparing apples and oranges. The British Columbia Utilities Commission ruled that the cost of clean energy was the same as that of independent power. Davidson estimates that for the dozens of EPAs negotiated under the Liberals, Hydro is paying $16.2 billion over twenty years for power that it is not likely to need. He calculates the unnecessary burden for ratepayers at $200 per year, or $4,000 over the twenty-year span. Additionally, he reports that many of the contracts include inflation protection, which could add billions more to the collective tab.

Clean Energy BC, which represents independent power producers in the province, has responded to debunk *Zapped*'s three allegations that (1) starting in 2007, BC Hydro bought too much energy; (2) BC Hydro overpaid for the energy it purchased; and (3) BC Hydro undertook these actions at the direction of the government.[73] This Clean Energy BC report is very misleading and inaccurate, which of course is what the BC government wanted.

What is very clear is that the price of clean energy has rapidly decreased. The government of Alberta bought wind power in December 2019 for $39 per MWh. Contrast that with the price of Site C energy at $95 per MWh (including the interest paid to borrow the money).[74] Alberta's Renewable Electricity Program states: "The road map for the Renewable Electricity Program (REP) includes interim targets to achieve 30 per cent renewable electricity by 2030, including Indigenous participation in the development of 1,500 megawatts of power, which is enough to power more than 700,000 homes."[75]

BC has put in place CleanBC and recently approved CleanBC's road map to 2030. Based on BC Hydro's Integrated Resource Plan (IRP), GHG Reduction Targets for 2025, 2030, and 2040 will not be met. There is an accelerated electrification plan in place to reduce GHG by the target dates but the road map does not take this into consideration.

BC Hydro's IRP has no new requirement for First Nations power generation until about 2032. If the IRP matched the road map, 1,000 GWh of new First Nations power generation would be needed by 2025 and 8,000 GWh by 2030. BC and BC Hydro are very short-sighted in their implementation of the First Nations' right to develop clean energy for the benefit of BC and the First Nations themselves. If BC would work with First Nations in clean energy development, this would also ensure BC met its own goals under the Climate Change Accountability Act[76] and Canada's Net Zero Emissions Act.[77] In any event, First Nations will remain tenacious in building capacity and being ready to develop power generation projects. Meanwhile, Alberta will see 5,000 megawatts of green energy generation, about $10 billion in new private investment, and the creation of 7,000 jobs by 2030.[78]

Contrast this initiative with BC, where there are no opportunities for First Nations to build for economic development purposes. Rather, they are limited to in-community clean energy projects to power their homes, community buildings, and businesses. As other provinces surge ahead on developing clean energy, in finding new innovations and technology, BC will trail behind, with BC First Nations looking in from the outside on an industry they believe would be important to their economic growth.

The clean energy industry is a sustainable one in the minds of First Nations in BC, but they have had that opportunity stymied by a short-sighted government that only cares about politics and maintaining a monopoly over power generation, and not about its relationship with First Nations. The government has announced, as well, that in the future, BC Hydro will build small clean energy projects—this from a corporation that does not have the skills or desire to build these kinds of projects. The government has written off an industry that has invested over $9 billion into the economy and created more than 20,000 jobs. If the power demand in BC increases beyond what Site C can produce, opportunities may open up again, but while BC Hydro retains a monopoly that opportunity may never surface. The BC government has never mandated BC Hydro to partner with First Nations or other companies, so for First Nations to partner with the government on clean energy projects within their territories is not a possibility until that mandate changes.

Other Businesses

First Nations in BC have invested in many varied businesses, from gas stations and stores on-reserve to industrial parks, tourism, forestry, fisheries, environmental services, farming, market housing, trailer parks, wineries, golf courses, traditional plants, maple syrup, fish products, interpretive centres, museums, and much more.

The forestry industry has also been embraced by First Nations, with higher environmental standards than are contained in the Forest Act and regulations. There is no clear-cutting, and often larger areas around streams and culturally modified trees are left untouched. Trees are replanted immediately so new growth can happen. Some First Nations have also adopted Forest Stewardship Council Certified standards to deal with the timber in their territories.

First Nations have been working to get tenures so they can participate in the forest industries. They have also worked with the government for revenue sharing from stumpage.

Climate Change and the Impact on Business
Climate change is having a major impact on First Nations businesses. Global warming has created droughts, flooding, and forest fires. All are devastating when forests are destroyed and all logging and non-timber forest products industries are put on hold for many years.

Climate change modelling has to occur before run-of-the-river projects can be developed to ensure there will be enough water for the project. Steady winds for wind power and enough sunlight for solar projects are also important for those types of clean energy.

Agricultural initiatives must be developed with plans to ensure that there is enough water and that the risk of flooding is minimal. Food sovereignty has become very popular with First Nations, and ensuring the right climate is key to the growth of the food industry for them.

Even tourism is affected by the effects of climate change. Wildlife tours, to see whales or grizzlies, for example, can be affected by shifting water levels, warming ocean temperatures, and declining animal populations.

First Nations have always been a part of the fishery industry. With ocean warming, acidification, and pollution, the run sizes of many fish species have diminished, and the Fraser River run has now been declared to have collapsed. This is a critical hit to the economies of coastal BC First Nations who rely on the fisheries for their economies and for their food. The realities of climate change are affecting many industries that First Nations rely on or are interested in developing.

Is Reconciliation an Opportunity to Advance Indigenous Economies?
The buzzword these days with governments is reconciliation. Since the Truth and Reconciliation Commission's Calls to Action were released in 2015,[79] governments have been committing to reconciliation. The problem is that they alone are trying to determine what reconciliation is and what their terms are, without consulting the First Nations they are meant to reconcile with.

First Nations must determine what they want from governments in order to achieve reconciliation, as it is not up to governments to define the term. Every First Nation will differ on what it will take to reach reconciliation.

For First Nations in BC without a treaty, it may be recognition of their title within their territories. It may be control and management of resources within their territories. It may be redress for sacred sites that may have been destroyed. It may be sufficient money to restore language and culture that were ravaged by residential schools and the potlatch ban. For First Nations with a treaty, it may be full implementation of that agreement.

Shortage of land for effective economic development is an issue, as is a lack of ownership of resources, including water and natural resources. The issue of title is unresolved for much of BC. First Nations own the land, everything that grows from the land and the water that runs through it and surrounds it. If governments would work closely with First Nations on reconciliation and resolving title to land, water, and natural resources, that would be an effective tool for development and there could be real progress.

The indefinite suspension of developing clean energy in BC is a real setback to reconciliation for those First Nations that were counting on developing clean energy projects, have invested money into their development, and now have no way of realizing that investment. When asked, the BC government responds that it intends to make up for that loss by working together on other types of development but offers no real solutions.

Right now, there is constant competition from the main sectors for forestry and water licences and permits, as well as for shares in the allocation of fish, birds, and other wildlife. Governments feel they need to give priority to the general public rather than to First Nations. Until First Nations become a priority and are given that priority, reconciliation will not happen.

Governments need to realize that when First Nations prosper, everyone else prospers, too. The benefits are regional, provincial, and federal. Stopping developments that First Nations are firmly against due to their negative impact or that involve abrogation or derogation of Aboriginal rights would be a strong act of reconciliation. Prioritizing constitutionally protected rights in the public interest would be a definite statement of reconciliation. First Nations have been looking for reconciliation since the colonizer arrived, an illustration of the strong tenacity First Nations have in all things, including economic development.

Realization of Benefits to First Nations

When First Nations drive their own sustainable economic development, they can maintain their values and set high environmental standards, which benefits everyone and works toward climate action.

First Nations form many strategic partnerships and alliances in order to move ahead. Sometimes those partnerships are with the actual business and sometimes they are strategic alliances to advance industries.

First Nations develop relationships locally, provincially, and federally. All relationships work toward reconciliation and moving First Nations ahead.

First Nations doing their own development and use of resources in their territory in a sustainable way will provide those resources for many generations to come. Business and development provide revenue, meaningful jobs, and diversification of the sustainable economy, which leads to economic revival throughout the province. First Nations' visions for sustainable living, development, and preserving and conserving all lands and resources for the future will slow down climate change and reduce greenhouse gases.

First Nations use their profits or own-source revenues to reinvest in businesses and supports for language and culture, education and health, housing, community facilities and infrastructure, sports and recreation, government services, facilities for Elders and youth, traditional forms of art, documenting histories and traditional use, and land use planning. Such investment can support the restoration and rehabilitation of their territories. Some First Nations provide a small percentage of profits for per capita distribution to their members. Other First Nations use the profits for buying strategic lands and resources. There are a myriad of uses and needs within First Nations communities.

Indigenous economies require tenacity to fight the barriers erected by existing laws, structures, attitudes, political unwillingness, and financing regulations. Dismantling those barriers requires innovation and a significant change of attitude. Reconciliation can be advanced in economic development through increased access to and recognition of authority over territorial lands, waters, and resources. Communities must make their own decisions and manage their lands and resources through their own systems of governance. A favourable climate must be created to attract investment and generate wealth for BC First Nations in keeping with community values and, in particular, in a sustainable manner. Relationships must be fostered with industry and government partners. There must be increased First Nations entrepreneurship and development of a skilled First Nations workforce. This includes both education and skills training at all levels. From generation to generation, First Nations leaders have fought to retain and implement their rights, including the right to self-determination and development. Tenacity has been the key to progress in First Nations communities and will continue to be central to overcoming other barriers and challenges with governments and third parties to pursue sustainable economic development.

Concluding Thoughts

Indigenous peoples are here to stay—they are committed to their lands and the resources that provide for their people. First Nations must engage in sustainable development in their way, with their values, and with the consent and support of all their members in order to be economically viable. First Nations are not opposed to development, but they are opposed to development that infringes upon or abrogates their rights and the ecosystems that support those rights. First Nations can lead and are leading the way in sustainable development that helps to mitigate climate change in whole or in part. Governments must have the political will to live up to reconciliation, which includes implementing UNDRIP and, in BC, the Declaration of Indigenous Rights Act. Third parties need to respect First Nations' right of consent and work to achieve reconciliation. Only then will First Nations realize true economic self-determination. First Nations are tenacious and have survived colonization, imposition of laws without their consent, government approvals of projects they are opposed to, and being kept out of industries they want to be a part of. It is this tenacity that underpins the economic success that First Nations want, in their own way and based on their own laws and values.

NOTES

✦

1   British Columbia, Declaration on the Rights of Indigenous Peoples Act [SBC 2019] Chapter 44, 28 November 2019, https://www.bclaws.gov.bc.ca/civix/ document/id/complete/statreg/19044; and Parliament of Canada, United Nations Declaration on the Rights of Indigenous Peoples Act, Bill C-15 (Royal Assent), 21 June 2021, https://parl.ca/DocumentViewer/en/43-2/bill/C-15/ royal-assent.

2   David Dodge and Duncan Kinney, blog, April 27, 2015, https://www.pembina. org/blog/judith-sayers-first-nations-run-of-river-hydro-trailblazer.

3   McGill Newsroom, "Indigenous Peoples around the Globe Are Disproportionately Affected by Pollution," 19 May 2020, https://www.mcgill.ca/newsroom/channels/ news/Indigenous-peoples-around-globe-are-disproportionately-affected- pollution-322211.

4   John McHugo, "How to Prove Title to Territory: A Brief, Practical Introduction to the Law and Evidence," in *Boundary and Territory Briefing*, ed. Clive Schofield, vol. 2, no. 4 (Durham, UK: University of Durham, Department of Geography, International Boundaries Research Unit, 1998), 2.

5   *Western Sahara Campaign UK v. Commissioners for Her Majesty's Revenue and Customs and Secretary of State for Environment, Food and Rural Affairs*, EUR-Lex: Access to European Union Law, doc. 62016CC0266, https://eur-lex.europa.eu/legal-content/EN/ TXT/?uri=CELEX percent3A62016CJ0266.

6   Union of BC Indian Chiefs, "Certainty: Canada's Struggle To Extinguish Abor-iginal Title," 1998, https://www.ubcic.bc.ca/ certainty_canada_s_struggle_to_extinguish_aboriginal_title

7   *Tsilhqot'in Nation v. British Columbia*, 2014 SCC 44, [2014] 2 S.C.R. 256.

8   First Nations Summit, News Release, https://fns.bc.ca/news/ fns-chiefs-support-first-nations-economic-development-action-plan.

9   Westbank First Nation, "Westbank First Nation Self-Government Agreement Between Her Majesty the Queen in Right of Canada and Westbank First Nation," 24 May 2003, https://www.wfn.ca/selfgovernment.htm; see parts 4, 10, 12, and 14.

10   Government of Canada, shíshálh Nation Self-Government Act, 1986, https:// laws-lois.justice.gc.ca/eng/acts/S-6.6/; see Sections 4, 10, and 14.

11 Government of Canada, First Nations Land Management Act, 1999, https://laws-lois.justice.gc.ca/eng/acts/F-11.8/.

12 Supreme Court of Canada, Judgment in *Haida Nation v. British Columbia (Minister of Forests)*, 18 November 2004, https://scc-csc.lexum.com/scc-csc/scc-csc/en/item/2189/index.do.

13 *West Moberly First Nation v. B.C. (Chief Inspector of Mines)*, 2010 BCSC 359.

14 Includes projects like Pacific GasLink, Enbridge, and Trans Mountain Pipeline.

15 Supreme Court of Canada, Judgment in *Delgamuukw v. British Columbia*, 11 December 1997, https://scc-csc.lexum.com/scc-csc/scc-csc/en/item/1569/index.do.

16 Ibid., para. 168; emphasis added.

17 *Haida v. BC*, https://scc-csc.lexum.com/scc-csc/scc-csc/en/item/2189/index. Paragraph 48; emphasis added.

18 *Tsilhqo'tin v. BC*, https://scc-csc.lexum.com/scc-csc/scc-csc/en/item/14246/index. do paragraph 97.

19 Huu-ay-aht First Nation, "Huu-ay-aht Citizens Vote to Continue to Explore Proposed LNG Project," https://huuayaht.org/2014/11/huu-ay-aht-citizens-vote-to-continue-to-explore-proposed-lng-project/.

20 Parliament of Canada, United Nations Declaration on the Rights of Indigenous Peoples Act, Bill C-15, Schedule (Subsection 2(1)), Annex.

21 Osoyoos Indian Band website, "Community," accessed 5 April 2023, http://oib.ca/community/; Kamloops (Tk'emlúps) Indian Band, "Business and Economic Develoment," accessed 5 April 2023, http://www.tkemlupsbusiness.ca/

22 First Nations On-Reserve Housing Program, https://www.sac-isc.gc.ca/eng/1100100010752/; Assembly of First Nations, "Additions to Reserve," https://www.sac-isc.gc.ca/eng/1465827292799/1611938828195, 12.

23 Indigenous Services Canada, "New Legislative Changes Improve First Nations Access to Lands and Financial Resources," 10 September 2019, https://www.sac-isc.gc.ca/eng/1544732060186/1544732109441.

24 Government of Canada, First Nations Land Management Act, 1999, https://laws-lois.justice.gc.ca/eng/acts/f-11.8/page-1.html.

25 Ts'uubaa-asatx (Lake Cowichan) First Nation, "Ts'uubaa-asatx Now," Ts'uubaa-asatx First Nation, 2021, https://www.lakecowichanfn.ca/who-we-are, accessed 5 April 2023.

26 Comprehensive Community Planning (CCP), https://www.sac-isc.gc.ca/eng/1100100021901/1613674678125].

27 Independent Electricity System Operator (IESO), "Indigenous Community Energy Plan Program Overview," accessed 5 April 2023, https://www.ieso.ca/en/Get-Involved/Indigenous-Relations/Indigenous-Community-Energy-Plan-Program/ICEP-Overview.

28 Susana Mas, "Trudeau Lays Out Plan for New Relationship with Indigenous People," CBC News, 8 December 2015, https://www.cbc.ca/news/politics/justin-trudeau-afn-Indigenous-aboriginal-people-1.3354747.

29   Indigenous Services Canada, "Water in First Nations Communities," https://www.
      sac-isc.gc.ca/eng/1100100034879/1521124927588.

30   Indigenous Services Canada, "Proponents' Guide to Environmental Review
      Process," https://www.sac-isc.gc.ca/eng/1403215245662/1613076676889].

31   Government of Canada, Indian Act, https://laws-lois.justice.gc.ca/eng/acts/i-5/.

32   Canadian Press, "First Nations Push for Greater Share of Forestry Industry as
      Policies Evolve," CBC News, 1 July 2019, https://www.cbc.ca/news/business/
      first-nations-forestry-1.5196318.

33   BC Hydro, "Filling the Site C Reservoir," accessed 5 April 2023, https://www.
      sitecproject.com.

34   Union of BC Indian Chiefs, "Approval of the Site C Dam Was Irresponsible and
      Must Be Reversed," accessed 5 April 2023, https://www.ubcic.bc.ca/reversesitec.

35   Taseko Mines Company, "New Prosperity," accessed 5 April 2023, https://www.
      tasekomines.com/properties/new-prosperity.

36   Amy Judd, "Federal Government Rejects New Prosperity Mine Project, West of
      Williams Lake," Global News, 27 February 2014, https://globalnews.ca/
      news/1175296/federal-government-rejects-new-prosperity-mine-project-
      west-of-williams-lake/.

37   David Beers, "Tsilhqot'in Finally Win Long Fight against Open Pit Mine," Tyee, 15
      May 2020, https://thetyee.ca/News/2020/05/15/
      Tsilhqotin-WinFight-Against-Open-Pit-Mine/.

38   "Lelu Island LNG Project Divides First Nations as Protest Continues," CBC News,
      12 November 2015, https://www.cbc.ca/news/canada/british-columbia/
      first-nations-lelu-island-lng-1.3316862.

39   Supreme Court of Canada, Applications for Leave, Coldwater Indian Band, et al. v.
      Attorney General of Canada, et al., 2 July 2020, https://decisions.scc-csc.ca/scc-csc/
      scc-l-csc-a/en/item/18411/index.do.

40   Tsleil-Waututh Nation Sacred Trust Initiative, "TMX: Supreme Court of Canada
      Denies Leave, as Tsleil-Waututh Announces Further Appeal," 5 March 2020,
      https://twnsacredtrust.ca/tmx-supreme-court-of-canada-denies-leave-as-tsleil-
      waututh-announces-further-appeal/.

41   Kathleen Harris, "Liberals to Buy Trans Mountain Pipeline for $4.5B to Ensure
      Expansion Is Built," CBC News, 29 May 2018, https://www.cbc.ca/news/politics/
      liberals-trans-mountain-pipeline-kinder-morgan-1.4681911.

42   Government of Canada, Transport Canada, "Oceans Protection Plan," https://
      www.tc.gc.ca/eng/oceans-protection-plan.html.

43   Tsleil-Waututh Nation, Assessment of the Trans Mountain Pipeline and Tanker Expansion
      Proposal (North Vancouver: Treaty, Lands and Resources Department, Tsleil-
      Waututh Nation, n.d.), https://twnsacredtrust.ca/wp-content/uploads/
      TWN_assessment_final_med-res_v2.pdf.

44   Canada Action, "Who Supports the Trans Mountain Pipeline Expansion in
      Canada?" 21 June 2019, https://www.canadaaction.ca/
      who_supports_trans_mountain_pipeline_expansion.

45 United Nations, Department of Economic and Social Affairs, United Nations Declaration on the Rights of Indigenous Peoples (UNDRIP), 13 September 2007, https://www.un.org/development/desa/Indigenouspeoples/declaration-on-the-rights-of-Indigenous-peoples.html. See Articles 18, 23, and 32.

46 Laura Dhillon Kane, "Projects Like Coastal GasLink Offer 'Life-Changing' Opportunities for First Nations: Haisla Councillor," 15 January 2020, https://www.cbc.ca/news/canada/british-columbia/coastal-gaslink-pipeline-life-changing-jobs-first-nations-haisla-1.5427666.

47 Supreme Court of Canada, Judgment in *Haida Nation v. British Columbia.*

48 Ben Cousins, "Wet'suwet'en: What's the Difference between the Elected Band Council and Hereditary Chiefs?" CTV News, 13 February 2020, https://www.ctvnews.ca/canada/wet-suwet-en-what-s-the-difference-between-the-elected-band-council-and-hereditary-chiefs-1.4811453.

49 Sean Boynton, "11 More Arrests Made as RCMP Expand Enforcement Area for Wet'suwet'en Pipeline Opponents," Global News, 8 February 2020, https://globalnews.ca/news/6525742/wetsuweten-enforcement-rcmp-day-3/.

50 Supreme Court of Canada, Judgment in *Delgamuukw v. British Columbia.*

51 Betsy Trumpener, "Gas Field Workers Push for LNG While Indigenous Protesters Vow to Stop It," CBC News, 27 September 2016, https://www.cbc.ca/news/canada/british-columbia/pacific-northwest-lng-opponents-dig-in-at-protest-camp-1.3780889.

52 United Nations, Department of Economic and Social Affairs, UNDRIP.

53 Parliament of Canada, Bill C-262 (Third Reading), 30 May 2018, https://www.parl.ca/DocumentViewer/en/42-1/bill/C-262/third-reading.

54 Parliament of Canada, Bill C-15 (First Reading), 3 December 2020, https://parl.ca/DocumentViewer/en/43-2/bill/C-15/first-reading.

55 Sarah Turnbull, "Systemic Racism Exists in All Institutions, Including RCMP: Trudeau," CTV News, https://www.ctvnews.ca/politics/systemic-racism-exists-in-all-institutions-including-rcmp-trudeau-1.4979878.

56 Parliament of Canada, Bill C-15.

57 Government of British Columbia, Declaration on the Rights of Indigenous Peoples Act.

58 Dana Cook, Eryn Fitzgerald, Judith Sayers, and Karena Shaw, *Survey Report: First Nations and Renewable Energy Development in British Columbia* (Victoria: BC First Nations Clean Energy Working Group, 2017), https://dspace.library.uvic.ca/handle/1828/7919.

59 New Relationship Trust, "BC Indigenous Clean Energy Initiative," accessed 5 April 2023, https://www.newrelationshiptrust.ca/initiatives/bcicei/.

60 BC Hydro, "Independent Projects History and Maps," https://www.bchydro.com/work-with-us/selling-clean-energy/meeting-energy-needs/how-power-is-acquired.html.

61 Hupačasath First Nation website, https://hupacasath.ca/upnit-power-corporation/.

62   David Dodge and Duncan Kinney, "Judith Sayers, First Nations Run-of-River Hydro Trailblazer," Green Energy Futures website, http://www.greenenergyfutures.ca/episode/judith-sayers-first-nation-run-river-hydro.

63   T'Sou-ke First Nation, "First Nation Takes Lead on Solar Power," http://www.tsoukenation.com/first-nation-takes-lead-on-solar-power/.

64   Barkley Project Group, "Projects," https://barkley.ca/projects/.

65   Kanaka Bar Indian Band, "Kwoiek Creek Resources Inc.," http://www.kanakabarband.ca/business/kwoiek-creek-resources-inc.

66   Bullfrog Power, "Kanaka Bar Indian Band Solar Project," https://bullfrogpower.com/projects/kanaka-bar-indian-band-solar-project/.

67   Trent Moraes, "Skidegate Band Council Heat Pump Video," YouTube, 14 December 2015, https://www.youtube.com/watch?v=f23JmolkhD4.

68   *Maa-nulth First Nations Final Agreement*, 2009, Section 8.6.1(a), Toquaht Nation website, http://www.toquaht.ca/wp-content/uploads/2021/11/Maa-nulth-Final-Agreement_2009.pdf.

69   BC Hydro, "Standing Offer Program," 20 March 2019, https://www.bchydro.com/work-with-us/selling-clean-energy/closed-offerings/standing-offer-program.html.

70   Government of British Columbia, *Clean Energy Act*; see Sections 2(l), 15, and 16 for objectives, http://www.bclaws.ca/civix/document/id/complete/statreg/10022_01.

71   Pembina Institute, "Clean Energy Jobs Map," https://www.pembina.org/bcjobsmap/.

72   Ken Davidson, *Zapped: A Review of BC Hydro's Purchase of Power from Independent Power Producers Conducted for the Minister of Energy, Mines and Petroleum Resources*, February 2019, https://www2.gov.bc.ca/assets/gov/farming-natural-resources-and-industry/electricity-alternative-energy/electricity/bc-hydro-review/bch19-158-ipp_report_february_11_2019.pdf.

73   https://www2.gov.bc.ca/assets/gov/farming-natural-resources-and-industry/electricity-alternative-energy/electricity/bc-hydro-review/bch19-158-ipp_report_february_11_2019.

74   Davis Swan, *True Cost of Electricity from the Site C Dam*, September 2017, British Columbia Utilities Commission website, https://www.bcuc.com/Documents/wp-content/09/DOC_90187_F131-1_Swan-D_Site-C-Submission.pdf.

75   Government of Alberta, "Long-Term Renewables Plan Powers Jobs, Investment," news release, 26 February 2019, https://www.alberta.ca/release.cfm?xID=62600ACA2C8C4-9C9C-1198-C73B9AB0471F6EDF.

76   Government of British Columbia, Climate Change Accountability Act, 29 November 2007, https://www.bclaws.gov.bc.ca/civix/document/id/complete/statreg/07042_01.

77   Government of Canada, Canadian Net-Zero Emissions Accountability Act, 29 June 2021, https://laws-lois.justice.gc.ca/eng/acts/C-19.3/FullText.html.

78 Government of Alberta, "Long-Term Renewables Plan Powers Jobs, Investment,"
    news release, 26 February 2019, https://www.alberta.ca/release.
    cfm?xID=62600ACA2C8C4-9C9C-1198-C73B9AB0471F6EDF.

79 Truth and Reconciliation Commission of Canada, *Calls to Action* (Winnipeg: Truth
    and Reconciliation Commission of Canada, 2015), https://ehprnh2mwo3.exactdn.
    com/wp-content/uploads/2021/01/Calls_to_Action_English2.pdf.

PART THREE

◆

Family Connections

The success of economic initiatives is essentially always intertwined with significant support from family and community. This has been and continues to be integral to many Indigenous businesses, particularly those described in this section. Their stories inspire, cultivate appreciation, and generate admiration for the diligence that has been applied over years of dedication.

In the Atlantic region, entrepreneurial resilience is honoured through lifetime achievement awards to businesses for contributions made to their communities over the last several decades. The stories documented by Chris Googoo, Catherine Martin, and Fred Wien reveal what was needed before government programs were available to support new businesses. For the award-winning entrepreneurs, this meant taking opportunities to serve their own community or the broader community with the gifts and talents handed down to them, and taking advantage of business opportunities that emerged from within their own families. The longevity of their businesses teaches passion, persistence through many challenges, thoughtful decision making, and other important lessons that are passed on to the benefit of ensuing generations.

In a case study from Inuvik Northwest Territories, Wanda Wuttunee captures the experiences of Métis businessman Jim McDonald, a partner in McDonald Brothers Electric. This service business succeeded not because of the owners' ethnicity but because of its stellar reputation, which opened up financing and project opportunities over time. McDonald offers encouraging advice to youth who want to start their own businesses, and is so pleased to pass on the business to the next generation. In his position as mayor of Inuvik, he demonstrated a people-first style, making space to hear people's concerns and opinions by standing front and centre in the community rather than only sitting behind a desk.

In the story of Neechi Commons, Wanda Wuttunee describes how the organization drew on the strength of relationships with its community in the North End of Winnipeg. Neechi Commons had a proud history of bringing in people from marginalized communities and beyond to build skills and work opportunities. The project was not only dedicated to bettering Indigenous food security but also offered a place to celebrate creativity through word, song, and visual expression. Although it closed after only five years, Neechi Commons left lasting and positive memories of the new and exciting opportunities it brought to the community, leaving members encouraged and more skilled than before. This legacy started in a small convenience store—Neechi Foods—and culminated in Neechi Commons. The Neechi story covers thirty-three years and ended in 2023 as the building's ownership changed hands and shifted focus to Indigenous youth programming.

CHAPTER 7

◆

Honouring Entrepreneurial Resilience: Atlantic Region Lifetime Achievers

◆

*Chris Googoo, Catherine Martin,
and Fred Wien*

As the introductory chapter of this book makes clear, much of Indigenous economic history has been a story about resistance, resilience, perseverance, and innovation under changing circumstances. Thus, one could jump in at almost any point in this historical trajectory and find examples to illustrate these themes. Our particular interest, however, is to take account of Indigenous entrepreneurship in the generation before contemporary businesses. This chapter describes entrepreneurs who are no longer as prominent as they once were but who started, expanded, and sustained their businesses for several decades, during a time of considerable adversity and without the benefit of extensive governmental support programs. These stories illustrate how tenacity and resilience were essential to the success these entrepreneurs achieved—they had to do it on their own, relying on their vision, determination, and commitment.

Our perspective on this world comes from the Atlantic region of Canada, where Ulnooweg Development Group has, for the past fifteen years, recognized and celebrated "lifetime achievers" from the Indigenous communities.[1] Twenty such awards have been made since 2005, and we set out to interview the recipients if they were still living, or, if they had passed away, their family members. We inquired into the nature of their business, how they got started and the barriers they encountered, how the business contributed to the wider community, and what accounted for their success in keeping a business going over several decades.

The Atlantic Aboriginal Entrepreneurship Awards

The Atlantic Aboriginal Entrepreneurship Award (Show) was created in 2005 as an opportunity to acknowledge and celebrate Aboriginal business successes in the Atlantic region. Ulnooweg believed that celebrating the accomplishments of the entrepreneurial sector was an important part of recognizing its impact within the Indigenous community and a key part in the process of building a stronger economy for our future generations.

The Award Show's objectives include recognizing the role of entrepreneurship as a building block on the path to self-determination, promoting entrepreneurship as a key to future economic growth for communities that struggle with employment, and providing a forum for fostering relationships and building new partnerships among both Indigenous and non-Indigenous businesses in the Atlantic region. A key consideration was the need to change the climate of opinion about Indigenous people and their communities by highlighting success and achievement.

In its inaugural year, the show gave awards in several different categories but these have been adapted over time. In the 2020 award show, for example, the following categories were recognized: Start-up Business (under two years), Cottage Craft, Youth, Female, Male, Resilient, Aboriginal Government Enterprise, and Lifetime Achievement.

In keeping with the Indigenous tradition of honouring Elders, Ulnooweg introduced the Lifetime Achievement Award in 2006. This is the highest honour given, bestowed upon an individual for their accomplishments in business and community throughout their life. Recipients of the award have included entrepreneurs who had been in business for more than twenty years, exemplifying qualities such as commitment to community through social and economic contributions as an entrepreneur. Candidates considered have been and continue to be living role models, whose lifelong careers in business have had a significant impact in their communities. One distinctive feature of the Lifetime Achievement Award, compared with the other awards, is that it is not a competition to identify the worthiest candidate. Instead, it is given to all who are nominated as long as they meet the criteria.

The process includes an invitation for nominations from across Atlantic Canada, including the region's Mi'kmaq, Wolastoqiyi, Innu, Inuit, and Métis communities. Nominators complete a nomination form, including a description of the candidate's entrepreneurial spirit, their accomplishments, and their impact upon and/or benefit to the Indigenous community. A biographical summary highlights the candidate's education, any awards or distinctions received, and participation in lectures and conferences. Letters of recommendation and any other supporting documentation are invited from the community. Once recommendations are forwarded from the jury, a film crew is engaged to interview recipients on camera, and the resulting video is played during the presentation of the awards.

Since 2005, Ulnooweg has hosted the show in each of the four Atlantic provinces. After four years of back-to-back shows, Ulnooweg decided to move to hosting the show biennially. The fall of 2020 marked the show's tenth anniversary and celebrated Ulnooweg's thirty-fifth anniversary.

Methodology

In the period 2006 through 2018, there were nine award shows held and twenty individuals were honoured for their lifetime achievement. They and their businesses are described below. To learn more about them, we drew on two information sources: the videos that were produced by the film crew and shown at the ceremonies, and an in-person, over-the-phone personal interview. Out of the twenty recipients, six had passed away since the time they were given the award, in which case we interviewed a close family member. We were successful in interviewing thirteen lifetime achievers or their family members.

We used an interview guide consisting of thirteen questions, and encouraged respondents to speak extensively about their experience and perspectives. In some cases, interviews were recorded, and in other instances extensive notes were taken to reflect the conversation. Ethics approval to undertake the research was obtained from the Ethics Review Board at Dalhousie University and also by the Mi'kmaq Ethics Watch administered through Unama'ki College at Cape Breton University.

The Historical and Community Context for Indigenous Entrepreneurship and Resilience

In the hundreds of years of recorded interaction between Indigenous peoples in the region and incoming Europeans and Americans, historians generally agree that the low point in Indigenous fortunes was reached in the early decades of the 1800s. At that time, the ravages of disease, starvation, loss of access to traditional lands and waters, and interference in traditional livelihood activities had reduced the Indigenous population almost to extinction.[2]

In the ensuing decades, the population gradually regrouped and found ways to regain its self-reliance, often working on the fringes of the settler economy, but this was precarious and often seasonal employment for low wages and incomes. Much of this activity involved self-employment and entrepreneurship. In this vein, some adults continued in their traditional ways, hunting, trapping, and gathering to the extent that they could. Others hired themselves out or made products for which there was some demand in the settler communities. Thus, accounts from the late 1800s and through the middle of the 1900s document people making barrels or hampers to contain agricultural products, crafting decorative baskets to be used in the home, or making wooden props to hold up mine shafts. Other individuals were employed to clean houses, guide visiting hunters or fishermen, work in road construction, pick seasonal produce such as blueberries or potatoes, or work in the emerging manufacturing businesses of the region.[3] Both of these two latter activities involved hundreds of people travelling to New England and beyond in search of employment.[4]

The lifetime achievers honoured by Ulnooweg did not, for the most part, chart a new path to entrepreneurship. They were, rather, part of an entrepreneurial tradition within the Indigenous communities of Atlantic Canada going back hundreds of years, including, of course, the pre-contact era. In the more recent past, stories of how lifetime achievers got started in their chosen business often reflect the fact they are continuing a family tradition—learning how to make baskets, for example, from their parents when they were children, or coming to understand the forests, game, and fish through family patterns, on the basis of which a business was established or maintained. In other cases, budding entrepreneurs were astute enough to recognize a service or product that was needed either in their own communities (such as a grocery store, gas station, or restaurant) or in the surrounding area (for example, providing goods or services to large-scale developments).

While being able to draw strength from a long entrepreneurial
tradition, the lifetime achievers nevertheless faced a daunting environment
in which to start and sustain their businesses. We give three examples of
events that occurred that strongly affected family and community life.

The Great Depression. Of course, the Great Depression affected
everyone in the region, but Indigenous people were especially impacted
because the foothold they had carved out was particularly vulnerable
to the forces unleashed by the Depression. Operating on the fringes of
the settler economy, the market for their goods and services quickly
dried up. There was also a belief at the time that Indians on-reserve
were a federal responsibility, and that the federal government would
look after any hardships that occurred. The federal government did
respond in the 1920s and later decades, but the response took the form
of what we would now call increased welfare payments to individuals
and families.[5] Fred Wien has argued elsewhere that this was an inadequate
policy response to the situation, one more focused on relief for individuals
and families than on tackling the more difficult assignment of rebuilding
Indigenous economies and societies.[6]

Centralization in Nova Scotia. In the 1940s, the federal government
became convinced that centralizing the forty or so Mi'kmaq communities
in the province and requiring people to move to two central locations
was a good idea. There were many reasons for forcing this move,
including the idea that it would be much more efficient to administer
the population and provide services if the people were gathered together
into larger centres. Promises were made and threats were issued, with
the result that many communities were abandoned, and others suffered
a sharp drop in population. In the process, patterns of subsistence living
were disrupted. In the end, centralization also came to be regarded as
a policy failure, causing trauma among those forced to move and creating
divisions between long-time residents and newcomers in the two

centralization destinations. It was also a failure on economic grounds. After a short boom period when new housing, nursing stations, band offices, and churches were constructed, residents were left without a substantial economic base in rural locations far removed from urban areas.[7]

Residential schools and the "Sixties Scoop." Especially since the recent work of the Truth and Reconciliation Commission, the damaging effects of residential schools on Indigenous family and community life have become better known.[8] In the Maritimes, many Mi'kmaq and Wolastoqiyik children were sent to the residential school at Shubenacadie, Nova Scotia, for extended periods of time.[9] Others attended what were known as Indian day schools located on-reserve. The Shubenacadie Residential School did not close its doors until 1967, but by that time another threat to family and community life was playing out. Known as the Sixties Scoop, it also involved Indigenous children being removed from families and communities, this time by way of adoption and foster care, and being placed into non-Indigenous homes. Children, families, and communities are still dealing with the after-effects of residential schools and out-of-community placements.

These three events affected many or all of the Indigenous communities of the region, but in addition, different parts of the region faced their own particular historic situations. The Mushuau Innu of Labrador, for example, were subject to a traumatic relocation in 2002. In Prince Edward Island, the Mi'kmaq were engaged in a protracted struggle to establish and retain their reserve lands. And in several parts of the region, recognition of First Nations under the Indian Act of Canada and qualification for federal services were much delayed.

It is in this context that the lifetime achievers grew into their businesses. As we will see in a later section, they reported additional obstacles to be overcome, such as the limited market available to them in their home communities, their relative isolation from urban areas, and the reality of discriminatory attitudes on the part of the surrounding population. They also observed that, for the most part, they did not have available to them the broad array of business and entrepreneurial support programs that have become more common in recent decades. These historical and community contexts serve to underline the achievements of the entrepreneurs honoured by Ulnooweg.

A Profile of the Lifetime Achievers and Their Businesses

Our lifetime achievers were a diverse group that included an almost equal balance between women (nine) and men (eleven). They came from all over the Atlantic region, with most having lived on lands reserved for the Mi'kmaq and Wolastoqiyik peoples but also including those who were on lands not recognized as reserves or who lived off-reserve. Since they were recognized for their achievements over a lifetime, they were of course not young in age, and indeed six of them had passed away by the time we undertook the interviews.

Identifying the year when a business was established was not always straightforward. Some of the entrepreneurs had learned the craft of basket making, for example, at the feet of their parents when they were small children. On that criterion, their "business" could be said to have started (or more accurately, continued from) as far back as the 1920s, when they were selling their own crafts as budding entrepreneurs. Several of the lifetime achievers gradually took over and continued what their parents, uncles, or aunts had started, while others started from scratch. In general, it could be said that the businesses under the direction of these entrepreneurs flourished in the second half of the 1900s, in the sense that the lifetime achievers were the principal drivers of their businesses, in the latter part of the 1900s. They were then more formally established (for example, home-based production might have developed into the creation of a retail store), and some signs of diversification became evident (for example, a heavy equipment construction business might have evolved into building and leasing apartments or offices). We do not wish to imply that these businesses did not also flourish or at least continue into this century, but it is the case that the lifetime achievers gradually drew back, selling their hunting/fishing camps, for example, or turning the operation over to younger family members. Evidently, it was their age rather than their passion that forced this transition.

Many types of business are represented, of course: everything from convenience stores/gas stations to fuel oil delivery, construction, making baskets, tea dolls, or canoes to operating restaurants and a cobbler shop. Customers tended to be largely from the reserve or other local community in which the entrepreneur was residing and therefore somewhat isolated from a wider market, but that was not always the case. A basket shop, for example, might be located on a major highway where bus tours stop for a shopping expedition, or a fly-in camp catering to hunters and fishers would have a client base that extends beyond the Atlantic region. A canoe builder's work (from Labrador) was in demand from as far west as British Columbia and as far south as New Hampshire. A diner in the middle of Newfoundland was renowned across the island for the home-cooked meals it provided.

Almost all of the businesses were still operating at the time this chapter was written, often having been taken over by family members. Even when the business associated with the lifetime achiever has ended, the tradition may continue. This was seen most often with basket makers, where a sibling might still be active in the craft, or children and grand-children have learned the skill. In time, the apprentice becomes the master, and the cycle continues. Crafters develop their unique traits, thereby identifying their own craft.

Main Themes from the Interviews

Starting Out

We asked the lifetime achievers when they got started with their business, but as noted above, that proved to be difficult to pin down in some cases. Several of the entrepreneurs inherited their business from their parents, and a new generation of entrepreneurs was seeded in the shops, perhaps starting by sweeping the floors or organizing the shelves. That was one route by which our entrepreneurs got started. A second route one might call a sideways shift, where the award winner learned a trade as a young person working for another company and gained experience in a particular industry, such as heavy equipment operation or construction. They then made the move to start their own business. A third route was what we call "import substitution," where a budding entrepreneur recognized there were business opportunities in their home community, meeting needs that were not being met or that could be organized to replace an external provider. In these cases, the Band Council was often instrumental in making this happen, providing a loan and a contract, for example, to provide bus transportation for students, to clear snow in the wintertime, or to prepare an area of land for house construction. There were also those who put their passions on hold for a regular day job, and early retirement gave them a chance to fulfill their lifelong aspirations. In one case, the downfall of an entire industry, the cod moratorium of the early 1990s, led to entrepreneurship as a means for survival.

What motivated the entrepreneurs to go into business in the first place? One theme that came through clearly was the passion they had for the work and how much they enjoyed devoting their life to it. The entrepreneurs also talked about their business as a community asset, a source of employment for youth in the community, a way to meet a need in the area, and a means to retain or reinvigorate traditional skills.[10]

Family influence seemed to play a big role as well. Entrepreneurship is not necessarily an inherited trait, but work ethic definitely is a learned trait that can be passed down. Of course, there is a practical side to it as well, with the business providing a source of income and a way to put groceries on the shelf. The entrepreneurs and their parents went to great lengths in order to be financially independent:

> There is no doubt that my mother was motivated at a young age by her parents to get monetary exchange for their baskets, as they did this throughout their lives. Her father would travel to New Brunswick, Prince Edward Island, Mainland Nova Scotia, and Newfoundland. She recalled that one time, her father walked all the way to North Sydney from Whycocomagh selling baskets. In the final good years of her life . . . she was the oldest paid employee in . . . teaching basket making to the youth in the community in the evenings. Some of those who had been taught by Mother tell me about when she helped them make their first basket.

Start-Up Challenges

Almost everyone we interviewed mentioned that obtaining financing to get their business established was a big challenge. We will discuss the role of government programs below, but suffice it to say here that, for the most part, government programs were either not available during this period or were not accessed. Sometimes a bank might have been approached for a loan and, after the mid-1970s, Ulnooweg became a source of start-up capital for some, but high interest rates were an issue, as was the difficulty in providing collateral to secure the loan. What is interesting is the creative means that the entrepreneurs used to surmount these obstacles. In a couple of cases, for example, the person from whom

the business was purchased—let's say a fishing or hunting camp—
provided favourable terms to make the sale possible. That could have
included selling off part of the business at one time and the rest later,
or providing a ten-year period during which the sale price could be paid
from the proceeds of the business itself. In another case, the entrepreneur sold some assets ("my toys") to supplement a small loan from
the bank. Or the entrepreneur had personal savings or investments that
could be used as collateral, or severance pay from a "city" job. The
message that came through from the interviews, in short, was that the
entrepreneurs had to be very creative and determined to overcome the
financing hurdle.

It is worth mentioning that there were differences between lifetime
achievers who lived on-reserve and those who did not. Financing, for
example, was more accessible off-reserve, as collateral would not be a
major issue. Home ownership was an asset and a foundation from which
to build up savings for personal finances to support entrepreneurial
ventures, and could lead to greater efforts to find funding programs to
support business development outside of the "Indigenous" envelope.

Establishing a market (finding customers) was mentioned by some
of the lifetime achievers as an issue, in two respects. First, they noted
that community residents would support a local business to some extent,
but it is in the nature of small communities that people regularly want
to escape and head for the nearest urban area. Travel of this nature
was driven as much by social needs as it was by a search to get a better
deal from a business operating on a larger scale and in a more competitive
environment. One lifetime achiever talked about how the opening of
a new road caused a downturn in business, because of the very fact of
community members wanting to escape. Ironically, the COVID-19
pandemic improved business, as more community members shopped
locally. Market limitations also arose if a reserve-based business was

constrained by the small size of the community itself and sought to break into the non-Indigenous market. In this case, geographic isolation was a factor, as were the attitudes of some elements of the non-Indigenous population who might be apprehensive about travelling to a reserve, or who would hold prejudicial views.

We asked the entrepreneurs about barriers and obstacles they faced after the initial start-up phase. Some that were mentioned were specific events that occurred affecting an individual business or its owner—for example, a major flood, a sharp change in the cost of providing the service, or a tragedy affecting the family. Other obstacles were more generic, being mentioned several times. These included the difficulty of obtaining black ash and other wood used in basket making, the lack of collateral on-reserve and the ongoing struggle for financing, and limitations in the market due to geographic isolation and racist attitudes in the surrounding region. As one lifetime achiever mentioned, "The most difficult issue was the attitudes of the people. They [entrepreneurs] were not looked at seriously by outsiders, who did not recognize their skills and understandings. [Their community] was looked down on and they always had to prove themselves by being better."

There were, of course, some internal struggles. A couple of entre-preneurs mentioned the lack of support from their own community members, noting that it took time for people to take pride in their own member's success. Tourism, for example, wasn't automatically acceptable in some areas, because tourists were seen as strangers. It wasn't until people started seeing their children employed by new tourism operators that they started to understand the positive impacts of the industry.

Notably, none of the entrepreneurs mentioned that they had diffi-culty recruiting or retaining employees. This was due in part to high unemployment in the communities, which provided a ready supply of labour, but also to the fact that the lifetime achievers knew pretty much everyone living in the neighbourhood and had the information base and the family relationships from which they could make wise personnel decisions.

Government Supports

As noted earlier, our lifetime achievers came of age, so to speak, at a time when there wasn't the range of government-sponsored financial and entrepreneurial support programs that have developed in the last few decades. It was also a time when court decisions were yet to have an impact in opening up economic opportunities, and before progress had been made in self-government. Indeed, our interviews revealed that the entrepreneurs needed to make their own way, and in none of the accounts we heard did government programs figure prominently in the life of the business. A particular enterprise may have made use of one government program to help get started or expand, but none of the respondents described more than one program being accessed, and several said "none" to this question. A few entrepreneurs attempted to make use of a program but backed away when they were asked to make more of a personal investment than they thought was safe under the circumstances, or when government encouraged them to become bigger than they wanted to be:

> Government and other people in the industry had the idea
> that big is always better but I was satisfied to keep it as a
> family business. Why take on something larger? I was satis-
> fied working hands-on with members of my family and
> community. And I didn't want to go against the stress factor
> that I had set out as an objective. As a small operator, though,
> I was always at the end of the line compared to the big guys
> who wanted to phase me out and who were well connected
> to government and the bureaucracy, playing golf with them.

Family and Community

The Ulnooweg Entrepreneurship Awards recognize individual achieve-ment for the most part, but in hearing the accounts about the lifetime achievers and their enterprises, one cannot escape the conclusion that family and community are deeply implicated. Indeed, one can surmise that these enterprises would not have succeeded without their contri-butions. These took different forms.

First, family and community provided the historical context and training ground in which the business develops. This was seen most readily in the case of those who built on traditional skills such as basket making, canoe building, or guiding for fishers, harvesters, and hunters. In the latter case, for example, the entrepreneur drew on skills and knowledge that had been practised by six generations of family members. This point also applied, of course, to those who inherited their business from parents, whether that was a construction business or a convenience store/gas station. As the saying goes, "a picture is worth a thousand words," and in this regard one can say a basket or a canoe is worth ten thousand words. Our Indigenous history in this sense is not learned from a textbook but from the stories of our ancestors, told through the teachings of how to use a carving tool, or weave sweetgrass into a miniature basket.

Second, family and community members contributed their skills and labour as employees. The spouse, for example, may have handled the books and banking transactions, a sister may have been involved in running the day-to-day operation of the business, and children and grandchildren may have served as employees on a part- or full-time basis. We were told that family members were not expected to donate their labour but were, rather, paid for their contributions. There were times, though, when community members willingly provided their skills and labour at no cost. "Back in the day, if your neighbours saw you putting shingles on, they'd show up, chip in and help you and wouldn't expect any payment. That's the way it was back then."

Finally, family and community members were also involved in a business sense. An uncle may have sold a business to the lifetime achiever, brothers may have been co-owners or partners, or other relatives may have owned a retail outlet where the crafts were sold. When it came time for the business to be sold, it was often a family or community member who took over the enterprise.

Giving Back to Community

All of the accounts of the lifetime achievers provide examples of giving back to the community, and this is not surprising in that community contribution is one of the criteria for the award. Nevertheless, one has the impression that this is also a cultural expectation and practice of most, if not all, entrepreneurs living in the community. We know of one business, not part of our sample, that annually makes a bicycle available to all high school graduates from the community. Giving back takes many forms. When the lifetime achievers hired employees, for example, they relied almost entirely on family and other community members. Providing employment, incomes, and work experience was an important part of their community contribution.

One can also imagine that anytime there is a fundraising initiative in a community, businesses in the community are among the first places to be contacted. While cash donations are always appreciated, in-kind contributions such as donating items that can be auctioned at community funerals are also appreciated. The lifetime achievers also contributed goods and services to their communities, taking part in the tradition of sharing that goes back many generations. If there was extra meat or fish available from an entrepreneur operating a hunting or fishing camp, for example, we were told that it was distributed within the community, with preference given to seniors and unwed mothers.

Several of the lifetime achievers were engaged in public service activities. They might have served as an elected Band Council member or Chief, they were involved in community or regional organizations such as tourism associations, and in a couple of cases they were active in the Aboriginal movement, seeking to advance the claims of their communities to formal recognition as First Nations.

Their businesses offered a place to socialize. Community members would come in and talk about current issues, often about the "good ol' days." Providing a safe and comfortable environment is a contribution that can easily be overlooked.

Finally, giving back also takes the form of passing along traditional knowledge and skills to family and other community members. This may happen through formal or informal classes, for example. One of the entrepreneurs provided an opportunity for community members to learn the ceremonies of the Mi'kmaq people, even purchasing a building for that purpose. In some cases, the entrepreneurs reinforced and passed on traditions through what they did, whether by building canoes or doing beadwork for the creation of regalia.

Lessons and Advice

We conclude this section by summarizing the advice that the lifetime achievers had for other entrepreneurs, including sharing their own secrets for success. One theme that recurred repeatedly in their remarks was *the need for persistence, dedication, and discipline* to be applied to the work. The entrepreneurs emphasized that running a business was a full-time job and could not be compartmentalized into a nine-to-five time frame. They said you need to stick with it over the long term and adopt a hands-on approach; a business will necessarily have its ups and downs. You need discipline to prevent yourself from going on vacation or to Las Vegas if you can't afford it, or if the business requires your attention.

You have to be able to say "no" to community requests if the funds are not available.

Other than discipline and persistence, the entrepreneurs mentioned other important factors for business success. One is to *research your product and market*, to understand what unmet needs exist in the community and who else is catering to them. Taking care of your customers is also a part of this—finding out what they want, being honest with them, giving them more than they expect, and keeping them happy. Another important aspect of running a successful business has to do with supplies and suppliers. The lifetime achiever's advice was to *make sure that you have the supplies you need, and that your suppliers are cared for*.

One lifetime achiever stressed the importance of *being aware of needs in a small community*, if people don't have access to services. For example, what happens if your hot water heater breaks down? As these points suggest, *the personal qualities of the entrepreneur* are also important. An entrepreneur needs to be someone who appreciates and respects their staff, who isn't afraid to develop themselves and learn new things, and who has a passion for the type of work that is the foundation of the business. Respecting your customers also includes *respecting your own work*. One entrepreneur put it this way: "If you're going to do something, do it the best way. To your satisfaction first, then to your customer's." *Get involved with the business community*. Find a mentor, be a mentor. Your success depends on the success of your business community and vice versa.

In sales of traditional arts and crafts, *know your product*, including the artisan and crafter behind it. There is a story to tell, and it is your responsibility as an Indigenous person to tell that story with as much humility and respect as possible. "The main thing that kept my mother going was her inborn passion to dream and create and to share those creations through the age-old traditions of basket making and intricate beadwork passed down through the centuries. To her, this was more important than the monetary benefits of this type of business."

Conclusion

We mentioned at the outset of this chapter that one can find examples of Indigenous economic resilience throughout history, but we chose to focus on individuals who have been awarded lifetime achievement awards by Ulnooweg Development Group in the Atlantic region. We did so for several reasons: these award winners are the precursors to the current generation of entrepreneurs, very little has been written about them, and they faced significant historical and contextual challenges that had to be overcome.

Our interviews and conversations revealed persons who were modest about their achievements ("Nobody starts out thinking they will get an award"). As one lifetime achiever reflected, "I really never thought about how much money this business would bring in, but [had] more interest in pleasing the people. Being there for people who needed the product that we offered. They were also very committed to their life's work and to their communities: "Retiring? I think I'll work until I have to stop. . . . Gives me a purpose in the morning to get up, to get moving and to get dressed."

It also became clear during the course of the interviews that these entrepreneurs did not accomplish what they did only through their own efforts. They were not alone, in other words, but at a minimum drew on family members ranging from grandparents to siblings to children and grandchildren. They also had a balanced relationship with their community, making many contributions to community life but also drawing resources from its members.

NOTES

✦

1   The Ulnooweg Development Group was established in 1986 to provide loans and
    services to Indigenous entrepreneurs throughout Atlantic Canada. In addition,
    the Ulnooweg Indigenous Communities Foundation builds capacity for children
    and youth, while the Ulnooweg Financial Education Centre assists First Nations
    decision makers in the areas of governance and financial administration.

2   Virginia P. Miller, "The Decline of Nova Scotia Micmac Population, 1600–1850"
    (paper presented at the Eleventh Algonkian Conference, Ottawa, 1979).

3   Fred Wien, *Rebuilding the Economic Base of Indian Communities: The Micmac in Nova
    Scotia* (Montreal: Institute for Research on Public Policy, 1986).

4   Jeanne Guillemin, *Urban Renegades: The Cultural Strategy of American Indians* (New
    York: Columbia University Press, 1975).

5   Declan Cullen, Heather Castleden, and Fred Wien, "The Historical Roots of
    Dependency: Social Assistance in the Mi'kmaq Communities of Nova Scotia,"
    article submitted to the *International Indigenous Policy Journal*, 2020.

6   Wien, *Rebuilding the Economic Base*, ch. 2.

7   Lisa Patterson, "Indian Affairs and the Nova Scotia Centralization Policy" (MA
    thesis, Dalhousie University, 1985); Ellice B. Gonzalez, *Changing Economic Roles for
    Micmac Men and Women: An Ethnohistorical Analysis*, Canadian Ethnology Service
    Paper 72 (Ottawa: National Museums of Canada, 1981); Tuma Young, Deborah
    Ginnish, and The Mi'kmaq Association of Cultural Studies, *Tptinewey: Mi'kmaq
    Elders' Perceptions of Social Assistance. Report for the Building a Social Policy Framework for
    Mi'kmaq Communities: A Two-Eyed Seeing Approach* (Sydney, NS: Cape Breton
    University, 2017).

8   Truth and Reconciliation Commission of Canada, *Honouring the Truth, Reconciling
    for the Future: Summary of the Final Report of the Truth and Reconciliation Commission of
    Canada* (Ottawa: Truth and Reconciliation Commission, 2015).

9   Isabel Knockwood, *Out of the Depths: The Experiences of Mi'kmaw Children at the Indian
    Residential School at Shubenacadie* (Black Point, NS: Fernwood Press, 1992).

10 One of the entrepreneurs explained that he made a point of not hiring youth
    from the community whose future was more or less assured as they pursued
    education in community colleges or universities. He said he did not want to
    distract them from their career path. Instead, he would offer jobs to those with the
    requisite experience and interest but who also were at risk in some way if
    opportunities were not made available to them.

CHAPTER 8

✦

A Métis Light in the Northern Darkness:
A Case Study

✦

Wanda Wuttunee

Jim McDonald of McDonald Brothers Electric, located in Inuvik, Northwest Territories, is a proud Métis businessman. His family-owned business has been operating for thirty-nine years. Like the accounts of "lifetime achievers" from the Atlantic region described in Chapter 7, his is a story of individual entrepreneurial achievement spanning several generations and highlighting the importance of perseverance, along with family and community connections. Interviews with Jim form the basis for this chapter.[1]

To appreciate the longevity of this business, it is important to begin with some of the context of operating a business in the Northwest Territories. The Northwest Territories is a unique region that has faced a number of challenges to economic development. The population is sparse and widely distributed, and there is a dependence on natural resource development, which is subject to cyclical downturns and reliant on expensive energy and labour market challenges.[2]

The health of the overall northern economy has been weakened by declining commodity prices. Mineral extraction and public administration make up more than 40 percent of the northern economy, resulting in susceptibility to cyclical economic downturns. More than 70 percent of communities rely on expensive diesel generators, resulting in higher energy costs and higher environmental risks. Infrastructure gaps cause significant challenges, as well as a workforce characterized by low levels of education.[3]

In 2016, the community of Inuvik had a total population of 3,140 people. There were 1,700 individuals available to work and 195 individuals in construction.[4] From a national perspective, it is interesting that despite the hurdles to entrepreneurial development, the number of Métis entrepreneurs is growing the most out of all Indigenous groups. This phenomenon has been noted in the National Indigenous Economic Development Board reports for the past several years.[5]

The Early Years

The McDonald family has its roots in Clandeboye, Manitoba, where Jim's father, Alexander James (Jim Sr.) McDonald, was born. His family travelled by train to Edmonton and Fort McMurray, Alberta, eventually settling in Fort Chipewyan where they lived on the land, hunting and trapping. Jim Sr. gradually moved north, looking for a new life. In Fort Norman (Tulita), Northwest Territories, he met and married Alestine Lennie before moving to the Mackenzie Delta. He couldn't get a licence to hunt and trap so he worked for the Hudson's Bay Company in Aklavik.

Jim Sr. and his wife moved from Aklavik when construction of the new community that was to eventually become Inuvik started in 1956. The community of Inuvik was built to accommodate the Canadian government's desire for an administrative centre in the western Arctic. They lived in a small house known as a five-by-twelve, which was the square footage of cabins originally built to house construction workers.

With nine children in the family, quarters were cramped but life was good. Jim recalls, "We grew up close. We weren't poor. We didn't have everything but Mom and Dad gave us all the basics that we needed. We were never short of food, schooling, or the basic necessities of life." Jim has fond memories of spending time in the Mackenzie Delta hunting and fishing to augment the family's food supply. Inuvik was an exciting place at that time, with government workers, military personnel and their families from southern Canada, and local Aboriginal youth, many of whom became good friends. Jim notes, "Growing up in a mixed community and being friends with all types broadens the mind about who your friends can be. Inuvik's population was around 5,000 to 6,000 in the '70s and there was a lot to do. We weren't really isolated and we were quite rich in many ways."

Jim's parents were a huge influence on his grounding in his Métis heritage. "We were independent, as we didn't get the same rights as treaty Indians. We were proud but sometimes it was hard. Sometimes when one of us was sick we had to wait until Dad's payday to get medicine." Overall, Inuvik was a pleasant and friendly place to live, and Jim never faced blatant prejudice in the culturally diverse and resilient community. People from southern Canada, the Filipino community, the Middle East, and North Africa raise families and make Inuvik their home.

Particular mentors who impacted Jim's character were his father, Jim, and his brother Ken McDonald, who brought Jim into the electrical trade when he was young, as well as Tom Butters, former MLA and founder of *The Inuvik Drum*, the local newspaper that is still published today. These individuals were particularly encouraging and had a major influence on Jim over the course of his life.

McDonald Brothers Electric—Reflections
on Thirty-Nine Years

Jim started his electrical apprenticeship in Inuvik but soon both he and his brother Ken took an opportunity to work in Edmonton and Fort McMurray, where they spent five years in the mid-1970s. Jim earned his journeyman's ticket from Northern Alberta Institute of Technology and thoroughly enjoyed his experience working in Alberta. Work in the Beaufort Sea brought him back to the North at the beginning of the 1980s. By the end of 1980 McDonald Brothers Electric Ltd. was formed and as of 2020 was still operating.

With a small market, the company successfully bid on contracts in a broad area, underlining their approach of meeting the needs of as much of the market as possible. Projects have included housing, commercial buildings, maintenance, and small industrial projects. When the company started, much of the work was in the oil industry on drill rigs, supply ships, and camps as well as in remote radio sites.

It was tough in the early days, Jim recalls: "The challenge of a small, northern company was that people didn't feel that we had the experience and knowledge to do a lot of these projects. There were a lot of years where we had to prove ourselves. Over the years we got a lot of experience and with that our reputation grew due to the wide range of projects we successfully completed, from wiring houses to office buildings to alarm systems and water plants as well as runway lighting." Very few banks wanted to deal with a new company lacking a track record. Jim reflects that this issue resolved itself over time.

The company is able to offer steady work to ten to twelve people, with large projects expanding this to twenty people. It has been a challenge to locate qualified people regardless of their heritage. The company has always invested in training Aboriginal apprentices through to their journeymen qualifications. There is no guarantee that these people will stay with McDonald Brothers, but the investment is worth it.

Although the company's employment strategy focuses on Aboriginal trainees, the company was not built on the owners' Métis heritage. Instead, they have completely built their company on their reputation. "We tried to maintain a high standard of quality. We stood by our work so if there were any issues we would always go back and make sure we corrected things. There always will be problems but it is how you deal with your customers that is important."

Ken has retired, while Jim is still involved in the company. The brothers' sons are learning the business, and Jim hopes that they will take the company over and continue. Passing a successful enterprise from one generation to the next is important. It is harder to start a new business now because there is not a lot of industry in the region. However, there is a lot of opportunity that people don't see unless they focus on the local economy. Jim states that business owners have to be creative and keep an eye open for opportunities and be proactive in pursuing them.

Political Leadership

In addition to his work with McDonald Brothers Electric, Jim was town councillor for three terms and served one term as mayor, for a total of twelve years. His leadership approach reflects his appreciation for his community:

> I used common sense with a no-nonsense attitude. I listened more than I spoke. It's important for any leader to listen. Most of the time people just want to be heard. The most important part of my role as mayor was that I was very visible in the community and was always there to listen to

people and hear them out. Rather than giving them my
opinion, I took the time to hear their opinion. I wasn't
always able to solve everyone's problems but I dedicated
my time to do what I could. I gave issues a lot of thought,
usually at three or four in the morning, and did my best
to resolve them. People appreciate that. They realize that
at times there is not too much that can be done but you've
made the effort and you've heard them out. It worked well
for me and I enjoyed my time in the mayor's office.

I never really got a lot of calls on the mayor's phone. I
attribute that to the fact that I was always out in the
community. I was always speaking to people so if people
wanted to see me they didn't have to come into the office
or to town hall because I was out and visible in the community. You don't have to spend all your time in the office.

Jim challenged young people who want to enter politics to "get an
education. They [young people] need to be dedicated and committed
to what they are doing. It is more than just about wages or a job, they
have to be dedicated."

The work that gave Jim great satisfaction was the $40 million in
infrastructure projects, including a new water treatment plant and
water reservoir that will ensure Inuvik has clean water for the next half
century. An unexpected meeting occurred when Jim travelled to China
as the only mayor from Canada for the International Mayors' Forum
on Tourism in 2018. Jim notes:

Three or four years earlier a young man from Australia
had lost his life in a tragic construction accident and I had
worked with the family through their difficulties with the
bureaucracy, we also did a memorial to remember him.

The site where the accident happened was being developed for a satellite tracking station and we named the road that led onto the site after the community of Longreach where he was from in Australia. It so happened that the mayor from that community was also attending the forum. What were the chances of meeting the mayor from Longreach, Australia, in China? The mayor was planning to come up to Inuvik on a holiday soon. I hope that we meet again.

Jim has thoughts about the future of Inuvik and the role that politicians have:

Our leaders need to get our resources developed in the region. The future of our next generation rests on the resources in the ground. There is a lot of oil and gas here. We struggle economically because we don't have ways to get it to market; it also contributes to the high cost of living in the community. We are sitting on 3 trillion cubic metres of natural gas in the ground that has been discovered and proven.

We are trucking natural gas from BC right now to heat our homes and to generate our power. That is ludicrous, [and] until we get access to those resources we will continue to struggle to build a sustainable economy. It will give us a secure source of energy. We are doing a lot on green alternate sources of energy—wind and solar—but it is not cheap and it can't meet all of our needs. Our leaders need to focus on finding a market and develop those resources that are in the ground.

Conclusion

A northern entrepreneur, grounded in his culture, offers some valuable insights. Isolated areas such as Inuvik still offer a quality of life that builds community and supports small businesses. Leaders are acknowledged for their wisdom and care for the well-being of the community.

Jim has never let his Métis heritage go away, and it is ingrained in his independent spirit that has taken him from the Northwest Territories to Alberta and back again. He has shared this independence with his children, the next generation, by including his love for the land in their upbringing. Two young men are in training to take over the business that Jim and his brother Ken built, if they desire. This is a business with a solid foundation based on skill and reputation, two keys to a business's longevity, even when the market shrinks.

Jim's approach to leadership demonstrates his love for the community. The most important part of his work as mayor was to ensure he had his fingers on the pulse of Inuvik. He brought his integrity to the position, with care and follow-up at the centre of his leadership style, letting constituents know their voices were being heard. The connection with an Australian mayor brightened a sad memory and reflected the friendly community attitude that stretches far beyond Inuvik.

NOTES

✦

1   Jim McDonald (Métis citizen and businessman), in discussion with the author, April 2019.

2   Canadian Northern Economic Development Agency, *Canadian Northern Economic Development Agency: 2016–2017 Report on Plans and Priorities,* written by Navdeep Bains (Ottawa: Canadian Northern Economic Development Agency, 2016), 8.

3   Ibid., 9.

4   "Gross Domestic Product," NWT Bureau of Statistics, Government of Northwest Territories, https://www.statsnwt.ca/economy/gdp/, 10 June 2019.

5   National Indigenous Economic Development Board, *The Indigenous Economic Progress Report* (Ottawa: The National Economic Development Board, 2019), 59, http://www.naedb-cndea.com/wp-content/uploads/2019/06/NIEDB-2019-Indigenous-Economic-Progress-Report.pdf.

CHAPTER 9

◆

Neechi Commons Case Study:
A Lost Love Letter to Winnipeg

◆

Wanda Wuttunee

Indigenous economic tenacity is in part a story about the commitment, creativity, and persistence of individual entrepreneurs. But as the "lifetime achievers" in Chapter 7 illustrated, Indigenous tenacity is also a story about connection to a wider universe, to family and community. These ties help to sustain individual businesses while at the same time allowing the businesses to contribute back to these collectivities. This is brought to the forefront by the story of Neechi Commons in Winnipeg, Manitoba.

Building community in a place that has very little to speak of takes vision beyond that reality, and hope that all the pieces will come together for a sustainable future. This place is filled with people who are on the margins and mostly invisible. Most are Indigenous and newcomers, in a rundown section of the city that includes skid row. This place is one of Canada's urban areas most densely populated with Indigenous people—and was home to a team, headed by Louise Champagne (Métis), focused on making a positive difference in the lives of their neighbours.

Neechi Commons was a place of community, located in the heart of Winnipeg's inner city. It hired community members to staff its Three Sisters Fruit and Vegetable Courtyard, Kookum's Bakery, Neechi Niche, and the Come N' Eat restaurant. The "Three Sisters" refers to corn, beans, and squash, the physical and spiritual sustainers of life for people of the Haudenosaunee.[1] "kookum" means grandmother in the Anishinaabe language, and "neechi" means friend, sister, or brother in Cree and Anishinaabe.

As Neechi Co-op president, Louise Champagne had worked tirelessly with supporters and worker-owners for more than twenty-eight years in Neechi Co-op Limited, the original grocery store that served the inner-city community. With the community's continued support, Neechi Commons was opened in March 2013 to broaden the vision of the co-op and was located a few blocks away from Neechi Co-op. By 2018, under the weight of a $3.9 million debt, Neechi Commons had closed its doors.[2] Forty jobs were lost but important lessons remain.

The Commons drew in the disenfranchised and the marginalized and gave them hope through employment if they needed work or a sense of community if they were customers. "Neechi" and "kookum," words of community, underlined the value placed on Indigenous customers while Come N' Eat reflected the friendly and open atmosphere throughout the Commons by extending an open hand beyond the inner city to Winnipeggers who wanted to support a wonderful initiative that enriched their city.

The community network of relationships that had been nurtured by the original Neechi Foods Co-op offered a foundation for Neechi Commons that allowed a leap into a new reality for their community. The original Neechi Foods Co-op (renamed Neechi Foods Community Store) remained open as a convenience to its regular inner-city customers but closed soon after Neechi Commons closed.

History of Neechi Foods Community Store

Neechi Foods Community Store is an ideal example of a sustained Indigenous community economic development initiative. Its history provides insight into the Neechi Commons launch. The grocery store had operated since 1990 and was an associate member of Federated Co-operatives Ltd. (FCL). Neechi Foods joined 225 other co-ops located in western Canada, all member-owners of FCL. FCL offers important central wholesaling, manufacturing, marketing, and administrative services to its member-owners.[3]

Neechi Foods Community Store was committed to ensuring customer satisfaction through quality products and services and encouraged its workers to take an equity position in the store, thus building a meaningful cooperative. Local Indigenous suppliers of handicrafts and products were supported through a focus on local community economic development and maximized opportunities for Indigenous people. Neechi Community Store offered its customers fresh bannock, wild rice, wild blueberries, freshwater fish, and other Indigenous specialty foods, "home-made" deli products, regular grocery products, and Indigenous crafts, books, and music. The Community Store became commercially self-reliant and profitable. It survived severe economic crises through the dedication and persistence of its management and worker-owners.

Louise recalled "the nineties where the economy was depressed, and we called a meeting about closing the store. It was the women who said, we are prepared to take a cut in salary so we can keep the store open and demonstrated stick-with-it-ness. Everyone went on minimum wage rather than go on welfare. There was a sense of pride of having a job."[4]

When the store's annual sales exceeded $600,000, a decision was taken to develop ideas for expanding into the Neechi Commons business complex.

Neechi Principles for Community Economic Development

Louise described conversations with bankers who did not grasp the concept of a business that earned profit for the benefit of the community. It was not until the term "social enterprise" came into use, linked closely with social economy, that Louise had a term to describe the approach to development used by Neechi Community Store.[5] This term encapsulated some of the core desires and challenges facing a project that placed people at its heart.

Out of a discussion with the community soon after Neechi Co-op started, a set of principles were identified that would guide Neechi's approach to community development. They became known as the Neechi Principles and were embraced by the provincial government of Manitoba and the local community economic development (CED) community.[6] These principles include:

1. Use of local goods and services: By using local goods and services, a community creates greater self-reliance and less dependence on outside markets while at the same time supporting local producers.

2. Production of goods and services for local use: Focusing on local goods and services results in producing goods and services that are needed and produced within the community.

3. Local reinvestment of profits: CED encourages businesses to invest their profits toward community-building activities rather than keep them for their own profit so that in this way the whole community benefits.

4. Long-term employment of local residents: This provides long-term jobs for people within a community.

5. Local skill development: CED also encourages local skill development.

6. Local decision making and ownership: Many CED businesses are collectively owned, which means that all people who work at the business have a part in the decision making and become part owners of the business.

7. Healthy citizens: The CED model invests in community development that brings physical, mental, and emotional health and well-being to community members at home, in the workplace, and in the community at large.

8. Positive physical environment: CED projects encourage healthy, safe, and attractive neighbourhoods.

9. Neighbourhood stability: CED encourages development that brings stability and health to a whole community.

10. Human dignity: Essentially, CED works for the self-respect and dignity of all members of the community.

11. Support for other CED projects: CED projects strategically support other CED projects by buying from each other.[7]

Neechi Commons set these principles as the foundational strategy to accomplish their vision for the community. The Commons was an expansion of an idea that outgrew its original space. It was a move forward that honoured the community that had supported it for twenty-eight years by maintaining a presence and meeting community needs. The next section discusses Neechi Commons and its presence in the city of Winnipeg.

Launching Neechi Commons

Financing was difficult, which compromised Neechi Commons attempts to build a solid footing. Louise noted,

> One of the hardest things in this project has been getting
> the financing. When you are poor you live from hand to

mouth and that's Neechi too. We struggle and live from hand to mouth and have survived in a very competitive food industry. It has not gotten any easier in the 25 years we have been here. The level of sales you have to earn to survive has quadrupled. If you aren't hitting those sales levels, then suppliers don't even want to look at you because you aren't going to survive. It's very tough for small businesses but that is who we are in the wider world. We are still here despite all the challenges because of stick-with-it-ness.[8]

Sales climbed to over $2 million after the move from the Neechi Co-op store to the Commons, and projections were for sales to double in the following years. Neechi was the largest commercial employer of Indigenous people in Winnipeg when staffing increased from twelve to fifty people, mostly drawn from the inner city as was their intent. This early success underlined the *economic* healing that was needed to support sustained personal and social healing. This awareness was the context from which Neechi Commons was born. It inspired a much higher level of effort than had been achieved through Neechi Co-op, with greater benefits for community members.[9]

The start-up financing for the Neechi Commons dream was a collaboration made up of partners from both municipal and provincial levels of government and support from a local credit union and a provincial co-op loans board. Another component was the sale of investment shares that eventually resulted in a multi-stakeholder co-op. This strategy brought the Co-op's vision to the broader community and was meant to ensure a solid foundation for stability and growth.[10]

Neechi was the first co-op in Manitoba to sell shares to the public, so the process involved a steep learning curve for government agencies that facilitated the process. According to Russ Rothney, Neechi Commons

Treasurer, while there was considerable interest in their strong business plan from their targeted audience—institutions in Winnipeg and other major centres—in the end $350,000 came from individuals with no institutional support.[11] This was insufficient to cover the debt load, so a second share offering was planned but never materialized. Efforts were made to attract a partner interested in purchasing the real estate from the Commons in order to lessen their debt load.[12]

Educating customers about Neechi Commons, their scope of target market, and building support for the Co-op Harmony brand was an ongoing project of educating and trust building, and was a two-way process. Since customers responded to sales, that was an effective way to get people to try new products. It was challenging to interest people on low incomes to try new products because their families did not embrace new items very easily, an important consideration for customers on a limited budget. Advertising had a strong influence. Of note, it was the middle-class people who could afford to buy more expensive food who looked for deals and often were more price conscious than people on low incomes.[13]

As a worker co-op, Neechi Commons introduced an entrepreneurial aspect to its staff through ownership by the workers. This was a slow process, but if local workers had a say in the Commons' operations, there was a strong likelihood that neighbourhood family interests would be represented. The theme of pride and cultural awareness was woven throughout all the components of Neechi Commons, including the grocery and food services, the art store, and the restaurant. This hallmark of the Commons was both an attempt to make the Commons stronger and a way to draw in the citizens of Winnipeg.[14]

While it was tough going, the Commons had the support of vol-unteers: some fifty Winnipeg residents helped with business planning and development on a volunteer basis through their participation in ongoing Neechi Commons work groups. In all, well over 9,500 volunteer hours, equivalent to five years of full-time work, were invested in the project because of its unique social value that was clear from the start-up phase.

In reflecting on the broad picture at that moment, Louise noted, "The impact that is unexpected is the sense of pride that Indigenous people have when they come into Neechi Commons no matter where they are from. It is a beautiful place and awesome to see all these Indigenous workers in a reasonable-sized business. It has made it worth it. We really do need some winners. We count and look what we can do."[15]

Russ added that people's first impression was that something different was happening. One striking feature was the large number of Indigenous people who worked in the Commons, particularly Indigenous youth. A lot of the food offerings were local and promoted nutrition. The word that tied these impressions together was "community."[16]

Lived Experience

While Neechi Commons could have been located anywhere in Winnipeg, choosing to keep it in the inner city made a clear statement about the strong connection the Commons wished to continue forging with local residents, especially youth. The Commons also took advantage of the opportunity to increase its impact on the larger city of Winnipeg. The opportunities for revitalization, employment, and training were focused on neighbourhoods that were hard hit economically and socially. Winnipeggers in general experienced a warm, welcoming community at Neechi Commons, which hosted special events and gatherings that were dressed richly in artistic and literary garb, often saturated in song.

For local neighbourhoods, Neechi Commons provided an alternative perspective for residents who had aspirations other than gang activity and social assistance. The very limited grocery options in the area were expanded. Those who were hired developed job skills that they could build on for their future and that directly increased personal and community esteem. Staff learned to work successfully in a team environment, an important skill to carry to other workplaces. Neechi Commons nurtured this approach. Co-operation with other employment and training programs created a strong environment of opportunity. In Louise's words, "We operate a self-reliant business venture that has a strong commitment to social and environmental well-being."[17]

The Three Sisters Fruit and Vegetable Courtyard continued a tradition of healthy food choices and a wellness approach begun by Neechi Foods Community Store more than twenty-eight years earlier. Harmony Co-op brand foods were the centrepiece of Three Sisters' products, augmented by fresh produce. Regional, local, and Indigenous co-ops and food producers rounded out the healthy offerings. The emphasis on local products also permeated the Come N' Eat restaurant and the art store, Neechi Niche.

A creative partnership existed between the courtyard, which supported physical well-being, and Neechi Niche, which drew in other gifts Indigenous people had to offer. Books, beadwork, and sculpture, clothing, and Indigenous artwork were all part of the range of creations that could be purchased. Artists worked at the site so customers could witness their creative process. It was an inviting and pleasant atmosphere with friendly staff.

The restaurant offered a menu of solid favourites ranging from Three Sisters soup to bannock to bison burgers. This area attracted various forms of engagement, commentary, and appreciation. Schoolchildren were invited to offer their projects, which were displayed in the same space in which professional artists mounted installations. Book launches, film discussions, and guest speakers graced Neechi Commons from the beginning. Many Winnipeggers were welcomed to regular event offerings. In the summer, a farmers' market ran on Saturdays with outdoor films offered in the evening for the community.

Neechi Commons was a part of the community and contributed to building community by celebrating the richness of Indigenous gifts and talents. The Commons made space for children's visions of the future, and for new and emerging artists and writers who shared their projects in respectful ways that invited interaction, curiosity, and under-standing. A Neechi Commons Newsletter from December 2013 described one such project:

> Inner City Youth Alive invited the children and youth between the ages 5–25, from Winnipeg's North End to create a piece of art that expresses their dreams. The artists were asked to use art as a means of self-expression to show the world what their dream future would look like, regard-less of the challenges they face today. The call for art was open to accepting any type of artistic medium whether it be drawing, painting, sculpture, poem or craft as long as the piece expresses their hopes, visions, and dreams.
>
> Fifty-six works were created and submitted and Neechi Niche is so pleased to bring this explosion of creativity to the community. The children didn't hold back and their work is an incredible sampling of the varied dreams that the kids in our community share full of vibrancy and life. Some dream of owning a farm, some of being a shoe designer, others a soccer player or to become an astronaut,

still others dream of seeing their departed parents again
if only for a moment. This art installation encapsulates
all the joy, sadness, heartfelt messages and dreams of our
community's children.[18]

Literary works were launched, including *The Winter We Danced*,
which captured writings and images from the Idle No More movement,[19]
and *Kimiwan* (an Indigenous words and art magazine) in partnership
with the Native Youth Sexual Health Network. A "bead-in" wall recognized residential school pupils by offering a regular time to learn
beading and enjoy being together. A gift for Neechi Commons neighbours was a free lunch celebration in the parking lot in cold, cold
months of winter. Youth had regular weekly opportunities to learn
their language and to hear from Elders.[20]

Nurturing community connections was inherent in the way that
Neechi Commons chose to impact its neighbours. The Commons
introduced literature and art that were not easily accessed by people
in their local neighbourhood and demonstrated the vitality of the
Indigenous community to the rest of Winnipeg by welcoming everyone
in. This was a unique gift that was distinctive in the city.

Leadership

Working in the Neechi Co-op as key leaders in its success over twenty-
eight years allowed Louise and Russ to draw on many personal values
and perspectives. A common theme was that of a person having
problems in their life but still being able to be successful in meeting
their ambitions. Going against the statistics and labels placed on
Indigenous employees in particular had made the co-op the largest
Indigenous employer in Winnipeg, as previously mentioned.

In reflecting on the journey from the small store to Neechi Commons, Louise saw that community development in the context of feminism denoted a different experience. For women, the vision was in terms of small projects that drew in people with skills to accomplish needed tasks quickly. Once a project grew it seemed that it became a man's responsibility, aligning with what the business world expected. In particular, Louise noted at that time that the small store (Neechi Community Store) epitomized the low self-image that many Indigenous people carry. It was dilapidated, crumbling, and perhaps could not be conceived as something better because of internalized oppression. "This negative attitude is hard to overcome but then we saw the opportunity to move the project forward and it was liberating. We can make this work in the middle of skid row. We want to be a profitable business and we are also about building strength, pride, and success in the inner city."[21]

Conclusion

Neechi Commons was set to leave a unique legacy in the city that had often been called "Canada's Crime Capital." No citizen wanted that label attached to their city. Most of the crime was in the North End of Winnipeg, where Neechi Commons deliberately chose to plant something much better than fear or disruption. The gift they offered did everything to challenge that mindset. While many businesses come and go, Neechi Commons left a legacy that changed lives individually and in the community. All were important lessons lived, for all to benefit from what was perhaps, in the end, a lost love letter to those living in the North End and an even more important one to the city of Winnipeg.

Postscript

On 30 June 2018, Neechi Commons closed its doors because of its debt load.[22] Time will tell if the lessons learned from its experience will stand. Sscope (Self-starting Creative Opportunities for People in Employment), a local non-profit organization, announced that Neechi Commons would be turned into social housing, with a thrift store employing residents. It has secured a one-year lease.[23]

NOTES

◆

1   M.C. Bol, *Iroquois Confederacy of the North-East*, Carnegie Museum of Natural History, 27 February 2014, accessed 14 September 2023, https://nsew.carnegiemnh.org/iroquois-confederacy-of-the-northeast/.

2   Bryce Hoye, "Neechi Commons to Close Due to $3.9M Debt, Board Says," CBC News, Manitoba, 29 June 2018, https://www.cbc.ca/news/canada/manitoba/neechi-commons-closing-winnipeg-1.4727871.

3   Federated Co-operatives Ltd., 2014, https://www.fcl.crs.

4   Louise Champagne, President, Neechi Commons, personal communication, 15 May 2014.

5   Louise Champagne, President, Neechi Co-op Ltd., interview, 14 April 2013.

6   Manitoba adopted Neechi Principles in 2004 under Premier Gary Doer. Kirsten Bernas and Brendan Reimer, *Building a Federal Policy Framework and Program in Support of Community Economic Development* (Saskatoon: University of Saskatchewan, 2011), https://ccednet-rcdec.ca/sites/ccednet-rcdec.ca/wp-content/uploads/2022/09/Federal_Policy_Framework_Report_1.pdf, p 6–7.

7   Neechi Principles, Canadian CED Network, https://ccednet-rcdec.ca/resource/neechi-principles/#:~:text=The%20guiding%20CED%20principles%20of%20Neechi%20Foods%20Worker,Long-term%20employment%20of%20local%20residents%20Local%20skill%20development.

8   Champagne, personal communication, 15 May 2014.

9   Champagne, "2013 Excellence in Indigenous Leadership Award," Winnipeg, 10 October 2013.

10 Ibid.

11 Russ Rothney, Treasurer, Neechi Commons, personal communication, 22 May 2014.

12 Rothney, personal communication, 22 May 2014.

13 Champagne, personal communication, 15 May 2014.

14 Rothney, personal communication, 22 May 2014.

15 Champagne, personal communication, 15 May 2014.

16 Rothney, personal communication, 22 May 2014.

17 Champagne, "2013 Excellence in Indigenous Leadership."

18 Neechi Commons, *Supermarket Deals and Neighbourhood Delights Newsletter*, Winnipeg, 11–17 December 2013.

19 Kino-nda-niimi Collective, *The Winter We Danced: Voices from the Past, the Future, and the Idle No More Movement* (Winnipeg: ARP Books, 2014).

20 Neechi Commons, *Supermarket Deals and Neighbourhood Delights Newsletter*.

21 Champagne, personal communication, 15 May 2014.

22 Hoye, "Neechi Commons to Close."

23 Ben Waldman, "Former Neechi Commons Transformed into Housing," *Winnipeg Free Press*, 25 August 2020, A1–2.

PART FOUR

◆

Partnering for Success

When economic opportunities present themselves, partnerships can make sense: each partner brings something unique to the table that contributes to the overall success. In this part, two examples are presented that offer wisdom in navigating these relationships to the benefit of all partners.

Tahltan Nation, British Columbia, has moved from poverty and discrimination to a deliberate reclamation of livelihoods on its own terms, with exceptional success. In 2021, the Tahltan Nation Development Corporation reported $70 million in revenue and $80 million in assets with 500+ employees (73 percent Indigenous), earning recognition as the largest First Nations business in the province. Today, the Tahltan Heritage Trust holds $160 million for future generations. In Chapter 10, Jerry Asp reports on the Tahltan Nation Development Corporation. Asp points to a foundational strategy composed of a vision, a strategy, and a vehicle to achieve the vision. With these in place, Tahltan Nation took on the challenge of building its business reputation by partnering with companies that passed its due diligence process. Capitalizing on this experience led to a strong negotiating position in building partnerships directly with resource developers, leading to housing, mining, and hydropower projects. These projects met the First Nation's needs, centring on protection of the land, creating equity positions, managing social impacts, and providing employment, training, and business opportunities. The chapter concludes with a summary of insights for other First Nations, resource developers, and all levels of government.

Intriguing partnerships between First Nations communities and municipalities are profiled by Wanda Wuttunee in Chapter 11. Community Economic Development Initiatives (CEDI), operating under the guidance of its founding partners, Council for the Advancement of Native Development Officers and the Canadian Federation of Municipalities, accepts applications for support from municipalities and their partner First Nations communities. The success of these partnerships relies on trust-building relationships that are often recognized in friendship accords. Areas for planning that will result in mutual benefits to the partners are identified and implementation plans are outlined based on consensus. These partnerships often begin with first-ever meetings, and often within a context of a history of animosity. Meetings build relationships based not only on trust but also on open attitudes, curiosity, and strong listening skills, which then sensitize the partners in planning for future collaborations. These relationships also help in the face of inevitable setbacks. "Stronger together" is the CEDI motto.

CHAPTER 10

◆

Tahltan Economic Tenacity:
From Affluence to Poverty to Affluence

◆

P. Jerry Asp

Firstly—We claim the sovereign right to all the country of our
tribe—this country of ours which we have held intact from
the encroachments of other tribes, from time immemorial, at
the cost of our own blood. We have done this because our
lives depended on our country. To lose it meant we would lose
our means of living, and therefore our lives.

—*Declaration of the Tahltan Tribe, 1910*[1]

A s this chapter's epigraph indicates, the Tahltan people were
proud, fierce defenders of their territory and resources. Situated
in northwestern British Columbia, Tahltan territory extends from the
Coast Mountains in the west to the lower parts of the Yukon's boreal
forest in the north, the Cassiar Mountain range in the east, and the
sacred headwaters of the Nass, Skeena, and Stikine rivers in the south.

Our people have always been entrepreneurs. Before contact with
Europeans, the Tahltan people capitalized on their location and

established themselves as middlemen between coastal nations and interior nations. Along with furs, fish, and dried berries, the Tahltan traded obsidian, jade, and copper, which they mined in their territory. The Stikine River was the conduit for their thriving trading economy.

The reputation of the Tahltans as fierce defenders of their territory coupled with the remoteness of their lands delayed European contact. It wasn't until 1838 that the first white man, seeking to set up a trading post for the Hudson's Bay Company, made contact with the Tahltans but he was encouraged neither to stay nor to return.[2]

The inter-tribal trading economy that had sustained the Tahltans for so long ended with the discovery of gold along the Stikine (1861–62), in Cassiar (1874 to 1876), Atlin (1892 to 1900), and in the Yukon (1898 to 1903).[3] The lure of gold triggered massive waves of miners and equipment, the majority of which were transported on the Stikine River. This invasion into their territory had a significant impact on the traditional way of life of the Tahltans: their trails became roads, their traditional trading economy and relationships with other trading nations were disrupted, disease and alcohol took a toll, foreign foods were introduced to their diets, and the stability of the stocks of fish and game that had sustained them for millennia was impacted by reckless overharvesting and a disregard for fragile ecosystems.

In terms of participation in these gold rushes, Tahltans were trained as prospectors and employed as guides and providers of some camp services. And so, the era of solely relying on a "bush economy" for physical, cultural, and spiritual survival ended as our people entered the "wage economy."

The Indian Act, introduced in 1876 in the midst of the upheaval of the gold rushes, imposed the most drastic and enduring change in the traditional life of the Tahltan people. Government policies forced them into permanent dwellings on two small reserves, at Dease Lake and Telegraph Creek. As part of the assimilation policy, the children were sent to distant residential schools, where their connections to family, community, culture, and language were severely impacted. In 1896, a federal count registered just 296 Tahltans.[4]

Unbeknownst to the remote Tahltan, while their traditional territory was invaded by thousands of Europeans in search of gold, the governor of British Columbia laid claim to all land north of the sixtieth parallel in 1863. When this disturbing news reached the Tahltan they composed the 1910 Declaration of the Tahltan Tribe, quoted at the beginning of this chapter. In the Declaration, the Tahltan asked for a treaty with the federal and provincial governments to resolve land and rights issues. Over 100 years have passed and the Tahltans still do not have a treaty.

The mineral exploration and mining sector enjoyed the benefits of the resource-rich Tahltan lands for decades but did little in the way of sharing those benefits beyond casual employment during construction and operation of the mines. The boom-and-bust cycle of the sector and ensuing cycles of relatively large incomes followed by periods of no income had an overall negative impact on the community. There was no long-term net gain for the Tahltans from the mining taking place on their territory.

By 1985, our people were struggling with serious drug and alcohol problems and a high suicide rate—we were losing three to four community members to suicide every year. There was 98 percent unemployment in the winter and 65 percent unemployment in the summer; 80 percent were on welfare, and education standards were low. Our people lived in houses that did not have electricity or water. And there were no business opportunities or a local economy with which we could change the status quo. Our once-proud people who fiercely defended their lands were in dire straits.

Like Membertou First Nation described in an earlier chapter in this volume, Tahltan leadership knew that government programs and projects were band-aid solutions that were never going to leverage the community out of poverty and back to a foundation of self-sufficiency and pride. The transition to the wage economy was incremental and individual, not community-wide. Small businesses such as gas stations and convenience stores elevated individual families to self-sufficiency but contributed little to the economy or the social well-being of the greater community.

We needed three things: a vision, a strategy, and a vehicle to bring the vision to reality. Our vision was a return to our former self-sufficient, entrepreneurial, healthy glory.

In January 1985, I was working in Whitehorse for the Council of Yukon Indians as a business service officer. Three Tahltan leaders, Chief Ivan Quock, Chief Pat Edzerza, and Vernon Marion, President of the Tahltan Tribal Council, were in Whitehorse for meetings with the Yukon First Nations, and we discussed some upcoming federally funded housing projects for Telegraph Creek. I saw an opportunity and suggested we start a company so that we could act as the contractors and build the houses with Tahltan labour. The leaders agreed to talk about it. Four months later, on 5 April 1985, the Tahltan Nation Development Corporation (TNDC) was formed. We had our vehicle.

The first project for TNDC was to negotiate a contract with the Department of Indian Affairs (now Indigenous Services Canada) and Canada Mortgage and Housing Corporation to build new houses in Telegraph Creek and Iskut. But in order to build houses, you need qualified carpenters. TNDC negotiated with the provincial government to enroll eighteen journeymen carpenters in an apprenticeship program. Within five years, eighteen carpenters graduated with interprovincial tickets. Over the next few years, TNDC built a total of ninety-eight new homes, two band offices, two health centres, and a fire hall, and developed a subdivision. The work was spread between the communities of Dease Lake, Telegraph Creek, and Iskut. While these on-reserve building projects were good for individual members of the community, they were still tied to federal funding and did not contribute substantially to nation building.

So, we looked to the land. Tahltan territory is rich in resources below ground (gold, silver, and copper) and above ground (forests and hydroelectric potential). The richness of our resources was a big draw for mineral exploration and mining companies, as well as logging operations. Our lands were being exploited all around us and others were benefiting. We realized we had to establish the terms to which extractive industries must adhere. We needed a policy that would protect the land, restrict the negative social impacts of resource projects, ensure that training and employment for Tahltan people were part of every project, ensure equity participation, and provide business development opportunities.

The Tahltan Resource Development Policy was drawn up and came into effect on 7 April 1987:

> Before a resource development project can commence within Tahltan tribal territory, it will be necessary for the developer and the Tahltan Tribal Council to enter into a project participation agreement that encompasses the following elements and basic principles:
>
> 1. assurance that the development will not pose a threat of irreparable environmental damage;
>
> 2. assurance that the development will not jeopardize, prejudice or otherwise compromise the outstanding Tahltan aboriginal rights claim;

3. assurance that the project will provide more positive than negative social impacts on Tahltan people;

4. provision for the widest possible opportunity for education and direct employment-related training for Tahltan people in connection with the project;

5. provision for the widest possible opportunity for employment opportunities for Tahltan people with respect to all phases of the development;

6. provision for substantial equity participation by Tahltans in the total project;

7. provision for the widest possible development of Tahltan business opportunities over which the developer may have control or influence;

8. provision of the developer to assist the Tahltans to accomplish the objectives stated above by providing financial and managerial assistance and advice where deemed necessary.[5]

We had our strategy.

One year later, TNDC and North American Metals Corp. signed the first ever Impact and Benefits Agreement (IBA) in British Columbia; it was only the fourth of its kind in Canada. The IBA (at the time referred to as a Native Participation Agreement) became a template many other First Nations used in their negotiations with resource development companies.

The Tahltan/North American Metals Corp. IBA, which was heavily weighted toward training and employment, included contracting opportunities that opened the door for TNDC to start a heavy construction division, which they did. TNDC then negotiated work to help build a portion of the 160-kilometre road to the Golden Bear Mine site plus a three-year road upgrading and maintenance contract on the road following its construction. The work required $3 million worth of equipment, which TNDC raised through a $1.8 million grant from the Native Economic Development Program and financed the remaining $1.2 million with equipment dealers.

Mine construction is a massive, labour-intensive, prolonged process, and the Tahltans wanted more than a small piece of the action. They began negotiating for site work, mill construction, settling ponds, and the open pit. But they ran into a hurdle common to all new contract-ors—the need for validation. For newly minted First Nations contractors, especially back in the late 1980s, it was a significant hurdle. The mine owners insisted TNDC have a joint-venture partner, in other words, a company that had a good track record. TNDC was only considered for the work if it had a non–First Nations company as a partner.

To truly appreciate the significance of what the Tahltan leadership and TNDC were accomplishing, you must look at it in the context of where Canada was in its relationship with First Nations. Up until 1951, under the Indian Act, a "person" was "an individual other than an Indian, unless the context clearly requires another construction."[6] Before 1982, Aboriginal peoples (First Nations, Inuit, Métis) were not recognized as having Aboriginal rights in the Canadian Constitution. In 1987, the Tahltan Tribal Council drew up its Resource Development Policy, dictating the terms that resource companies had to agree to if they expected to work on Tahltan land. That's just five years after Aboriginal and treaty rights were formally entrenched in the supreme law of Canada via Section 35 of the Canadian Constitution Act, 1982. First Nations were just beginning to use the courts for affirmation of their rights. At the time British Columbia, unlike most of the rest of

Canada, did not have treaties outside of the Douglas Treaties for Vancouver Island.

The Tahltan/Golden Bear IBA was primarily a socio-economic agreement that included a 20 percent employment target for the mine. At the peak of the mine's operation, Tahltans made up 39 percent of the workforce through direct employment and contract work. And the turnover rate of 2 to 4 percent was much lower than the 20 to 24 percent experienced by most mines.

By 1991, six short years after being launched, TNDC was the largest First Nations–owned and –operated heavy construction company in Western Canada. TNDC went on to sign an IBA for Eskay Creek for road, mine, mill, and camp construction. It then formed a joint-venture with a transport company to haul mill concentrate from the mine. And it formed Spatsizi Remote Services Corporation, a wholly owned subsidiary, to provide cooking and housekeeping at the mine site.

Building on its success with the mining companies and keeping true to the tenets of the Tahltan Resource Development Policy, TNDC began to include hydropower projects. It negotiated the first First Nations–owned independent power project with BC Hydro in 1992 and has an agreement with AltaGas on the three hydro projects it has in Tahltan territory. TNDC also represents the first First Nation to sign an agreement with the Province of British Columbia under the Clean Energy Act for land and water rentals—for sixty years. This agreement alone brings in $2.5 million for each of those sixty years.

Tahltans, as do most First Nations, place a high importance on protecting their lands. Our world view holds that we are stewards of the land and as such must protect the resources for future generations. Our 1987 Resource Development Policy only went so far in terms of ensuring protection of the land. As our experience expanded in working with mining companies, we realized we needed to place more emphasis on protecting the land and resources. With so much mineral activity in our lands we needed a mining plan that capitalized on our local traditional knowledge and created an organization for our people to participate in mining development activities. In 2005, the Tahltan Heritage Resources Environmental Assessment Team (THREAT) was formed. The roots of THREAT lie in the 1987 policy.[7]

With THREAT, nation building became nation rebuilding. We were returning to the core values that our ancestors had lived by. We were revitalizing our culture, stating our responsibility to the land, and honouring our traditional knowledge, to continue the Tahltan way of life by protecting our values. These include

> Recognizing the importance of Tahltan spirituality: reincarnation, we are all connected,
>
> Valuing our connection to the land,
>
> Demonstrating our value and respect for other beings' fish/wildlife,
>
> Realizing that "we belong to the land," and
>
> Supporting our bonds, kinship, roots, and belonging.
>
> Respecting each other: Tahltans will show respect for all people and Beings.
>
> We will practise our beliefs and show respect by asking permission, using all that we take and not wasting, sharing what we take, providing offerings, and leaving things properly.

I was elected Chief of the Tahltan Nation in 2002 and again in 2004. I was President of the TNDC from 1985 to 1993. When I left in 2006, the Tahltan people had 95 percent employment in the winter and 100 percent employment in the summer. We graduated twenty-one journeymen carpenters, six welders, three heavy duty mechanics, dozens of heavy equipment operators and truck drivers with Class 1 licences, chefs, kitchen staff, camp and office managers. Our high school completion rate was way up. We had implemented drug and alcohol programs in the communities and on the job sites. And our suicide rate had dropped to zero. The root of this success is best summed up in a quote by Ronald Reagan: "I believe the best social program is a job."[8]

There were hurdles along the way. One of the greatest, but least surprising given the era and where Canada was with its relationship with Indigenous peoples, was the ongoing stereotyping of First Nations. The common belief, at the time, was that First Nations were good at fancy beadwork and carving and not much else. But as proven with the success and hard work that went into developing the TNDC and our mutually respectful relationship with resource developers, we have much, much more to offer. We have continued to grow and in 2021 achieved a revenue of more than $70 million and employed a significant number of Tahltan Nation members and associates.[9] We have engaged in a range of sectors, including mining, forestry, and airport services, running one of only four BC provincial airlines operated by an Indigenous organization. We've brought fibre optics to our communities, worked with seven business partners, and supported community services through the Tahltan Central Government (TCG). TCG has focused efforts on wildlife and fisheries management, on language, culture, and heritage supports, as well as on education and training, employment and contracting.[10]

For First Nations:

- Learn all you can about proposed projects. That is the only way you can effectively weigh the advantages to your community against the potential long-term negative impacts.

- Learn all you can about the company behind the project. Talk to other First Nations that have worked with them or been approached by the company.
- Develop a policy that reflects your core values and provides a framework for companies to negotiate within.
- Develop a land use plan.
- Form a development corporation that operates outside the politics of your nation.
- Understand your Aboriginal rights.
- Understand the rules and laws associated with the industry that wants to work with you.

For resource developers—tips from the trenches:

- You are asking to work in our backyard. Therefore, I suggest you do your due diligence regarding our culture, our rights and title, where our traditional or treaty lands are, and our history as you would do when you embark to work in a jurisdiction outside of Canada.
- You also need to be fully informed and up to date on rights and title court cases.
- You should also have a working knowledge of the United Nations Declaration on the Rights of Indigenous Peoples.
- You need an engagement strategy that starts early in your project plans.
- You need a communications strategy. Don't just contact the community when you need something.
- You need to mitigate expectations—promise less and deliver more. Do not, under any circumstance, think offering more than you can actually deliver is a way to open doors. First Nations have a long history of being offered more than is delivered.

- You need to realize the power of social media. There are no
  dark corners. Anywhere.

For governments of all levels:
- Get to work on settling land claims. Investor confidence is at
  stake. Canada's reputation is at stake.

While economic development may not be a panacea for all our
problems, it does have the ability to move our communities, people,
and our nations from poverty to affluence. If the Tahltans can do it,
any First Nations or Aboriginal group can do it. Start with what you
have, and move forward with a vision, a strategy, and a vehicle to take
the strategy to fruition. This lesson is being applied by a number of
First Nations, including those described in this volume, who have made
a successful transition from poverty and dependence to building a
self-reliant economic base.

NOTES

◆

1   *Mehodihi: Well-Known Traditions of Tahltan People, "Our Great Ancestors Lived That Way,"*
     exhibition booklet prepared by Pam Brown and Shawnaditta Cross (Vancouver:
     UBC Museum of Anthropology, 2003), 4, moa.ubc.ca/wp-content/
     uploads/2014/08/Sourcebooks-Mehodihi-TAHLTAN-PEOPLE.pdf.

2   "Historical Events in the Stikine River Area," http://archpress.lib.sfu.ca/index.
     php/archpress/catalog/download/61/31/1273-1?inline=1#:~:text=It%20
     was%20not%20until%201838,contact%20with%20the%20Tahltan%20tribe.

3   Ibid.

4   International Institute for Sustainable Development, and Tahltan First Nation,
     Out of Respect, The Tahltan, Mining, and the Seven Questions to Sustainability, Report of
     the Tahltan Mining Symposium, 4–6 April 2003, Dease Lake, British Columbia,
     accessed 14 September 2023, https://www.iisd.org/publications/
     out-respect-tahltan-mining-and-seven-questions-sustainability.

5 *Tahltan Tribal Council Resource Development Policy Statement*, 7 April 1987, www.tndc.ca/pdfs/Tahltan%20Resource%20Development%20Policy.pdf.

6 An Act to Amend and Consolidate the Laws Respecting Indians (Indian Act), 1876, Term 3.12, https://www.sac-isc.gc.ca/eng/1100100010252/1618940680392.

7 Tahltan Heritage Resources Environmental Assessment Team (THREAT), "Organization, People, and Workflows" (Tahltan Central Council, 2005), 5.

8 Quoted by Barry Popik, *The Big Apple* (blog), 20 August 2009, https://www.barrypopik.com/index.php/new_york_city/entry/the_best_social_program_is_a_job.

9 Deena Tokaryk, *We Are Tahltan Nation Development Corporation—2022 Annual Report* (Tahltan Nation, BC: Tahltan Nation, 2022).

10 Tahltan Central Government, *2020–2021 Annual Report* (Tahltan Nation, BC: Tahltan Nation, 2021), https://tahltan.org/2020-2021-annual-report/.

CHAPTER 11

✦

Stronger Together: First Nations–Municipality Community Collaborations[1]

✦

Wanda Wuttunee

My experience is that it takes time, patience and resilience
to build successful partnerships; as municipalities we have a
lot to offer and more to receive.
—*Vicki Blanchard, Economic Development Manager,*
Municipality of Sioux Lookout, Ontario[2]

Partnerships work well when each partner brings something to the table and is committed to the success of the project. Sometimes history, distance, or other obstacles effectively remove any thought of working together and achieving mutual benefits. First Nations communities are struggling, for the most part, in areas that promote well-being and form the basis for a vigorous economic profile. Physical, mental, emotional, and spiritual health are often taxed to the limit. When individuals are not healthy, this impacts family, community, and ultimately the ability to engage in work successfully. The Indian Act, residential schools, poverty, and their corollaries of suicide, drugs, and gangs have a long legacy that continues to negatively affect communities today. To be accurate, there are some First Nations communities across the country that are bright economic lights for supporting their citizens and benefiting surrounding communities.³ Examples include Westbank First Nation, Osoyoos Indian Band, Tahltan First Nation (see Jerry Asp, Chapter 10), Tsawwassen First Nation (Daniel Millette, Chapter 2), all located in British Columbia; Membertou First Nation, Nova Scotia (see Mary Beth Doucette and Fred Wien, Chapter 1); and Lac La Ronge Indian Band, Saskatchewan. Judith Sayers (Chapter 6) also explores issues faced by British Columbia's Indigenous communities.

The Calls to Action from the national Truth and Reconciliation Commission (TRC) specifically recognize municipalities as essential to successful reconciliation with Indigenous peoples. Eight recommendations focus on "all levels of government," and five refer to municipal governments. "The context for working together is positive and encouraging with a means to set the stage for collaboration discussions. Most of the Calls to Action require federal, provincial and territorial government leadership, and municipal governments to roll up their sleeves to support reconciliation as a national challenge that is felt deeply at the local level."⁴

Communities have been reaching out to their neighbours to explore potential partnerships when doors are open and attitudes are positive. The Federation of Canadian Municipalities (FCM) built on its own history to develop a program that supports First Nations communities and neighbouring municipalities in developing collaborations, partnering with the Council for the Advancement of Native Development Officers (Cando) in the Community Economic Development Initiative (CEDI). FCM has a 2,000-municipality membership base, while Cando has a broad membership of more than 500 Indigenous economic development officers, economic organizations, and academics interested in all aspects of Indigenous community economic development.

In reflecting on FCM's history, FCM's CEDI Program Manager Helen Patterson identified FCM's long interest in First Nations government as their neighbours. A joint workshop in 2004 with Indigenous organizations and FCM members on Indigenous land management sparked interest in other topics, such as identifying points of collaboration in service agreements with Indigenous participants and provincial and federal governments. In 2012, CEDI was developed as a result of an FCM/Cando survey that prioritized joint economic development initiatives. A foundation for success through CEDI is "[acknowledging] the importance of history, culture and relationship building before anyone can start doing business transactions," according to Patterson.[5]

CEDI presents an opportunity to bridge the divide that often exists between a First Nations community and a neighbouring municipality. A venue is offered where the two groups come together, lines of communication are opened, and a partnership nurtured. Patterson described a situation where the City of North Battleford, Saskatchewan, and the Battlefords Agency Tribal Chiefs had to deal with the impact a tragic death of a local young man had as they tried to build a partnership. Chief Lori Whitecalf of Sweet Grass Reserve brought forward the idea to do a "blanket exercise" to bring the two councils closer together. It involved members of the First Nations sharing their history and painful personal stories in a circle with both groups. With the assistance of an elder and two Indigenous youth facilitators from Canadian Roots Exchange, meaningful conversation and educating occurred that set the basis for a solid relationship and partnership.[6]

The six-partner collaborations for CEDI Phase One were geographically diverse and demonstrated a likelihood that they would lead to successful collaboration. These are enumerated below. Two of the collaborations will be explored more thoroughly in the next section of this chapter from perspectives of two project champions for each collaboration. An evaluation report on CEDI Phase One offers useful insights into all the experiences and will inform the chapter's concluding summary.

Phase One—CEDI Collaborations

British Columbia: Seabird Island Band and District of Kent
Ten minutes separate these two communities in the Fraser Valley that came together in 2009 at a Union of BC Municipalities meeting. The result was a memorandum of understanding that acknowledged a willingness to work together. Involving CEDI was the next step in developing this relationship. Top priorities for this partnership included a river management strategy, a new salmon hatchery, a regional strategy to bring in new investors and build tourism, and improved emergency access for those using logging roads. Seabird Island's Chief Clem Seymour observed, "We are collectively the largest landowners in the Fraser Valley and our lands are well situated near critical infrastructure required for development and transport. Now more than ever in history is an opportune time for partnerships between First Nations and the business community to flourish. Business relationships built on honesty, trust and respect will enrich our community and your organization."[7]

Alberta: Sawridge First Nation, Town of Slave Lake, and Municipal District of Lesser Slave River
After a 2011 forest fire ravaged the town of Slave Lake, these three partners came together to rebuild what had been lost. A tri-council was formed and a Friendship Accord signed to mark the important relationship. Planning meetings determined that priorities were housing, joint land development, business development, including improved

employment, and labour opportunities with a focus on tourism development.[8] Relationship-building workshops took place, a regional growth
strategy was developed, and a joint tourism officer was hired, followed
by a family canoe trip with the leaders and their families to shape
stronger relationships.[9]

*Quebec: Kebaowek (Formerly Eagle Village) First Nation, Town of Témiscaming,
and Municipality of Kipawa*

The overriding priority for these communities has been tourism development that highlights the natural beauty of the region. It was a natural
fit for their economic development departments to coordinate these
efforts, which were recognized with a Friendship Accord. Trips to
neighbouring communities to learn how they approached tourism
opportunities included visiting a Chamber of Commerce and a local
park, as well as a First Nations community and the local national park.
The three communities were thus well-informed to prepare themselves
to be the gateway to a new provincial park, Opemican, in their region.
Since the formation of the partnership, relationship building and joint
planning have built trust and resulted in a joint tourism strategy. While
the journey has brought trials along with satisfaction, the partners have
stuck with it and each now knows more about the others, which has
built a strong foundation for collaboration.[10]

New Brunswick: Madawaska Maliseet First Nation and City of Edmundston

With a history of little contact with each other, the community of
Madawaska (pop. 134 on-reserve, 116 off-reserve) and the City of
Edmundston (pop. 22,000) came together for the CEDI needs assessment
in 2013. They discovered shared interests, which were enhanced by
educating local residents and businesses that included ratification in a
Friendship Accord. "Today we are meeting to begin discussing our
shared vision for the future and how to plan for it. This is the first time

in history that we have done so together," said Richard Lang of the Madawaska Maliseet Economic Development Corporation. The communities' joint long-term strategy is to preserve their distinct Acadian and Maliseet identities and cultures through promoting their local businesses and unique business culture, drawing in new businesses and investors, and enhancing regional tourism and branding.[11]

Ontario: Lac Seul First Nation, Municipality of Sioux Lookout, and Kitchenuhmaykoosib Inninuwug

When FCM suggested these three communities form a partnership, Lac Seul First Nation (LSFN) Elder Garnet Angeconeb said, "This feels like you are asking us to get married. This is only our first date."

Starting Conditions

A collaborative attitude beginning with a Friendship Agreement between LSFN Slate Falls and Sioux Lookout was codified five years later with a Friendship Accord in 2012. LSFN lies forty kilometres from Sioux Lookout and is home to 860 citizens, with 2,500 living off-reserve.[12] As with many Indigenous communities, LSFN must deal with social disintegration that manifests as loss of culture, substance abuse, mental health issues, suicide, family breakdown, unemployment, crime, and physical and sexual abuse.[13] The First Nation's goal was to achieve social recovery that embraced their culture and traditions, creating a healthy, resilient community. This perspective takes a wider view of some Indigenous community issues that are often placed under the rubric of economic development.

In discussions leading to the Friendship Accord, the issue of racism was raised by LFSN's Chief Clifford Bull, and the question was how all partners could work together to deal with it in a good way. He noted,

"We're all Canadians, we all live in the same country and we all have to live and work together."[14]

Sioux Lookout, a municipality of 5,000 people, is described as the "Hub of the North," with connections to health care and essential services for thirty-one remote Indigenous communities.[15] It is important for Sioux Lookout to have strong relationships, as its main industry is supplying goods and services to the communities in the region. On the topic of racism, Vicki Blanchard, Economic Development Manager for Sioux Lookout, observed that an anti-racism committee had been in existence for many years. In her opinion, some people have racism embedded in them through generations, even though more than 70 percent of the municipality's population is Indigenous. "It is important to remember that we have no tragic events similar to those faced by other communities in Canada and because we are the hub of services for the communities, many members feel welcomed as they often visit other family members who live in Sioux Lookout."[16]

The Municipality of Sioux Lookout and the First Nations communities of Slate Falls and LSFN determined that formally recognizing key relationships was important to working together for the future of their communities. The Sioux Lookout Friendship Accord recognizes that the municipality's planning process includes First Nations leaders and communities, and "honours our ancestors, traditions and the spirit of Sioux Lookout which first drew First Nations people together. We acknowledge and honour the long history of service to the community that continues to be embodied by the Municipality of Sioux Lookout and its employees."[17] Further, it acknowledges the traditions and spirit needed to nurture a respectful and lasting relationship between the municipality and First Nations communities. Values of "honesty, respect, mutual sharing and contribution" are the basis for good relationships on all levels, which are marked by "accountability, transparency, inclusiveness, responsiveness and shared stewardship."[18]

The Friendship Accord sets out a framework for constructing agreements based on protocols for improved communication, acknowledging First Nations government, focusing on regional leadership, health and education, and offering investment opportunities and increased participation for First Nations communities in Sioux Lookout. Blanchard has used these guiding principles in the way she conducts business dealings every day. This sets a protocol of respect that has underscored her business with Indigenous communities and partners. Projects flow through her office, so she regularly approaches partner communities with opportunities to participate.

LSFN was particularly interested in the Friendship Accord, according to Sam Manitowabi, LSFN's Director of Employment and Training,[19] as the First Nation had not been able to garner support in Sioux Lookout for an urban reserve or economic development zone. The municipality's leadership had supported the concept and organized open houses, but to no avail. Negative comments from community members were based on lack of understanding of the shared benefits such a project would bring. Some Sioux Lookout citizens made it known that they didn't want reserve housing with broken windows in their town, nor did they want drunk people hanging around. With that experience in mind, the timing was right to reach out to build a stronger and positive relationship. Kichenuhmaykoosib Inninuwug (KI) was interested in joining the Accord as it looked for ways to reduce all costs, including food costs, and build its community. KI also took the lead in applying to be part of CEDI in 2013 on its own, with LSFN and Sioux Lookout eventually becoming partners, too.

Institutional Design

Each of the CEDI partners brought an interest in drawing on each other's strengths to benefit their own communities. Sioux Lookout plays a central role in the region by providing needed goods and services for Indigenous communities, while LSFN and KI wanted to improve their communities economically and socially with opportunities that could not be accomplished without partners committed to developing the region. LSFN brought business sensitivity resulting from work on forestry, hydroelectric dams, and impact benefit agreements from resource development, while KI brought the knowledge of living on the land, traditions, and needs arising from isolation.

After LSFN, Sioux Lookout, and KI completed a needs assessment, the partnership focused on a food distribution centre that would decrease the cost of shipping food to the North. All partners agreed that they should go to a consulting firm to assess the feasibility of such an undertaking. The consultant's report set out project costs that were beyond the abilities of the collaboration. A new building would be built at the airport, but leasing costs and taxes were very expensive.

While LSFN withdrew from the project, KI and Sioux Lookout continued working to put together a much larger partnership. New partners included Health Canada, the Ontario Ministry of Health and Long-Term Care, Universities of Toronto and Guelph, and Lakehead University. It was a labour of love, according to Blanchard, a social enterprise that would not bring in a lot of revenue but would give northern communities needed support. This included northern entrepreneurs who want to buy in bulk and then sell the food in their communities. Blanchard shared projections of 40 percent savings based on full planes flying to the North.

Their competitor was Northwest Company, which rejected an offer to partner on this project, according to Blanchard, but instead announced a similar project with a newly purchased small airline. Blanchard observed that part of their project would require ground transportation, a potential opportunity for LSFN, which wanted to grow that business. This move indicates a healthy and respectful partnership, where differences in goals are recognized so a partner can withdraw participation in one project while other possibilities are still open to them.

Other projects under discussion by the CEDI working committee included a medicinal marijuana factory and addressing issues involving food security. There was a familiarity with each partner's needs and wants, with meetings characterized by camaraderie and open, respectful discussions interspersed with humour, leading to decisions based on consensus. This respectful and trusting environment allowed for tough discussions that may not have been broached or settled in different circumstances.

It is clear that the benefits of investing in relationships outweigh the costs. As committee members have changed, the Friendship Accord has been the anchor that brings new people up to speed on the vision and guiding principles. Over several changes in leadership the Friendship Accord and partnership continues to be supported.

Collaborative Process

The Friendship Accord offers a context for understanding why community leadership embraced the CEDI partnership opportunity. A trust-favouring partnership was set out in the Friendship Agreement that preceded the Accord. In 2013, Cat Lake First Nation joined the Accord, followed by KI in 2014 with a trust-building process through meetings by invitation over several years. Ideally, all the northern Ontario communities would join the Accord in the future, according to Manitowabi.[20] Further, a Shared Territory Protocol between LSFN, Cat Lake, and Slate Falls, signed in 2017, brought these communities together as potential gold deposits were being explored in their area.

Decision procedures outlined in the protocol strengthen the process of project development and benefit distribution for affected communities.[21]

Mayor Doug Lawrance of Sioux Lookout has worked with his Chief Administrative Officer and Blanchard to breathe new life into the Friendship Accord by organizing regular meetings and bringing partners to the table. A new First Nations Economic Development office allowed KI and LSFN to use desk space when they come to town. There was now meeting space available to support Sioux Lookout's effort to offer infrastructure and a welcoming atmosphere as part of the collaboration.

Sioux Lookout took the positive and bold step of declaring 2017 the Year of Reconciliation after the TRC's Calls to Action, focusing on municipalities. A series of events to raise awareness were undertaken, including a screening of *The Secret Path*, an animated film based on the life and death of twelve-year-old Chanie Wenjack, who died after running away from a residential school in Ontario.[22] The topic brings hard questions forward, allowing community members to go beyond a superficial, feel-good experience. Manitowabi recalled that when asked by a Sioux Lookout committee as to how LSFN citizens could be made to feel more welcome in the community, a request was made that the local *Sioux Bulletin* refrain from printing a column called "Courts and Briefs," which named individuals who were in court. A large majority were Indigenous names, which did not leave positive feelings. The column was dropped, an example of small gestures indicating a paradigm shift that could be very meaningful to all concerned.

What further impacts have blossomed from the collaboration and investment in relationships? A number of promising projects and events have reinforced relationships and built new ones. Reaching out to communities has value, so Sioux Lookout worked to establish a connection with the township of Pickle Lake and, according to Blanchard, provided opportunity and support by involving it with the Shared Territory Protocol, framework agreements with mining corporations and First Nations. Sioux Lookout was the facilitator in the process and Blanchard functioned as the glue by assisting in capacity building.

An annual regional mayor/chief gathering is held in LSFN each fall. Manitowabi noted that it is a great opportunity for chiefs to sit down with mayors for the first time or to renew acquaintances at a neutral gathering with no agenda. Questions can be asked without repercussions, which increases comfort levels over time. Making a space for these things to happen is very rewarding for all participants.

When communities come forward saying they want to know the best way to create a Friendship Accord, Blanchard advises that they begin by mapping their history, recognizing and owning it. Next, present it to the other community, which will prompt the next conversation to where relationship building begins. Blanchard observed that the government was now encouraging a regional lens, and the old way of working one-on-one was no longer effective. Essential to success is having someone in the municipality who can facilitate, understand, and build on those relationships with strong support from the mayor and Chief Administrative Officer, or no progress will occur.

The Calls to Action issued by the TRC are another reason to consider the role of collaborations. Blanchard noted that Sioux Lookout formed a Truth and Reconciliation committee that took the Calls to Action focusing on municipalities and broke them down into economic, health, and education streams, and so on. These were being studied and committees tasked with carrying out sections of the work. This effort supported the overarching Friendship Accord, with the CEDI project acting as a springboard to relationship building and business activity. The Shared Territories Protocol is more regionally inclusive and the exploration framework agreement guides all resource development. Truth and reconciliation efforts have been one of many underlying influences.

Facilitative Leadership

The following quotations capture the perspectives of various leaders who have been involved in collaborations, including that of Slave Lake, Sawridge First Nation, and Lesser Slave Lake Municipal District in Alberta, as well as the Ontario partnerships examined thus far. Similar sentiments were echoed by leaders in the Manitoba partnership that is examined in the next section.

> You're trying to keep score all the time and you can't do that. . . . Everything we do as an individual project is not going to benefit us all equally—it never will. And if we're trying to do that, we'll never get anything done. But collectively as a whole, all those projects can be a benefit for all of us.
>
> —Mayor Tyler Warman, Town of Slave Lake[23]

> Muster your courage; take that leap of faith. The other levels of government aren't actually the enemy—they can become your best allies.
>
> —Chief Roland Twinn, Sawridge First Nation[24]

> We didn't just learn to work together, we became friends, and that's what was missing before.
>
> —Reeve Murray Kerik, M.D. of
> Lesser Slave Lake[25]

This project is more than a feasibility study. It is a coming together of our Municipality and regional First Nations to work on an initiative of mutual interest with support from Cando and the FCM. We look forward to working on this project and it is our hope to work on many more initiatives such as this.

—Mayor Doug Lawrance, Municipality of Sioux Lookout[26]

With a representation of First Nations and municipal governments, you have a stronger voice at Queen's Park, at the federal buildings in Ottawa, and you're apt to be listened to more.

—Chief Clifford Bull, Lac Seul First Nation[27]

Community champions in the Ontario partnership have been Sam Manitowabi and Brian King in LSFN, Bruce Sakakeep in KI, and Vicki Blanchard in Sioux Lookout. These individuals were part of the process from the beginning, forming the core group. This is a critical element for success but in addition they have the respect of the Chiefs. The core group brings stability and an understanding of relationship building for new partners. Blanchard's passion for the success of these partnerships has led her to "live it, eat it and drink it every day." She acknowledged that gratitude is regularly expressed for her efforts at all levels.

Sioux Lookout's commitment has been extraordinary in offering the needed funding and infrastructure to enable partnerships to move forward. Blanchard provides funds for all meeting travel by leveraging CEDI funds into a large enough portfolio that allows communication with northern communities. The cost of the initial meeting that brought the KI leader and staff in was borne by Sioux Lookout. Blanchard's funding applications include the costs of taking partner members to an annual Prospectors and Developers Association of Canada, the largest mining conference in the world. Nine members went in 2015 and twelve attended the 2016 conference. Blanchard manages the funds and completes the conference expense report.

Blanchard stated that Sioux Lookout is the only municipality with the ability to make funding applications for the collaboration because the Province of Ontario recognizes the Friendship Accord as a treaty. The Shared Territory Protocol between LSFN, Cat Lake, and Slate Falls means they have one territory with one trapline and can move about it without asking each other's permission. They all come to the table to make large decisions about resource development. Mining companies all come through Blanchard's office, so she completes the travel arrangements for the Shared Territory Protocol members and sends one bill to the mining company, then reimburses the communities. The first exploration framework agreement was signed several years earlier with the First Nations Mining Corporation. Blanchard tries to schedule other meetings around the same time as the meetings with the First Nations Mining Corporation, in order to ensure that travel costs of First Nations leaders are covered and good use is made of their time.

Manitoba: Opaskwayak Cree Nation, Town of The Pas, and Rural Municipality of Kelsey

Background Conditions

These communities came together despite a history of independence and some animosity. On behalf of The Pas, a community of 5,500 people, a municipal employee took up FCM's offer of applying to be part of CEDI. Surrounding communities were then required to send letters of support with the application. Both Opaskwayak Cree Nation

(OCN) (pop. 3,198 on-reserve, 2,099 off-reserve) and the Rural Municipality (RM) of Kelsey (pop. 2,272) determined that it was a great opportunity with possibilities of mutual benefit. The Pas and OCN play roles in meeting the needs of communities in the northern region. Struggles have resulted from the closure of Tolko's paper and lumber mill and the IGA store, and the possibility of other business closures. The Pas is landlocked, with Kelsey and OCN on three sides as well as across the river, so if The Pas wants to expand it must work with both partners.

The CEDI process brought various ideas to the table, which were narrowed down to ways to attract investors and joint strategies for attending to infrastructure issues. Without a clearly framed relationship, the brainstorming process got bogged down. A suggestion was made to consider a Friendship Accord, which was agreed to and eventually signed by the parties in 2014. The key terms of the Accord ("Three Communities, One Heart") strengthen the social, spiritual, and economic ties that support a mutual respect of interests that are beneficial to all communities, including the signatories and neighbours. This agreement acknowledges government-to-government relations, where wisdom can be shared for a better future for children and grandchildren. It also commits to building mutual trust and respect while acknowledging their history, past experiences, and differences that impact current perspectives and opinions. These communities agree to come together twice a year for open dialogue and to agree on priorities.

Duncan Lathlin, OCN member and Special Projects officer for Paskwayak Business Development Corporation, called the Friendship Accord a strong foundation for a partnership that opened needed dialogue.[28] Town Councillor Brian Roque noted, "There has always been a need to help each other but bad feelings from the past got in the way"; the Friendship Accord turned the page and allowed each partner to move forward.[29] Lathlin pointed out that the OCN and The Pas high schools studied their community Friendship Accord, then created their own Friendship Accord that was signed by students in both communities as they met on a symbolic walk to the middle of the bridge that divides the two communities.[30] The students were developing relationships through joint activities, a remarkable step for them as future leaders. This was also very exciting for the town, according to Roque.[31] He noted that an earlier Reeve report shed some light on the shifting young family demographics where an equal number live in The Pas and work in OCN and vice versa. This ties the two communities together in a newly recognized way. Roque concluded that the Friendship Accord was moving forward, although not in the ways that everyone might have expected.[32]

Institutional Design

The collaborative attitude launched quarterly meetings under the purview of a tri-council in 2015. The tri-council's main CEDI-supported projects were an investor-focused brochure and website. At the launch of these efforts, Town Councillor Brian Roque noted, "It has been a learning process, but I found it exciting and have enjoyed the networking and the connections I've made with other participants. You learn more about them and how they feel. There is a positive energy here. Tonight is called a launch because it's just a beginning. Now with what we learned today we can move forward and continue on with the process. The ultimate goal is let's make a better community, let the tri-Council region become stronger because of working together and sharing our resources and situations."[33]

Lathlin shared further benefits from the collaboration. He characterized the initial relationship with The Pas and Kelsey as neighbourly but from a distance and where you really didn't know each other well.[34] That improved from feeling like OCN was operating in a bubble, as described by Lathlin, to one where each knows more about the way their neighbours do business, their organizational structure, and their operating environment. Despite the differences, the partnership greatly expanded what OCN factors into decisions on something that might impact one or the other of their partners. For example, if they have a large project they ask questions about the capacity of The Pas to handle the project and are prepared to help improve needed changes to the infrastructure.

Unfortunately, the change in economic climate referred to earlier made some of these efforts obsolete. The brochures were archived and the website removed. There was a communication issue around the website at the time these interviews took place. Lathlin said that an agreement existed where OCN was to pay for the website in the first year, which was honoured, The Pas was to bear the financial costs in the second year, and Kelsey agreed to carry the costs in the third year. Unfortunately, OCN did not know why the website was not continued after the first year as there was no communication with The Pas on this decision. Lathlin hypothesized that the reason might include recent economic impacts with the mill and other businesses closing.[35]

The lack of communication about the website had not impacted Lathlin's to-do list, which included a call to the appropriate person at The Pas. In the past, this lack of communication could have been chalked up to something potentially more detrimental, but the strength of the relationship meant the doors of communication remained open.[36] Another example of the collaboration's impact, according to Roque, has been the way they do business. For example, The Pas's community development corporation (CDC), which focuses on municipal business, was resurrected but with discussions on ways to bring in OCN to broaden the scope of CDC's work.[37]

The tri-council identified a landfill as a critical project to replace other landfills in the area that had aged out, and alternatives that were up to code were needed. When the partners discussed this mutual issue, it was determined that OCN had an appropriate parcel of land that would be the best option for a regional landfill that expanded the area of concern to approximately twenty other communities. Roque outlined the steep learning curves that occur in such discussions.[38] He pointed to relationships with other governments, including the federal government's relationship with OCN and the municipal government's relationship with the provincial government. That meant that for this project, OCN would work with the federal government and the town would work with the provincial government, so that a master plan could be developed that worked most effectively for all involved.

Collaborative Process

The tri-council meetings are attended by general managers from each community, where relevant issues are discussed and recommendations passed to the leadership. Once a consensus is reached, then recommendations are ratified by the respective leadership. If there are such things as by-laws or government permits involved, then the leadership makes final decisions. Lathlin felt that each person's commitment was to do the best they could, and "what we got out of it was a really great relationship."[39] A leadership approach that is most effective, according to Roque, is to listen. While it is easy to talk about one's own issues, it is more valuable to listen first to what the other party wants. The partnership is strengthened as independent decisions disappear in situations that are more suited to the collaboration. As the relationships are strengthened, identifying where overlaps occur will be streamlined.

An important part of the relationship was the RM of Kelsey. OCN now had a more complete idea of where mutual interests lie. The First

Nation had thought that Kelsey was only involved in agriculture that occurred on land that was quite removed from OCN. It was surprised to find out that Kelsey owns land close to OCN. The two partners are now working on coordinating commercial development on contiguous land that each was developing separately until the partnership opened up discussions. Lathlin noted, "We have similar goals that we had no idea of before."[40]

Facilitative Leadership

Lathlin stated that changes in leadership impact the success of the tri-council.[41] One challenge to the collaboration's health was how new leaders are introduced to the partnership. Some perceptions of change in leadership, for example, occurred when an eager champion who connected well with the partners was replaced with a new leader who had a more hands-off style. This is not a deal breaker so long as the lines of communication are open. There are always pressures that are hidden to outsiders, and as Lathlin stated, "Because we are friendly doesn't mean that I can poke my nose in their business."[42]

Roque added that changes in leadership had not stopped the momentum, because each partner had goals to accomplish that drove the process. Methods of communication can cause issues when one is setting meetings. For example, efforts to schedule a meeting may not be successful because there is no response to the email invitation. Roque stated, "Call me old-fashioned but there is such a thing called the telephone. Problems occur when assumptions are made that others prefer to do things the same way that I do. It is better to realize that some people might do things a little differently."[43]

Both Lathlin and Roque are collaboration champions. They have worked hard to inspire others and bring their experience to the table to help the tri-council move forward. Roque thought a meet-and-greet after the new Chief of OCN was elected made sense. He organized it himself, despite difficulties in setting tri-council meetings. Fifteen out of twenty-two leaders across the three partnerships showed up at the meet-and-greet. The new Chief met the mayor and many useful contacts were made for the benefit of all concerned.[44]

At OCN, Lathlin and another employee were enthusiastic and passionate about building relationships, so they modelled this behaviour to others in various departments. This was picked up as the value became clear, so it became a common means of doing business and people from OCN felt comfortable to include the town in the process. This is being done independently without leadership having to give directions.[45]

The future of the collaboration looked promising, according to Lathlin and Roque, as it could only improve, grow, and become stronger. The inevitable shift as young people step into leadership roles will require space for the wisdom of experienced, older citizens who have much to offer. It makes sense to access all assets even while generational practices, communication, and use of technology may stretch older people's abilities. It is a work in progress that will adapt from generation to generation.

Roque's advice to municipalities interested in developing collaborations was to know their list of projects well enough so that opportunities for working together are quickly identified.[46] This is a collaborative process that relies on relationship building rather than going in with a demanding attitude where the focus is on venting, with the goal of winning disagreements. Speaking up quickly without the facts or bringing gossip into the picture are injurious.

Lathlin's advice to First Nations communities interested in this type of partnership was to pursue it persistently. "You will find common interests and goals. The paths that lead to achieving those goals will be vastly improved with collaboration. No one loses anything from collaboration. Instead it is multiplied for the better."[47]

Summary

Collaborations between First Nations and municipalities in the further-ance of community goals are of interest for many reasons. The variety of similar goals is apparent in the CEDI project profiles. Targeted projects include tourism, support for business development, and meeting local needs that sometimes extend to regional challenges. Developing relationships prior to important decisions were important in the Lac Seul and KI collaboration with Sioux Lookout and were visible in the OCN, The Pas, and Kelsey collaboration. Both of these partnerships were formed after a history of some negativity. It was clear in these collaborations that knowing how to work with each other for mutual benefit was important.

The CEDI Final Report surveyed participants, and one key finding reinforced the need to build trust-based relationships, as these were "key sustainable outcomes, building a foundation for long-term success in this work."[48] The overall strength of these relationships was described as an unintended outcome by CEDI but cannot be highlighted enough in these collaborations that lead to a "shared sense of unification, while working to reconciliation."[49]

Within both the Manitoba and Ontario partnerships discussed here, individual partners had very different ways of doing business, but with open communication and opportunities to get to know other leaders beyond their jobs, it was possible to construct a framework to complete the work. The OCN formed a collaboration with Kelsey and The Pas developed a Friendship Accord as the basis for working together in a tri-council arrangement. For the Lac Seul, KI, and Sioux Lookout collaboration, a Friendship Accord was the basis for a variety of partnerships, with membership depending on specific goals. For example, the Shared Territory Protocol focused on resource development, while the CEDI partnership looked at projects with shared interest. The distribution centre expanded to include a number of new partners, with one original partner withdrawing.

The CEDI Final Evaluation Report notes that CEDI had helped increase capacity in developing joint economic strategies both for organizations and for elected officials, in the first capacity-building support of this sort.[50] Through the types of agreements developed in the Manitoba and Ontario collaborations discussed here, the ability to seek out joint efforts has flourished.

Leadership was critical to both collaborations, despite some players changing with elections. Useful collaboration characteristics include consistency in the level of interest despite change, open attitudes, curiosity, and the ability to listen and observe when it is clear when other groups do business differently. Relationships need attention so that robust business decisions can be made from a strong foundation. Building consensus needs time and an understanding that the big picture is important while still including individual issues. Consensus means impactful decision making with all partners equally committed.

The CEDI Final Evaluation Report noted that collaboration champions had increased knowledge of the governance models, structures, and cultural practices of their partners. Better understanding of issues impacting First Nations partners was a "valuable, yet unintended, outcome."[51] This outcome offsets initial capacity limitations that might have stalled the new relationships.

The champions were evident in both collaborations and brought their own levels of commitment. All were supportive of the collaborations and worked hard to support success. The Ontario collaboration had a municipality as champion that consistently funded travel to meetings, handled many administration details, and brought a strong level of coordination by involving new business and levels of government to support collaboration at a regional level. One important finding in the CEDI Final Evaluation Report was that often support staff was insufficient, which challenged critical supportive communication between partners and impeded work on resolving key partnership issues.

At a 2015 Cando conference, the Ontario collaboration was presented to an audience that included economic development officers from across Canada. Members of the audience indicated that they were ready for collaborations with neighbouring municipalities but had met with rejection. With the growing number of success stories across the country from CEDI and those collaborations that occur without outside attention, it is possible that more partnerships will form for the benefit of all. Getting all levels of government on board to support and sustain growing relationships between communities as they encourage a regional focus will have a decided impact, especially with communities that have unused capacity to become more self-sustaining in partnership.

The CEDI Final Evaluation Report recommended that the second phase of CEDI projects include mentors who would share their experiences and success. These might be Phase One CEDI partners who would reach out beyond the CEDI group as peer mentors to help overcome problems mentioned at the Cando conference. The CEDI application process acted as initiator for many of the collaborations that were highlighted in this chapter. The supportive role played by FCM with necessary resources, training, and relevant information in the initial and continuing stages of these partnerings added value to the collaborative processes outlined here, which indeed builds from strength to strength.

NOTES

◆

1 This material originally appeared in *Building Bridges: Case Studies Collaborative in Governance in Canada*, edited by Claude Rocan (Ottawa: Invenire, 2018). Revised March 2022. Permission to use has been granted by Invenire "the idea factory."

2 Federation of Canadian Municipalities (FCM), *Building First Nations–Municipal Community Economic Development Partnerships*, http://www.fcm.ca/Documents/reports/CEDI/cedi-tkag-en-screen.pdf.

3 Assembly of First Nations Make Poverty History Expert Advisory Committee, *The State of the First Nation Economy and the Struggle to Make Poverty History* (Ottawa: Assembly of First Nations, 2009), 6.

4 FCM, *Pathways to Reconciliation: Cities Respond to the Truth and Reconciliation Commission Calls to Action* (Ottawa: Federation of Canadian Municipalities, 2016), 3, accessed 8 June 2017, https://fcm.ca/en/resources/pathways-reconciliation.

5 Helen Patterson, personal communication, 18 May 2017.

6 Ibid.

7 FCM, First Nations–Municipal Community Economic Development Initiative, "Seabird Island Band, and District of Kent, BC," accessed 25 August 2016, https://www.cedipartnerships.ca/partnerships/past-partnerships/british-columbia/.

8 Town of Slave Lake, Municipal District of Lesser Slave River, and Sawridge First Nation, *Slave Lake Regional Tri-Council Economic Development Strategic Plan: 2012–2015*, https://www.fcm.ca/Documents/reports/CEDI/Tri_council_economic_development_strategic_plan_EN.pdf.

9 FCM, First Nations–Municipal Community Economic Development Initiative, "Sawridge First Nation, Town of Slave Lake, and Municipal District of Lesser Slave River, AB," accessed 25 August 2016, https://www.cedipartnerships.ca/partnerships/past-partnerships/sawridge-first-nation/.

10 FCM, "First Nations Municipal Updates," June 2017.

11 FCM, First Nations–Municipal Community Economic Development Initiative, "Madawaska Maliseet First Nation and City of Edmundston, NB, accessed 25 August 2016, https://www.cedipartnerships.ca/partnerships/past-partnerships/madawaska-maliseet-first-nation/.

12 Lac Seul First Nation, "Lac Seul First Nation," 2017, https://lacseulfn.org/.

13 Lac Seul First Nation, "Social Recovery Strategy," 2017, https://lacseulfn.org/.

14 Christian Quequish, "Friendship Agreement Brings Communities Together in Respect, *Wawatay News*, 1 December 2015, 1, http://www.wawataynews.ca/home/friendship-agreement-brings-communities-together-respect.

15 "About Sioux Lookout," Sioux Lookout: Hub of the North, 2014, http://www.siouxlookout.ca/en/living-here/about-sioux-lookout.asp.

16 Vicki Blanchard, personal communication, 20 June 2017.

17 *Sioux Lookout Friendship Accord*, 2013, https://slfa.ca.

18 Ibid.

19 Sam Manitowabi, personal communication, 9 June 2017.

20 Ibid.

21 Mike Aiken, "Sioux Lookout Expands Friendship Accord," *Kenora Online*, 3 March 2017, https://www.kenoraonline.com/local/sioux-lookout-expands-friendship-accord.

22 *The Secret Path* is an adaptation of the 2016 album of the same name by Canadian singer-songwriter Gord Downie and accompanying graphic novel by Jeff Lemire. The film was first aired by the CBC in 2017. See https://anticaproductions.com/film-tv/the-secret-path/.

23 FCM, First Nations–Municipal Community Economic Development Initiative, "Sawridge First Nation."

24 Ibid.

25 Ibid.

26 FCM, First Nations–Municipal Community Economic Development Initiative, "Lac Seul First Nation, Municipality of Sioux Lookout, and Kitchenuhmaykoosib Inninuwug, ON," accessed 25 August 2016, http://www.fcm.ca/home/programs/community-economic-development-initiative/participating-communities/ontario.htm.

27 Cando (Council for the Advancement of Native Development Officers), *CEDI First Nations—Municipal Community Economic Development Initiative*, 2017, http://www.edo.ca/cedi.

28 Duncan Lathlin, personal communication, 9 June 2017.

29 Brian Roque, personal communication, 9 June 2017.

30 Lathlin, personal communication, 9 June 2017.

31 Roque, personal communication, 9 June 2017.

32 Ibid.

33 "Tri-Council.ca Launched," *Opaskwayak Times*, 1 April 2016, 1.

34 Lathlin, personal communication, 9 June 2017.

35 Ibid.

36 Ibid.

37 Roque, personal communication, 9 June 2017.

38 Ibid.

39 Lathlin, personal communication, 9 June 2017.

40 Ibid.

41 Ibid.

42 Ibid.

43 Roque, personal communication, 9 June 2017.

44 Ibid.

45 Lathlin, personal communication, 9 June 2017.

46 Roque, personal communication, 9 June 2017.

47 Lathlin, personal communication, 9 June 2017.

48 FCM and Cando: Community Economic Development Initiative, "Evaluation Report," 10 May 2016 (unpublished), 5.

49 Ibid.

50 Ibid.

51 Ibid.

CONCLUSION

♦

What Have We Learned about Indigenous Tenacity?

♦

Wanda Wuttunee and Fred Wien

I f the dialogue on Indigenous economic activity in Canada is focused on tenacity, then it must begin by considering the "continued existence of Indigenous peoples in Canada" as one part of the tenacity conversation as well as considering what "continued existence" looks like. The historical and contemporary context in which Indigenous peoples demonstrate tenacity has been explored in these chapters. Tenacity is not a word commonly associated by the general public with Indigenous economic history and contributions to Canada. Yet the contributors of each chapter point to various facets of Indigenous tenacity, often showcasing common experiences that bind these stories together and engaging the reader in a deeper appreciation for the journey that has led to where we find ourselves today.

David Newhouse's introduction recaps a history in which Indigenous leaders have struggled to maintain the well-being of their communities through different periods, striving to create or recreate conditions where economic activity and community life can flourish. Newhouse describes the many trials that traditional and elected leaders have overcome and the continued push for meaningful change that really defines a nation-building process. The push forward demonstrated here encompasses all levels, from individual and family enterprises through community economic development initiatives and on to nation-building exercises seeking to attain economic success in line with community values.

In the case studies featured in this book, entrepreneurship is important but so is the role played by political leaders who are on the front lines, helping to shape the community's vision for development, securing and exercising treaty and other rights, negotiating for funding and for business opportunities, and putting in place a strong public service. Thus, the often-heard refrain that business should be separated from politics (erroneously attributed to the Harvard Project on American Indian Economic Development) is much too simplistic. As our chapters reveal, what is important is not to deny the role of the political leadership but rather to understand what the proper division of labour between business and political leaders needs to be, and where the boundaries are—where politics inappropriately interferes with day-to-day decisions that should be made on economic grounds, for example. One can't understand the success that Membertou has had, for example, by simply describing its various business ventures, especially since many of them are in fact owned and led by the Membertou Development Corporation, a creation of Chief and Council (Chapter 1). The importance of political leadership is also demonstrated by the Muskeg Lake Cree Nation case study (Chapter 3), which highlights its role in establishing an urban economic development zone.

In the introductory chapter, Newhouse describes times when external threats and pressures were almost overwhelming. Even in more recent decades, the challenges have been formidable. The chapter focusing on lifetime achievers, for example, describes a context where First Nations entrepreneurs in the Atlantic region had to make their way largely on their own, without the support of government programs or the recognition of treaty and Aboriginal rights (Chapter 7). At present, the situation facing Indigenous businesses remains difficult, with factors such as small community size, geographic isolation, and racism playing a role, but there have also been significant positive developments. We note especially some favourable court decisions that have opened up opportunities, much more robust government programming, and the development of a web of institutions designed to support Indigenous economic development. Just looking at what has been mentioned in our case studies, we are impressed with the range of mechanisms and vehicles that communities have developed to advance their interests. These have included the creation of community economic development corporations (Chapter 10), negotiating impact benefit agreements, securing treaty land entitlements, building urban economic development zones, turning to cooperative forms of organization (Chapter 9), and developing municipal–First Nation partnerships (Chapter 11). These institutional developments contribute to tenacity in that they provide a collective and often legally buttressed mechanism to protect and advance Indigenous forms of economic activity.

What is also impressive is that the Indigenous communities profiled here have not opted for economic development at any cost, despite high levels of need for employment and income. The evidence is that, historically and today, they have tried to pursue a culturally informed approach to economic development, examples of which are found throughout this book. Given the assimilative pressures coming from mainstream society, this is not an easy path to follow, as Isobel Findlay notes (Chapter 4). There is, in fact, a lively debate among Indigenous and other scholars about how much room there is within capitalism to advance and maintain an approach to development that is consistent with Indigenous culture. Clifford Gordon Atleo (Chapter 5) is skeptical, for example, while Daniel Millette's Tsawwassen case study (Chapter 2) shows that in practice, considerable cultural congruity is possible. Judith Sayers (Chapter 6) describes the tension evident within and between British Columbia First Nations over how to take advantage of economic opportunities but also to do so in a manner that is consistent with sustainable development. Sayers summarizes the intricate nuances underlying polar positions held by British Columbia First Nations in the debate. Self-government means leadership must govern as its citizens see fit. Sustainable development holds a place in discussions but the weight given to priorities can and does differ across stakeholders.

At the core of Indigenous economic tenacity are the entrepreneurs who have struggled to establish and sustain their businesses. We get a sense of this journey from the stories of Jim McDonald (Chapter 8), Neechi Commons (Chapter 9), and the lifetime achievers (Chapter 7). One of the lessons that has emerged from these case studies is that individual entrepreneurs do not do this work on their own. They draw on previous generations to teach them about particular businesses and to help them get started. They draw in family members to do everything from sales to accounting to truck driving, and they rely on their communities to provide the principal market for their goods and services, to provide contracts, and to furnish their labour force.

It is notable that the relationship between communities and their entrepreneurs is a two-way street. While entrepreneurs draw sustenance from their families and communities, they also give back in many ways—through providing employment and charitable contributions, serving in elected positions, volunteering in community organizations, and even in providing a place for community members to "hang out." These contemporary businesses, of course, are also the training ground for the next generation of entrepreneurs.

In closing, the rich history and numerous contributions from individuals operating in different and connected spheres of influence and impact add meaning to what Indigenous tenaciousness brings to the Canadian economic experience. It is the actions of those who think for themselves and act for others. Over time, opportunities are often handed to the next generation for their continued efforts. These stories of tenacity in Indigenous economic endeavours do not stand apart from the Canadian experience. They are integral.

In speaking to Canadians, John Ralston Saul states unequivocally: "Most of the problems faced by Aboriginal people are solvable. And our pessimism—our guilt, sympathy, and dismissal—blocks these perfectly achievable resolutions. Aboriginal people are in the process of solving them. We are still getting in the way. . . . We must reinstall a national narrative built upon the centrality of the Aboriginal peoples' past, present, and future. And the policies of the country must reflect the centrality, both conceptually and financially."[1]

Problems are being solved, and Indigenous tenacity needs to be recognized as a demonstration that "we are more than our problems."

NOTES

◆

1   John Ralston Saul, *The Comeback* (Toronto: Penguin, 2014), 8, 14.

ACKNOWLEDGEMENTS

In the early 1980s, I was working with my friend the late Chief Noel Doucette, who was at the time the president of the Union of Nova Scotia Indians. Supported by a grant from the Donner Canadian Foundation, our task was to shape an economic development strategy for the Mi'kmaw communities of Nova Scotia. Our starting point for that assignment was to talk with the long-standing entrepreneurs in the community who had developed and sustained their businesses during an era when there was very little support available for First Nations businesses. The story of these entrepreneurs and their tenacity is captured in one of the chapters of this book. It wasn't long after that when Chief Terry Paul of Membertou First Nation and his team began what would turn out to be at least a two-decades' effort to turn around the fortunes of his community, something he accomplished with outstanding results, impacting not only the members of his community but also the wider Cape Breton region and beyond—the subject of another chapter. I have learned so much from these and other stories of determination, commitment, and resilience, and am happy that we are able to share them—and others like them—in this publication.

My collaboration with Wanda Wuttunee (Charles) also goes back several decades, especially in our working together on the editorial board for the *Journal for Aboriginal Economic Development*, beginning in the early 1990s. More recently, we were co-principal investigators for the CIHR-funded Poverty Action Research Project, in which we worked with five First Nations from different parts of the country on the development and implementation of strategies for addressing poverty in their communities. In these projects, as well as in the work of putting this book together, one could not ask for a better partner. There is some tenacity evident in her character as well, notably when we made an unforgettable road trip to northern Manitoba in minus-40-degree weather. I will always cherish the times we have worked together.

Let me also express my appreciation to the contributors to this book, and to Jill McConkey, our outstanding editor with the University of Manitoba Press. Well, hopefully not out standing in minus-40-degree weather—but then Manitobans scarcely seem to notice.

—*Fred Wien*

◆

Celebrating Indigenous economic resilience and tenacity has been at the heart of my teaching and research for the past thirty-eight years. There are many stories of obstacles, but the story I have always wanted to share was how well many of our Indigenous leaders and citizens have risen to all the challenges and how they did so with persistence and brilliance. Often their accomplishments were achieved with the support of numerous allies, who did so with respect and sensitivity. This has been accomplished most vigorously in this project with the help of each and every one of our contributors. Each story has impacted their communities and beyond.

It has been a pleasure to work with my dear friend Fred Wien, who has worked for many years in this field. He is incisive, witty, and a class act always, willing to step in wherever needed. Jill McConkey, our editor, shared our vision from the beginning and was patient and insightful, totally engaged and supportive.

I am grateful for my husband Phil's quiet, loving patience, his support of my work and protection of my writing time and space. Kian and Willow are the glitter stars in my heart always. Drew, Cody, and Erin are true blessings in my life. All glory to God who has my heart and my life forever.

—*Wanda Wuttunee*

CONTRIBUTORS

P. JERRY ASP, Tahltan Nation, is Co-Founder, Chair, and CEO of Global Indigenous Development Trust, and President of Gray Wolf Solutions Limited.

CLIFFORD GORDON ATLEO, PhD, Tsimshian and Nuu-chah-nulth, is Assistant Professor at Simon Fraser University, British Columbia.

DR. CHARLOTTE BEZAMAT-MANTES, PhD, is Associate Researcher at the French Institute of Geopolitics, Université Paris Vincennes-Saint-Denis, France. She was also a visiting PhD student at the Department of Indigenous Studies, University of Manitoba.

MARY BETH DOUCETTE, PhD, Membertou Band, is Associate Professor and Purdy Crawford Chair at the Shannon School of Business, Cape Breton University, Sydney, Nova Scotia.

ISOBEL M. FINDLAY, PhD, is Professor Emerita, Edwards School of Business; Fellow in Co-operatives, Diversity, and Sustainable Development, Canadian Centre for the Study of Co-operatives; and University Co-Director, Community-University Institute for Social Research, University of Saskatchewan.

CHRISTOPHER GOOGOO, BBA, We'koqma'q First Nation, is CEO of Ulnooweg Development Group, Millbrook, Nova Scotia. Chris has over twenty-five years of experience working with Indigenous businesses and communities.

CATHERINE MARTIN, BA, BEd, CM, Millbrook Mi'kmaq First Nation Community, is an independent producer and the first woman Mi'kmaw filmmaker from the Atlantic Region. Catherine is also the Director of Indigenous Community Engagement at Dalhousie University.

DANIEL M. MILLETTE, PhD, has travelled to over 250 Indigenous communities documenting land use planning, traditional planning, and architecture. He formerly taught at different universities and continues to work directly with numerous Indigenous communities.

DAVID NEWHOUSE, MBA, Onandaga, is Professor and Director at the Chanie Wenjack School for Indigenous Studies at Trent University, Peterborough, Ontario.

JUDITH SAYERS, Hon LL.D, Hupacasath First Nation, is President of the Nuu-Chah-nulth Tribal Council and Chancellor at Vancouver Island University. Judith is also Adjunct Professor at the Gustavson School of Business and the School of Environmental Studies at the University of Victoria, British Columbia.

FREDERIC WIEN, PhD, Professor Emeritus at Dalhousie University, Nova Scotia, is highly regarded for collaborating with Indigenous leaders and scholars to undertake the research they need in order to create evidence-based policies and practices.

WANDA WUTTUNEE, PhD, Red Pheasant Cree Nation, is Professor Emerita, Department of Indigenous Studies, University of Manitoba.

SELECTED BIBLIOGRAPHY

Legal Cases

Calder et al. v. Attorney-General of British Columbia, [1973] SCR 313.

Coldwater Indian Band, et al. v. Attorney General of Canada, et al., Case #3911, dismissed.

Delgamuukw v. British Columbia, [1997] 3 SCR 1010.

Guerin v. The Queen, [1984] 2 SCR 335.

Haida Nation v. British Columbia (Minister of Forests), [2004] SCC 73.

Mikisew Cree First Nation v. Canada (Governor General in Council), [2018] 2 SCR 765.

R. v. Marshall, [1999] 3 SCR 533.

R. v. Mitchell, [2001] SCC 33.

R. v. Sparrow, [1990] 1 SCR 1075.

R. v. Van der Peet, [1996] 2 SCR 507.

Tsilhqot'in Nation v. British Columbia, [2014] SCR 257.

West Moberly First Nation v. B.C. (Chief Inspector of Mines), [2010] BCSC 359.

Western Sahara Campaign UK v. Commissioners for Her Majesty's Revenue and Customs and Secretary of State for Environment, Food and Rural Affairs, EUR-Lex: Access to European Union Law, doc. 62016CC0266.

Williams Lake Indian Band v. Canada (Aboriginal Affairs and Northern Development), [2018] 1 SCR 83.

Legislation

An Act to Amend and Consolidate the Laws Respecting Indians (Indian Act), RSC, 1985, c. I-5, 22 December 2017. Accessed 14 September 2023. https://laws-lois.justice.gc.ca/eng/acts/I-5/page-1.html.

Bill C-15 (Royal Assent). An Act respecting the United Nations Declaration on the Rights of Indigenous Peoples, 21 June 2021. Accessed 14 September 2023. https://parl.ca/DocumentViewer/en/43-2/bill/C-15/royal-assent.

Bill C-262 (Third Reading). An Act to ensure that the laws of Canada are in harmony with the United Nations Declaration on the Rights of Indigenous Peoples. House of Commons of Canada, 30 May 2018. Accessed 14

September 2023. https://www.parl.ca/DocumentViewer/en/42-1/
bill/C-262/third-reading.

Canadian Net-Zero Emissions Accountability Act, S.C. 2021, c. 22. Accessed 14
September 2023. https://laws-lois.justice.gc.ca/eng/acts/C-19.3/FullText.
html.

Clean Energy Act, [SBC 2010], c. 22. Accessed 14 September 2023. http://www.
bclaws.ca/civix/document/id/complete/statreg/10022_01.

Climate Change Accountability Act, [SBC 2007] c. 42, 29 November 2007.
Accessed 14 September 2023. https://www.bclaws.gov.bc.ca/civix/document/
id/complete/statreg/07042_01.

Constitution Act, 1867, 30 & 31 Vict, c. 3. Accessed 14 September 2023. https://
www.canlii.org/en/ca/laws/stat/30---31-vict-c-3/latest/30---31-vict-c-3.html.

Declaration on the Rights of Indigenous Peoples Act, [SBC 2019], c. 44, November
2019. Accessed 14 September 2023. https://www.bclaws.gov.bc.ca/civix/
document/id/complete/statreg/19044.

First Nations Land Management Act, (S.C. 1999), c. 24. Accessed 14 September
2023. https://laws-lois.justice.gc.ca/eng/acts/f-11.8/page-1.html.

shíshálh Nation Self-Government Act (S.C. 1986, c. 27), 1986. Accessed 14
September 2023. https://laws-lois.justice.gc.ca/eng/acts/S-6.6/.

Published Sources

Adams, Howard. *Prison of Grass: Canada from a Native Point of View*. Rev. ed.
Saskatoon: Fifth House Publishers, 1989.

Alfred, Taiaiake. *Wasáse: Indigenous Pathways of Action and Freedom*. Peterborough:
Broadview Press, 2005.

Anderson, Robert B., Leo Paul Dana, and Theresa Dana. "Indigenous Land Rights,
Entrepreneurship, and Economic Development in Canada: 'Opting-in' to the
Global Economy." *Journal of World Business* 41, no. 1 (2006): 45–55.

Anderson, Robert B., Robert Kayseas, Leo Paul Dana, and Kevin Hindle.
"Indigenous Land Claims and Economic Development in the Canadian
Experience." In *ANZAM 2003: Surfing the Waves: Management Challenges,
Management Solutions: Proceedings of the 17th ANZAM Conference*. Joondalup,
Western Australia: School of Management, ECU, 2003.

ARCAS Consulting Archaeologists. *Archaeological Investigations at Tsawwassen, BC*.
Vols. 1–4. Delta, BC: ARCAS Consulting Archaeologists, 1992–96.

Atleo, Clifford Gordon. "Aboriginal Capitalism: Is Resistance Futile or Fertile?"
Journal of Aboriginal Economic Development 9, no 2 (2015): 41–51.

Bargh, Maria. "A Blue Economy for Aotearoa New Zealand?" *Environment,
Development and Sustainability* 16, no. 3 (2014): 459–70.

Bargh, Maria, Sarsha-Leigh Douglas, and Annie Te One. "Fostering Sustainable
Tribal Economies in a Time of Climate Change." *New Zealand Geographer* 70,
no. 2 (2014): 103–15.

Barron, F. Laurie. "The Indian Pass System in the Canadian West, 1882–1935." *Prairie Forum* 13, no. 1 (1988): 25–42.

Barron, F. Laurie, and Joseph Garcea. "The Genesis of Urban Reserves and the Role of Governmental Self-Interest." In *Urban Indian Reserves: Forging New Relationships in Saskatchewan*, edited by F. Laurie Barron and Joseph Garcea, 22–52. Saskatoon: Purich Publishing, 1999.

Baumol, William J., Robert E. Litan, and Carl J. Schramm, eds. *Good Capitalism, Bad Capitalism, and the Economics of Growth and Prosperity.* New Haven: Yale University Press, 2007.

Beatty, Bonita. "Beyond Advising: Aboriginal Peoples and Social Policy-Making in Saskatchewan." In *New Directions in Saskatchewan Public Policy*, edited by David P. McGrane, 201–23. Regina: Canadian Plains Research Center, 2011.

———. "A Distributive Aboriginal Political Culture Is Alive and Well in Northern Saskatchewan." *Journal of Aboriginal Economic Development* 10, no. 1 (2016): 38–53.

———. *Straining a Gnat but Swallowing a Camel: Policing First Nation Fishers in Northern Saskatchewan.* Yellowhead Institute Policy Brief 22, 13 February 2019. Accessed 13 September 2023. https://yellowheadinstitute.org/2019/02/13/policing-first-nation-fishers/.

Beaver, Jack. *To Have What Is Our Own.* Ottawa: National Indian Socio-Economic Development Committee, 1979.

Bernas, Kirsten, and Brendan Reimer. *Building a Federal Policy Framework and Program in Support of Community Economic Development.* Report prepared for the Northern Ontario, Manitoba, and Saskatchewan Regional Node of the Social Economy Suite. Accessed 14 September 2023. https://ccednet-rcdec.ca/sites/ccednet-rcdec.ca/wp-content/uploads/2022/09/Federal_Policy_Framework_Report_1.pdf.

Big-Canoe, Katie, and Chantelle A.M. Richmond. "Anishinabe Youth Perceptions about Community Health: Toward Environmental Repossession." *Health Place* 26 (2014): 127–35.

Bol, M.C. *Iroquois Confederacy of the North-East.* Carnegie Museum of Natural History, 27 February 2014. Accessed 14 September 2023. https://nsew.carnegiemnh.org/iroquois-confederacy-of-the-northeast/.

Borrows, John. *Law's Indigenous Ethics.* Toronto: University of Toronto Press, 2019.

British Columbia Hydro. "Independent Projects History and Maps." Accessed 14 September 2023. https://www.bchydro.com/work-with-us/selling-clean-energy/meeting-energy-needs/how-power-is-acquired.html.

———. "Standing Offer Program," 20 March 2019. Accessed 14 September 2023. https://www.bchydro.com/work-with-us/selling-clean-energy/closed-offerings/standing-offer-program.html.

British Columbia Papers—Indian Land Question 1850–1875. Victoria, BC: R. Wolfenden, 1875.

Brown, Keith, Meghan Finney, Janice Esther Tulk, Mary Beth Doucette, Natasha Bernard, and Isabella Yuan. "Membertou Always Wanted to Succeed: The Membertou Business Model." *Journal of Aboriginal Economic Development* 8, no. 1 (2012): 32–48.

Brown, Keith G., and Janice Esther Tulk. "Membertou Pedway: A Case Study of Challenges in Aboriginal Economic Development." Purdy Crawford Chair in Aboriginal Business Studies, Case Studies in Aboriginal Business, Cape Breton University, Sydney, NS, March 2012. Accessed 13 September 2023. https://cbufaces.cairnrepo.org/islandora/object/cbu%3A1924.

Calliou, Brian. "A Wise Practices Approach to Indigenous Law, Governance, and Leadership: Resistance Against the Imposition of Law." In *Wise Practices: Exploring Indigenous Economic Justice and Self-Determination*, edited by R. Hamilton, J. Borrows, B. Mainprize, R. Beaton, and J.B.D. Nichols, 19–43. Toronto: University of Toronto Press, 2021.

Canada. Aboriginal Affairs and Northern Development Canada and Inuvialuit Regional Corporation. *Evaluation of the Impacts of Comprehensive Land Claims and Self-Government Agreements—Federal and Inuvialuit Perspectives.* Ottawa: Aboriginal Affairs and Northern Development Canada and Inuvialuit Regional Corporation, 2013.

———. Canadian Northern Economic Development Agency. *Canadian Northern Economic Development Agency: 2016–2017. Report on Plans and Priorities.* Ottawa: Canadian Northern Economic Development Agency, 2016.

———. Crown-Indigenous Relations and Northern Affairs Canada. "Treaty Texts," 29 August 2013. Accessed 13 September 2023. https://www.rcaanc-cirnac.gc.ca/eng/1370373165583/1581292088522.

———. Department of Indian Affairs and Northern Development. *Statement of the Government of Canada on Indian Policy, 1969* (White Paper). Ottawa: Queen's Printer, 1969.

———. House of Commons. *Report of the Special Committee on Indian Self-Government* (Penner Report). Ottawa: House of Commons, 1983. Accessed 14 September 2023. https://parl.canadiana.ca/view/oop.com_HOC_3201_22_6.

———. House of Commons. *Indigenous Land Rights: Towards Respect and Implementation. Report of the Standing Committee on Indigenous and Northern Affairs.* Ottawa: House of Commons, 2018.

———. Employment and Social Development Canada. *Indicators of Well-being in Canada: Canadians in Context—Aboriginal Population,* 2014. http://www4.hrsdc.gc.ca/.3ndic.1t.4r@-eng.jsp?iid=36.

———. Indigenous Services Canada. "Additions to Reserve/Reserve Creation." *First Nations Land Management Manual.* Accessed 14 September 2023. https://www.sac-isc.gc.ca/eng/1465827292799/1611938828195.

———. Indigenous Services Canada. Proponents' Guide to Aboriginal Affairs and Northern Development Canada's Environmental Review Process. Accessed

14 September 2023. https://www.sac-isc.gc.ca/eng/1403215245662/16130
76676889.

———. Indigenous Services Canada. "Water in First Nations Communities."
Accessed 14 September 2023. https://www.sac-isc.gc.ca/eng/110010003487
9/1521124927588.

———. Royal Commission on Aboriginal Peoples. *Report of the Royal Commission
on Aboriginal Peoples.* 5 vols. Ottawa: Minister of Supply and Services Canada,
1996.

———. Standing Committee on Indigenous and Northern Affairs. *Indigenous Land
Rights: Towards Respect and Implementation.* Ottawa: House of Commons, 2018.

———. Statistics Canada. "Adult and Youth Correctional Statistics in Canada,
2016/2017." *Juristat,* 19 June 2018. Accessed 14 September 2023. https://
www150.statcan.gc.ca/n1/pub/85-002-x/2018001/article/54972-eng.htm.

———. Statistics Canada. *First Nations People, Métis and Inuit in Canada: Diverse
and Growing Populations.* Catalogue no. 89-659-x2018001. Ottawa: Minister
of Industry, 20 March 2018. Accessed 14 September 2023. https://
www150.statcan.gc.ca/n1/en/pub/89-659-x/89-659-x2018001-eng.
pdf?st=B9cnxlDd.

———. Statistics Canada. *National Household Survey,* 2011. Accessed 14 September
2023. https://www12.statcan.gc.ca/nhs-enm/index-eng.cfm.

———. Truth and Reconciliation Commission of Canada. *Calls to Action.*
Montreal: McGill-Queen's University Press for the Truth and Reconciliation
Commission of Canada, 2015. Accessed 14 September 2023. https://
ehprnh2mwo3.exactdn.com/wp-content/uploads/2021/01/Calls_to_
Action_English2.pdf.

———. Truth and Reconciliation Commission of Canada. *Final Report of the Truth
and Reconciliation Commission of Canada.* 6 vols. Montreal: McGill-Queen's
University Press for the Truth and Reconciliation Commission of Canada,
2015.

———. Truth and Reconciliation Commission of Canada. *Honouring the
Truth, Reconciling for the Future: Summary of the Final Report of the Truth and
Reconciliation Commission of Canada,* 2015. Ottawa: Truth and Reconciliation
Commission of Canada, 2015. Accessed 14 September 2023. http://caid.ca/
TRCFinExeSum2015.pdf.

Cardinal, Harold, and Walter Hildebrandt. *Treaty Elders of Saskatchewan: Our
Dream Is That Our People Will One Day Be Clearly Recognized as Nations.* Calgary:
University of Calgary Press, 2000.

Carter, Sarah. "Controlling Indian Movement: The Pass System." *NeWest Review*
10, no. 9 (1985): 8–9.

———. *Lost Harvests: Prairie Indian Reserve Farmers and Government Policy.* Montreal:
McGill-Queen's University Press, 1993.

Champagne, Duane. *Social Change and Cultural Continuity among Native Nations*. Lanham: Altamira Press, 2007.

Clark, Natalie. Cu7Mc7 q'wele'Wu-kt. "'Come On, Let's Go Berry-Picking': Revival of Secwepemc Wellness Approaches for Healing Child and Youth Experiences of Violence." PhD diss., Simon Fraser University, 2018.

Coates, Ken S. *Summary Report: Social and Economic Impacts of Aboriginal Land Claims Settlements: A Case Study Analysis*. Ottawa: ARA Consulting, 1995.

Conference Board of Canada. *Support for Success: Indigenous Entrepreneurship in Northern and Remote Canada*. Ottawa: Conference Board of Canada, 2020.

Cook, Dana, Eryn Fitzgerald, Judith Sayers, and Karena Shaw. *Survey Report: First Nations and Renewable Energy Development in British Columbia*. Victoria: BC First Nations Clean Energy Working Group, 2017. Accessed 13 September 2023. https://dspace.library.uvic.ca/handle/1828/7919.

Corcoran, Mary. "'Be careful what you ask for': Findings from the Seminar Series on the 'Third Sector in Criminal Justice.'" *Prison Service Journal* 204 (November 2012): 17–22.

Cornell, Stephen. "Accountability, Legitimacy, and the Foundations of Native Self-Governance." In *Rebuilding Native Nations: Strategies for Governance and Development*, 1–34. PRS 93-1. Cambridge, MA: Malcolm Wiener Centre for Social Policy, Harvard Kennedy School, Harvard University, 1993.

Cornell, Stephen E., and Joseph P. Kalt. *Reloading the Dice: Improving the Chances for Economic Development on American Indian Reservations*. Harvard Project on American Indian Economic Development 59. Cambridge, MA: Malcolm Wiener Center for Social Policy, Harvard Kennedy School, Harvard University, 1992.

———. "Sovereignty and Nation-Building: The Development Challenge in Indian Country Today." *American Indian Culture and Research Journal* 22, no. 3 (1998): 187–214.

Cornell, Stephen, Joseph P. Kalt, Miriam Jorgensen, and Katherine S. Contreras. "Seizing the Future, Why Some Native Nations Do and Others Don't." In *Rebuilding Native Nations: Strategies for Governance and Development*, edited by Miriam Jorgensen, 296–320. Tucson: University of Arizona Press, 2007.

Coté, Rochelle. "Networks of Advantage: Urban Indigenous Entrepreneurship and the Importance of Social Capital." In *Well-Being in the Urban Aboriginal Community*, edited by David Newhouse, Kevin FitzMaurice, Tricia McGuire-Adams, and Daniel Jettém, 73–112. Toronto: Thompson Educational Publishing, 2013.

Coulthard, Glen Sean. *Red Skin, White Masks: Rejecting the Colonial Politics of Recognition*. Minneapolis: University of Minnesota Press, 2014.

Council for Yukon Indians. *Together Today for Our Children Tomorrow: A Statement of Grievances and an Approach to Settlement by the Yukon Indian People*. Whitehorse: Council for Yukon Indians, 1973.

Daschuk, James W. *Clearing the Plains: Disease, Politics of Starvation, and the Loss of Aboriginal Life.* Regina: University of Regina Press, 2013.

Davidson, Ken. *Zapped: A Review of BC Hydro's Purchase of Power from Independent Power Producers Conducted for the Minister of Energy, Mines and Petroleum Resources*, February 2019. Accessed 13 September 2023. https://www2. gov.bc.ca/assets/gov/farming-natural-resources-and-industry/electricity-alternative-energy/electricity/bc-hydro-review/bch19-158-ipp_report_february_11_2019.pdf.

Dockstator, Jennifer S., Eabametoong First Nation, Misipawistik Cree First Nation, Opitciwan Atikamekw First Nation, Sipekne'katik First Nation, T'it'q'et, Lillooet BC, Gérard Duhaime, Charlotte Loppie, David Newhouse, Frederic C. Wien, Wanda Wuttunee, Jeff S. Denis, and Mark S. Dockstator. "Pursuing Mutually Beneficial Research: Lessons from the Poverty Action Research Project." *Engaged Scholar* 2, no. 1 (Spring 2016): 17–38.

Dodge, David, and Duncan Kinney. "Judith Sayers, First Nations Run-of-River Hydro Trailblazer." Green Energy Futures website. Accessed 13 September 2023. http://www.greenenergyfutures.ca/episode/judith-sayers-first-nation-run-river-hydro.

Donnelly, Gabrielle. *Women of Membertou. Indigenous Women in Community Leadership Case Studies.* Antigonish: Coady International Institute, 2012.

Doucette, Mary Beth. "Membertou Heritage Park: Community Expectations for an Aboriginal Cultural Heritage Centre." Research project, Cape Breton University, 2008.

Dust, Theresa. "Common Questions about Urban Development Centres in Saskatchewan." *Guide to Service Agreements*, Unit 3, June 2006. Accessed 13 September 2023. https://sarm.ca/wp-content/uploads/2022/03/first-nations-municipal-community-infrastructure-partnership-program-service-agreement-toolkit-unit-3-guide-to-service-agreements.pdf.

———. "The Impact of Aboriginal Land Claims and Self-Government on Canadian Municipalities: The Local Government Perspective." Intergovernmental Committee on Urban and Regional Research, September 1995. Accessed 13 September 2023. https://www.muniscope.ca/resource/dm/114858933216831725.pdf?n=file_Impact_of_aboriginal_land_claims.pdf&inline=yes.

———. "Urban Neighbours Land Entitlement and Urban Reserves," 10 February 1994. Speech presented at a Statistics Canada, Future Focus Conference on the First Nations Community at Regina, Saskatchewan, 10 February 1994.

Emberley, Julia V. *The Cultural Politics of Fur.* Ithaca: Cornell University Press, 1997.

Federation of Canadian Municipalities. *Building First Nations–Municipal Community Economic Development Partnerships.* Accessed 13 September 2023. http://www.fcm.ca/Documents/reports/CEDI/cedi-tkag-en-screen.pdf.

———. *Pathways to Reconciliation: Cities Respond to the Truth and Reconciliation*

Commission Calls to Action. Ottawa: Federation of Canadian Municipalities, 2016. Accessed 8 June 2017. https://fcm.ca/en/resources/pathways-reconciliation.

———. First Nations–Municipal Community Economic Development Initiative. "Lac Seul First Nation, Municipality of Sioux Lookout, and Kitchenuhmaykoosib Inninuwug, ON." Accessed 25 August 2016. http://www.fcm.ca/home/programs/community-economic-development-initiative/participating-communities/ontario.htm.

———. First Nations–Municipal Community Economic Development Initiative. "Madawaska Maliseet First Nation and City of Edmundston, NB." Accessed 25 August 2016. https://www.cedipartnerships.ca/partnerships/past-partnerships/madawaska-maliseet-first-nation/.

———. First Nations–Municipal Community Economic Development Initiative. "Sawridge First Nation, Town of Slave Lake, and Municipal District of Lesser Slave River, AB." Accessed 25 August 2016. https://www.cedipartnerships.ca/partnerships/past-partnerships/sawridge-first-nation/.

———. First Nations–Municipal Community Economic Development Initiative. "Seabird Island Band, and District of Kent, BC." Accessed 25 August 2016. https://www.cedipartnerships.ca/partnerships/past-partnerships/british-columbia/.

Federation of Canadian Municipalities, and Cando (Council for the Advancement of Native Development Officers). Community Economic Development Initiative. "Evaluation Report." 10 May 2016.

Findlay, Isobel M. "Weaving the Interdisciplinary Basket: Building Resilient and Knowledgeable Communities and Economies." In *Visioning a Mi'kmaw Humanities: Indigenizing the Academy,* edited by Marie Battiste, 107–22. Sydney, NS: Cape Breton University Press, 2016.

Findlay, Isobel M., and Len Findlay. "Co-operatives: After the Crisis and Beyond the Binaries." In *Genossenschaften im Fokus einer neuen Wirtschaftspolitik* [Cooperatives in the focus of a new economic policy], edited by Johann Brazda, Markus Dellinger, and Dietmar Rößl (Hg.), 809–20. 2012 XVII International Conference on Cooperative Studies, Assoc. of Cooperative Research Institutes, University of Vienna. Vienna: LIT Verlag AG, 2013.

Findlay, Isobel M., Clifford Ray, and Maria Basualdo. "The Ethics of Engagement: Learning with an Aboriginal Cooperative in Saskatchewan." In *Journeys in Community-Based Research,* edited by Bonnie Jeffery, Isobel M. Findlay, Diane Martz, and Louise Clarke, 29–49. Regina: University of Regina Press, 2014.

———. "Research as Engagement: Rebuilding the Knowledge Economy of the Northern Saskatchewan Trappers Association Co-operative." In *Community-University Research Partnerships: Reflections on the Canadian Social Economy Experience,* edited by Peter V. Hall and Ian MacPherson, 141–58. Victoria: University of Victoria Press, 2011.

Findlay, Isobel M., and Warren Weir. "Aboriginal Justice in Saskatchewan 2002–2021: The Benefits of Change." In *Legacy of Hope: An Agenda for Change.* Vol. 1, *Final Report from the Commission on First Nations and Métis Peoples and Justice Reform,* 9-1– 9-161. Saskatoon: The Commission on First Nations and Métis Peoples and Justice Reform, 2004.

"Fortress Louisbourg Association: Association de La Forteresse-de-Louisbourg | Cape Breton, Nova Scotia—History." Accessed 24 October 2019http://www.fortressoflouisbourg.net/Overview/mid/12. http://www.fortressoflouisbourg.net/Overview/mid/12.

Fur Institute of Canada. *Reconnecting with the Land: Beaufort-Delta Region Youth Trapper Training Program, 2005. Final Report: Evaluation and Recommendations,* 2005. Accessed 13 September 2023. https://www.enr.gov.nt.ca/sites/enr/files/reports/sitidgi_lake_2005.pdf.

Elias, Peter Douglas. *Development of Aboriginal People's Communities.* Toronto: Captus Press, 1991.

Fiscal Realities Economics. "Stage 2: Economic and Fiscal Benefits Generated in Urban ATRs." In *Improving the Economic Success of Urban Additions to Reserves.* Gatineau: National Aboriginal Economic Development Board, 2015. Accessed 14 September 2023. http://www.naedb-cndea.com/reports/IMPROVING-THE-ECONOMIC-SUCCESS-OF-URBAN-ADDITIONS-TO-RESERVES.pdf.

Garcea, Joseph. "The FSIN and FSIN/SUMA Task Force Reports: Purposes, Processes, and Provisions." In *Urban Indian Reserves: Forging New Relationships in Saskatchewan,* edited by F. Laurie Barron and Joseph Garcea, 137–38. Saskatoon: Purich Publishing, 1999.

Gee, Kar-Fai, and Alvin Sharpe. *Aboriginal Labour Market Performance in Canada: 2007–2011.* Ottawa: Centre for the Study of Living Standards, 2012. Accessed 13 September 2023. http://www.csls.ca/reports/csls2012-04.pdf.

Gonzalez, Ellice B. *Changing Economic Roles for Micmac Men and Women: An Ethnohistorical Analysis.* Canadian Ethnology Service Paper No. 72. Ottawa: National Museums of Canada, 1981.

Graham, Katherine, Carolyn Dittburner, and Frances Abele. *Dialogue and Soliloquy: Public Policy and Aboriginal Peoples, 1965–1992.* Ottawa: Royal Commission on Aboriginal Peoples, 1996.

Guillemin, Jeanne. *Urban Renegades: The Cultural Strategy of American Indians.* New York: Columbia University Press, 1975.

Hamilton, Robert, John Borrows, Brent Mainprize, Ryan Beaton, and Joshua Ben David Nichols, eds. *Wise Practices: Exploring Indigenous Economic Justice and Self-Determination.* Toronto: University of Toronto Press, 2021.

Harcourt, Mike, and Ken Cameron, with Sean Rossiter. *City Making in Paradise: Nine Decisions That Saved Vancouver.* Vancouver: Douglas and McIntyre, 2007.

Hawthorn, Harry Bertram, H.A.C. Cairns, S.M. Jamieson, K. Lysyk, M.A. Tremblay, F.G. Vallee, and J. Ryan. *A Survey of the Contemporary Indians of Canada: A Report on Economic, Political, Education Needs and Policies in Two Volumes* (Hawthorn Report). Ottawa: Government of Canada, Department of Indian Affairs and Northern Development, 1966.

Hogeveen, Bryan. "Toward 'Safer' and 'Better' Communities? Canada's Youth Criminal Justice Act, Aboriginal Youth and the Processes of Exclusion." *Critical Criminology* 15, no. 3 (2005): 287–305.

Huu-ay-aht First Nation. "Huu-ay-aht Citizens Vote to Continue to Explore Proposed LNG Project." Accessed 14 September 2023. https://huuayaht. org/2014/11/huu-ay-aht-citizens-vote-to-continue-to-explore-proposed-lng-project/.

Iacobucci, Frank. "Introduction." In *Uneasy Partners: Multiculturalism and Rights in Canada*, edited by Janice Gross Stein, ix–xiii. Waterloo: Wilfrid Laurier University Press, 2007.

Independent Electricity System Operator. "Indigenous Community Energy Plan Program Overview." Accessed 5 April 2023. https://www.ieso.ca/en/ Get-Involved/Indigenous-Relations/Indigenous-Community-Energy-Plan-Program/ICEP-Overview.

International Institute for Sustainable Development, and Tahltan First Nation. *Out of Respect, The Tahltan, Mining, and the Seven Questions to Sustainability.* Report of the Tahltan Mining Symposium, 4–6 April 2003, Dease Lake, British Columbia. Winnipeg: Interntional Institute for Sustainable Development, 2004. Accessed 14 September 2023. https://www.iisd.org/publications/out-respect-tahltan-mining-and-seven-questions-sustainability.

Irwin, Marty. "Municipal Perspectives from Saskatoon." In *Urban Indian Reserves: Forging New Relationships in Saskatchewan*, edited by F. Laurie Barron and Joseph Garcea, 213–230. Saskatoon: Purich Publishing, 1999.

Jackson, Michael. *Locking up Natives in Canada: A Report of the Committee of the Canadian Bar Association on Imprisonment and Release.* Vancouver: University of British Columbia, 1988.

Johnstone, Harvey. "Membertou First Nation Indigenous People Succeeding as Entrepreneurs," *Journal of Enterprising Communities, Bradford* 2, no. 2 (2008): 140–50.

Johnstone, Harvey, and Doug Lionais. "Depleted Communities and Community Business Entrepreneurship: Revaluing Space through Place." *Entrepreneurship and Regional Development* 16, no. 3 (May 2004): 217–33.

Kayseas, Bob, Kevin Hindle, and Robert B. Anderson. *Fostering Indigenous Entrepreneurship: A Case Study of the Membertou First Nation, Nova Scotia, Canada,*

2006. https://researchbank.swinburne.edu.au/file/1e5bc4bb-88fc-437b-8ffb-ee9041ac06ef/1/PDF%20(Published%20version).pdf.

Keewatin Career Development Corporation. *Northern Economic and Labour Market Trends Report,* November 2016. Accessed 13 September 2023. http://www.kcdc.ca/economicandlabourmarkettrendsreport.pdf.

Kelly-Scott, Karen. *Aboriginal Peoples: Fact Sheet for Saskatchewan. Aboriginal Peoples Fact Sheets*. Statistics Canada Catalogue no. 89-656-X2016009, 14 March 2016. Accessed 13 September 2023. https://www150.statcan.gc.ca/n1/en/pub/89-656-x/89-656-x2016009-eng.pdf?st=lyyakbFt.

Kino-nda-niimi Collective. *The Winter We Danced: Voices from the Past, the Future, and the Idle No More Movement.* Winnipeg: ARP Books, 2014.

Knight, Rolf. *Indians at Work: An Informal History of Native Labour in British Columbia 1858–1930.* Vancouver: New Star Books, 1996.

Knockwood, Isabel. *Out of the Depths: The Experiences of Mi'kmaw Children at the Indian Residential School at Shubenacadie.* Black Point, NS: Fernwood Press, 1992.

Lac Seul First Nation. "Lac Seul First Nation," 2017. Accessed 14 September 2023. https://lacseulfn.org/.

Lafond, Lester. "Creation, Governance, and Management of the McKnight Commercial Centre in Saskatoon." In *Urban Indian Reserves: Forging New Relationships in Saskatchewan,* edited by F. Laurie Barron and Joseph Garcea, 188–212. Saskatoon: Purich Publishing, 1999.

Locke, Wade, and Stephen G. Tomblin. "Good Governance, a Necessary but Not Sufficient Condition for Facilitating Economic Viability in a Peripheral Region: Cape Breton as a Case Study, a Discussion Paper." Sydney: Cape Breton Regional Municipality, 2003.

Loizides, Stelios, Robert Anderson, and Conference Board of Canada, eds. *Growth of Enterprises in Aboriginal Communities*. Ottawa: Conference Board of Canada, 2006.

Loizides, Stelios, and Wanda Wuttunee. *Creating Wealth and Employment in Aboriginal Communities*. Ottawa: Conference Board of Canada, 2005.

Loney, Shaun, with Will Braun. *An Army of Problem Solvers: Reconciliation and the Solutions Economy.* Preface by Grand Chief Sheila North Wilson. Winnipeg: Friesens, 2016.

Maa-nulth First Nations Final Agreement. Toquaht Nation, 2009. Accessed 14 September 2023. http://www.toquaht.ca/wp-content/uploads/2021/11/Maa-nulth-Final-Agreement_2009.pdf.

MacIntyre, Gertrude Anne. *Perspectives on Communities: A Community Economic Development Roundtable.* Sydney: University College of Cape Breton Press, 1998.

Mandel-Campbell, Andrea. "Rough Trade: How Canada's Diamond Bonanza Is Turning a Secretive Industry Inside Out." *Walrus.* Accessed 28 August 2015. http://thewalrus.ca/2004-04-society/.

Manitoba. Aboriginal Justice Inquiry of Manitoba. *Report of the Aboriginal Justice Inquiry of Manitoba*. 3 vols. Winnipeg: Province of Manitoba, 1991.

Manitoba Indian Brotherhood. *Wahbung: Our Tomorrows.* Winnipeg: Manitoba Indian Brotherhood, 1971.

Membertou Band Council. *Annual Report 2017–2018: Leading by Example.* Membertou, NS: Membertou Band Council, n.d. Accessed 16 September 2023. http://www.membertou.ca/wp-content/uploads/2019/06/membertou-annual-report-2017-2018.pdf.

———. *We Have Arrived: Membertou Annual Report 2015–2016*. Membertou, NS: Membertou Band Council, n.d. Accessed 16 September 2023. https://membertou.ca/2015-2016/.

McHugo, John. "How to Prove Title to Territory: A Brief, Practical Introduction to the Law and Evidence." In *Boundary and Territory Briefing*. Vol. 2, no. 4, edited by Clive Schofield. Durham, UK: University of Durham, Department of Geography, International Boundaries Research Unit, 1998.

Mehodihi: Well-Known Traditions of Tahltan People, "Our Great Ancestors Lived That Way." Exhibition booklet prepared by Pam Brown and Shawnaditta Cross. Vancouver: University of British Columbia Museum of Anthropology, 2003. Accessed 14 September 2023. moa.ubc.ca/wp-content/uploads/2014/08/Sourcebooks-Mehodihi-TAHLTAN-PEOPLE.pdf.

Miller, J. "The Historical Context." In *Continuing Poundmaker and Riel's Quest*, edited by R. Gosse, J.Y. Henderson, and R. Carter, 41–51. Saskatoon: Purich and College of Law, University of Saskatchewan, 1994.

Miller, Robert J. *Reservation "Capitalism": Economic Development in Indian Country.* Lincoln: University of Nebraska Press, 2013.

Miller, Virginia P. "The Decline of Nova Scotia Micmac Population, 1600–1850." Paper presented at the Eleventh Algonkian Conference, Ottawa, 1979.

Millette, Daniel M. "Land Use Planning on Aboriginal Lands—Towards a New Model for Planning on Reserve Lands." *Canadian Journal of Urban Research* 20, no. 2 (2012): 20–35.

———. *Reconstructing Culture: A Traditional Use Study of the Tsawwassen First Nation.* Delta, BC: Tsawwassen First Nation and British Columbia Ministry of Forests, 1998.

Natcher, David. "Subsistence and the Social Economy of Canada's Aboriginal North." *The Northern Review* 30 (Spring 2009): 83–98. Accessed 13 September 2023. https://thenorthernreview.ca/index.php/nr/article/view/6/5.

National Aboriginal Financing Task Force. *The Promise of the Future: Achieving Economic Self-Sufficiency through Access to Capital.* Ottawa: National Aboriginal Financing Task Force, 1996.

National Indigenous Economic Development Board. *The Aboriginal Economic Benchmarking Report.* Ottawa: National Indigenous Economic Development Board, 2012.

———. *The Indigenous Economic Progress Report 2019*. Ottawa: National Indigenous Economic Development Board, 2019. Accessed 13 September 2023. http://www.naedb-cndea.com/wp-content/uploads/2019/06/NIEDB-2019-Indigenous-Economic-Progress-Report.pdf.

———. *Reconciliation: Growing Canada's Economy by $27.7B*. Ottawa: National Indigenous Economic Development Board, 2016.

Newhouse, David. "Aboriginal Economic Development in the Shadow of the Borg." *Journal of Aboriginal Economic Development* 3, no. 1 (2002): 107–13.

———. "The Challenges of Aboriginal Economic Development in the Shadow of the Borg." *Journal of Aboriginal Economic Development* 4, no. 1 (2004): 34–42.

———. "The Development of the Aboriginal Economy over the Next 20 Years." *Journal of Aboriginal Economic Development* 1, no.1 (1999): 68–77.

———. "Modern Aboriginal Economies: Capitalism with a Red Face," *Journal of Aboriginal Economic Development* 1, no. 2 (2000): 55–61.

———. "Resistance Is Futile: Aboriginal Peoples Meet the Borg of Capitalism." In *Ethics and Capitalism*, edited by John Douglas Bishop, 141–55. Toronto: University of Toronto Press, 2000.

New Relationship Trust. "BC Indigenous Clean Energy Initiative." Accessed 5 April 2023. https://www.newrelationshiptrust.ca/initiatives/bcicei/.

Northwest Territories. Bureau of Statistics. "Gross Domestic Product," 10 June 2019. Accessed 13 September 2023. https://www.statsnwt.ca/economy/gdp/.

Nova Scotia Commission on Building Our New Economy. *Now or Never: An Urgent Call to Action for Nova Scotians*. Report of the Nova Scotia Commission on Building Our New Economy. Halifax: Nova Scotia Commission on Building Our New Economy, 2014. Accessed 13 September 2023. https://www.onens.ca/sites/default/files/editor-uploads/now-or-never.pdf.

Office of the Correctional Investigator. *Annual Report 2017–2018*. Ottawa: Correctional Investigator Canada, 2018. Accessed 14 September 2023. https://oci-bec.gc.ca/index.php/en/content/office-correctional-investigator-annual-report-2017-2018.

Passelac-Ross, Monique M. *The Trapping Rights of Aboriginal Peoples in Northern Alberta*. Canadian Institute of Resources Law Occasional Paper #5. Calgary: University of Calgary, April 2005. Accessed 14 September 2023. https://prism.ucalgary.ca/server/api/core/bitstreams/d09abcf8-cc8b-455e-9e40-1c217e7fc171/content.

Patterson, Lisa. "Indian Affairs and the Nova Scotia Centralization Policy." Master's thesis, Dalhousie University, 1985.

Pattison, Dwayne, and Isobel M. Findlay. *Self-Determination in Action: The Entrepreneurship of the Northern Saskatchewan Trappers Association Co-operative*. Research report prepared for the Northern Ontario, Manitoba, and Saskatchewan Regional Node of the Social Economy Suite. Saskatoon:

Centre for the Study of Co-operatives and Community-University Institute for Social Research, 2010. Accessed 14 September 2023. https://cuisr.usask.ca/documents/publications/2010-2014/Self%20Determination%20in%20Action-%20NSTAC%202010.pdf.

Peter Ballantyne Cree Nation. "The Opawakoscikan Reserve in Prince Albert." In *Urban Indian Reserves: Forging New Relationships in Saskatchewan*, edited by F. Laurie Barron and Joseph Garcea, 159–76. Saskatoon: Purich Publishing, 1999.

Rata, Elizabeth. "The Theory of Neotribal Capitalism." *Review* (Fernard Braudel Center) 22, no. 3 (1999): 231–88.

Ray, Arthur J. *Indians in the Fur Trade.* With new introduction. Toronto: University of Toronto Press, 2005.

Rocan, Claude, ed. *Building Bridges: Case Studies Collaborative in Governance in Canada.* Rev. ed. Ottawa: Invenire, 2022.

Rostow, Walt Whitman. *The Stages of Economic Growth: A Non-Communist Manifesto.* Cambridge: Cambridge University Press, 1965.

Saul, John Ralston. *The Comeback.* Toronto: Penguin, 2014.

Scott, Jacquelyn Thayer. *Doing Business with the Devil: Land, Sovereignty, and Corporate Partnerships in Membertou Inc.* Halifax: Atlantic Institute for Market Studies, 2004. Accessed 12 September 2023. http://www.aims.ca/wp-content/uploads/2016/03/membertou.pdf.

Settee, Priscilla. "Indigenous Perspectives on Building the Social Economy of Saskatchewan." In *New Directions in Saskatchewan Public Policy*, edited by David P. McGrane, 73–90. Regina: Canadian Plains Research Center, 2011.

Shewell, Hugh. "'Bitterness behind Every Smiling Face': Community Development and Canada's First Nations, 1954–1968." *Canadian Historical Review* 83, no. 1 (2002): 58–84.

———. *Enough to Keep Them Alive: Indian Welfare in Canada 1873–1965.* Toronto: University of Toronto Press, 2004.

Simpson, Leanne, ed. *Lighting the Eighth Fire: The Liberation, Resurgence, and Protection of Indigenous Nations.* Winnipeg: Arbeiter Ring Press, 2008.

Smith, Adam. *The Wealth of Nations.* Books 1–3. Markham: Penguin Books Canada, 1986.

Stanger-Ross, Jordan. "Municipal Colonialism in Vancouver: City Planning and Conflict over Indian Reserves, 1928–1950s." *Canadian Historical Review* 89, no. 4 (2008): 541–80.

Starks, Rachel, Janice Esther Tulk, Tamara Young, Mary Beth Doucette, Trevor Bernard, and Cheryl Knockwood. *Managing Land, Governing for the Future: Finding the Path Forward for Membertou.* Dartmouth: Atlantic Policy Congress of First Nations Chiefs Secretariat, 2013. Accessed 14 September 2023. https://www.cbu.ca/wp-content/uploads/2019/08/FINAL-ManagingLandGoverningfortheFuture-FindingthePathForwardforMembertouMarch2014.pdf.

Swan, Davis. *True Cost of Electricity from the Site C Dam*. British Columbia Utilities Commission, September 2017. Accessed 14 September 2023. https://www. bcuc.com/Documents/wp-content/09/DOC_90187_F131-1_Swan-D_Site-C-Submission.pdf.

Tahltan Central Government. *2020–2021 Annual Report*. Tahltan Nation, BC: Tahltan Nation, 2021. Accessed 14 September 2023. https://tahltan. org/2020-2021-annual-report/.

Tahltan Heritage Resources Environmental Assessment Team (THREAT). "Organization, People, and Workflows." Tahltan Central Council, 2005.

Tahltan Tribal Council. *Tahltan Tribal Council Resource Development Policy Statement*, 7 April 1987. Accessed 14 September 2023. www.tndc.ca/pdfs/Tahltan%20 Resource%20Development%20Policy.pdf.

Thompson, Shirley, Asfia Gulrukh, Myrle Ballard, Byron Beardy, Durdana Islam, Vanessa Lozeznik, and Kimlee Wong. "Is Community Economic Development Putting Healthy Food on the Table? Food Sovereignty in Northern Manitoba's Aboriginal Communities." *Journal of Aboriginal Economic Development* 7, no. 2 (2011): 14–39.

Tokaryk, Deena. *We Are Tahltan Nation Development Corporation—2022 Annual Report*. Tahltan Nation, BC: Tahltan Nation, 2022. Accessed 13 September 2023. https://www.tndc.ca/content/1120/TNDC_AR_Jun2023-WebSpreads.pdf.

Torjmann, Sheeri, and Ann Makhoul. *Community-Led Development*. Ottawa: Institute of Social Policy, 2012.

Tough, Frank. *As Their Natural Resources Fail: Native Peoples and the Economic History of Northern Manitoba, 1870–1930*. Vancouver: University of British Columbia Press, 1996.

Town of Slave Lake, Municipal District of Lesser Slave River, and Sawridge First Nation. *Slave Lake Regional Tri-Council Economic Development Strategic Plan: 2012–2015*. Accessed 14 September 2023. https://www.fcm.ca/Documents/ reports/CEDI/Tri_council_economic_development_strategic_plan_EN.pdf.

Tsawwassen First Nation, and Canada, Indian Affairs and Northern Development. *Tsawwassen First Nation Final Agreement*. Ottawa: Indian Affairs and Northern Development and Federal Interlocutor for Métis and Non-Status Indians, 2012. Accessed 14 September 2023. https://tsawwassenfirstnation.com/wp-content/ uploads/2019/07/1_Tsawwassen_First_Nation_Final_Agreement.pdf.

Tsleil-Waututh Nation. *Assessment of the Trans Mountain Pipeline and Tanker Expansion Proposal*. North Vancouver: Treaty, Lands and Resources Department, Tsleil-Waututh Nation, n.d. Accessed 14 September 2023. https://twnsacredtrust. ca/wp-content/uploads/TWN_assessment_final_med-res_v2.pdf.

T'Sou-ke First Nation, "First Nation Takes Lead on Solar Power." Accessed 14 September 2023. http://www.tsoukenation.com/first-nation-takes-lead-on-solar-power/.

Tulk, Janice Esther. *Guiding Principles for Aboriginal Economic Development*. Purdy Crawford Chair in Aboriginal Business Studies, Case Studies in Aboriginal Business Shannon School of Business, Cape Breton University, Sydney, NS, 2013. Accessed 13 September 2023. https://www.cbu.ca/wp-content/uploads/2019/08/Guiding_Principles_for_Aboriginal_Economic_Development_sm.pdf.

Union of BC Indian Chiefs. "Certainty: Canada's Struggle To Extinguish Aboriginal Title," 1998. Accessed 13 September 2023. https://www.ubcic.bc.ca/certainty_canada_s_struggle_to_extinguish_aboriginal_title.

United Nations. Department of Economic and Social Affairs. *United Nations Declaration on the Rights of Indigenous Peoples (UNDRIP)*, 13 September 2007. Accessed 14 September 2023. https://www.un.org/development/desa/Indigenouspeoples/declaration-on-the-rights-of-Indigenous-peoples.html.

Voyageur, Cora J., David Newhouse, and Dan Beavon, eds. *Hidden in Plain Sight: Contributions of Aboriginal Peoples to Canadian Identity and Culture*. Toronto: University of Toronto Press, 2005.

Walker, Rachel Durkee, and Jill Doerfler, "Wild Rice: The Minnesota Legislature, a Distinctive Crop, GMOs, and Ojibwe Perspectives." *Hamline Law Review* 32, no 2 (2009): 499–527.

Weir, Warren. *First Nations Small Business and Entrepreneurship in Canada*. Centre for First Nations Governance, 2007. Accessed 12 September 2023. https://fngovernance.org/wp-content/uploads/2020/10/First_Nation_Small_Business.pdf.

Wesley-Esquimaux, Cynthia, and Brian Calliou. *Best Practices in Aboriginal Community Development: A Literature Review and Wise Practices Approach*. Banff, AB: Banff Centre, 2010.

Westbank First Nation. *Westbank First Nation Self-Government Agreement Between Her Majesty the Queen in Right of Canada and Westbank First Nation*. 24 May 2003. Accessed 14 September 2023. https://www.wfn.ca/selfgovernment.htm.

Wicken, William. C. "Moving into the City: The King's Road Reserve and the Politics of Relocation." In *The Colonization of Mi'kmaw Memory and History, 1794–1928: The King v. Gabriel Sylliboy*, 202–28. Toronto: University of Toronto Press, 2012.

Wien, Fred. "Profile of Membertou First Nation, Nova Scotia." In *Growth of Enterprises in Aboriginal Communities*, edited by Stelios Loizides, Robert Anderson, and Conference Board of Canada, 19–20. Ottawa: Conference Board of Canada, 2006.

———. *Rebuilding the Economic Base of Indian Communities: The Micmac in Nova Scotia*. Montreal: The Institute for Research on Public Policy, 1986.

World Economic Forum. *The Global Risks Report 2019*. 14th ed. Geneva: World Economic Forum, 2019. Accessed 14 September 2023. http://www3.weforum.org/docs/WEF_Global_Risks_Report_2019.pdf.

Wuttunee, Wanda. "Aboriginal Perspectives on the Social Economy." In *Living Economics: Canadian Perspectives on the Social Economy, Co-Operatives, and Community Economic Development*, edited by J.J. McMurtry, 179–201. Toronto: Emond Montgomery Publications, 2010.

———. *In Business for Ourselves: Northern Entrepreneurs*. Montreal: McGill-Queen's University Press, 1992.

———. *Living Rhythms: Lessons in Aboriginal Economic Resilience and Vision*. Montreal: McGill-Queen's University Press, 2004.

Yeo, Denton. "Municipal Perspectives from Prince Albert." In *Urban Indian Reserves: Forging New Relationships in Saskatchewan*, edited by Laurie Barron and Joseph Garcea, 177–87. Saskatoon: Purich Publishing, 1999.

Young, Tuma, Deborah Ginnish, and The Mi'kmaq Association of Cultural Studies. *Tptinewey: Mi'kmaq Elders' Perceptions of Social Assistance. Report for the Building a Social Policy Framework for Mi'kmaq Communities: A Two Eyed Seeing Approach*. Sydney, NS: Cape Breton University, 2017.

INDEX

306; and Indigenous values,
154; and McDonald Brothers
Electric Ltd., 240–41, 244; in
Membertou, 47, 48; and Neechi
Commons, 252; non-Indigenous
attitude toward Indigenous,
224, 229; and public service,
233; recent growth in,
18–19; research on, 234; and
reservation capitalism, 151–52;
resilience of, 217; stories of
starting out, 226–30; Tahltan
Nation and, 263–64
environmental sustainability: and
BC's energy plan, 201–2; and
climate change, 203–4; and
economic development in BC,
170–71; and non-renewable
resource projects in BC, 181–
88; and Tsawwassen land use
planning, 79, 84
equity shares, 192

F

family traditions and
entrepreneurship, 221, 231–32,
235
Federation of Canadian
Municipalities (FCM), 277–78
First Nations. *See* Indigenous
communities
fishery industry, 204
food security, 132, 216
food sovereignty, 203
forced removals, x, 33, 222–23
forestry industry, 203
Fouquet, L. (missionary), 72
fracking, 186, 191
Framework Agreement on First
Nation Land Management,
75–76, 89n12, 89n13

Fraser, Scott, 191
Friendship Accords, 281–83, 285,
290, 291–92
fur tanning, 133
fur trade, 5

G

Garcea, Joseph, 104, 110
globalization, 124, 126–27
Great Depression, 6, 222

H

Haida Nation v. British Columbia, 176,
177, 185
Halbritter, Ray, 161
Harmony Co-op brand foods, 254
Harvard Project on American Indian
Economic Development, 9, 14,
28, 151, 162, 163
Hawthorn Report, 8
Helin, Calvin, 161
Hesquiaht First Nation, 198
Highway, Florence, 133
Horgan, John, 191, 200
human dignity, 250
Hupačasath Upnit Power
Corporation, 196
Huu-ay-aht First Nation, 178, 198

I

Idle No More movement, 256
Impact and Benefit Agreement (IBA),
192, 268–69, 270
Indian Act, 33, 95, 96, 181, 264–65
Indian day schools, 223
Indian reserves, 100
Indigenous communities: attitude
towards development of,
207–8; and business in forestry
industry, 203; Canadians' blind